Tyndale Old Testament Commentaries

Volume 7

Judges and Ruth

T0323730

To Maureen, Sylvia and Jo,
who have stood alongside through thick and thin,
and in thankful memory of Sheena

Tyndale Old Testament Commentaries

Volume 7

Series Editor: David G. Firth
Consulting Editor: Tremper Longman III

Judges and Ruth

An Introduction and Commentary

Mary J. Evans

Inter-Varsity Press

IVP Academic
An imprint of InterVarsity Press
Downers Grove, Illinois

InterVarsity Press, USA
P.O. Box 1400
Downers Grove, IL 60515-1426, USA
Website: www.ivpress.com
Email: email@ivpress.com

Inter-Varsity Press, England
36 Causton Street
London SW1P 4ST, England
Website: www.ivpbooks.com
Email: ivp@ivpbooks.com

© 2017 by Mary J. Evans

InterVarsity Press®, USA, is the book-publishing division of InterVarsity Christian Fellowship/USA® and a member movement of the International Fellowship of Evangelical Students. Website: www.intervarsity.org.

Inter-Varsity Press, England, is closely linked with the Universities and Colleges Christian Fellowship, a student movement connecting Christian Unions throughout Great Britain, and a member movement of the International Fellowship of Evangelical Students. Website: www.uccf.org.uk.

First published 2017

Image: © Erich Lessing/Art Resource, NY

UK ISBN 978-1-78359-563-1 (print)
UK ISBN 978-1-78359-564-8 (digital)
USA ISBN 978-0-8308-4257-5 (print)
USA ISBN 978-0-8308-9499-4 (digital)

Set in Garamond 11/13pt
Typeset in Great Britain by CRB Associates, Potterhanworth, Lincolnshire

British Library Cataloguing in Publication Data
A catalogue record for this book is available from the British Library.

Library of Congress Cataloging-in-Publication Data
A catalog record for this book is available from the Library of Congress.

P	18	17	16	15	14	13	12	11	10	9	8	7	6	5	4	3	2	1
Y	33	32	31	30	29	28	27	26	25	24	23	22	21	20	19	18	17	

CONTENTS

General preface   vii
Author's preface   ix
Chief abbreviations   xi
Select bibliographies   xiv

JUDGES

Introduction   1

1. Literary issues   2
2. Canonical context   11
3. Historical and political background   15
4. Geographical background   22
5. Theological themes   23
6. Ethical issues facing twenty-first-century readers   30

Analysis   37

Commentary   39

RUTH

Introduction   217

1. Background   218
2. Character studies   221

3. Theological themes   224
4. Literary issues   228

Analysis   237

Commentary   239

GENERAL PREFACE

The decision completely to revise the Tyndale Old Testament Commentaries is an indication of the important role that the series has played since its opening volumes were released in the mid-1960s. They represented at that time, and have continued to represent, commentary writing that was committed both to the importance of the text of the Bible as Scripture and a desire to engage with as full a range of interpretative issues as possible without being lost in the minutiae of scholarly debate. The commentaries aimed to explain the biblical text to a generation of readers confronting models of critical scholarship and new discoveries from the Ancient Near East, while remembering that the Old Testament is not simply another text from the ancient world. Although no uniform process of exegesis was required, all the original contributors were united in their conviction that the Old Testament remains the Word of God for us today. That the original volumes fulfilled this role is evident from the way in which they continue to be used in so many parts of the world.

A crucial element of the original series was that it should offer an up-to-date reading of the text, and it is precisely for this reason that new volumes are required. The questions confronting readers in the first half of the twenty-first century are not necessarily those from the second half of the twentieth. Discoveries from the Ancient Near East continue to shed new light on the Old Testament, whilst emphases in exegesis have changed markedly. Whilst remaining true to the goals of the initial volumes, the need for contemporary study

8

of the text requires that the series as a whole be updated. This updating is not simply a matter of commissioning new volumes to replace the old. We have also taken the opportunity to update the format of the series to reflect a key emphasis from linguistics, which is that texts communicate in larger blocks rather than in shorter segments such as individual verses. Because of this, the treatment of each section of the text includes three segments. First, a short note on *Context* is offered, placing the passage under consideration in its literary setting within the book, as well as noting any historical issues crucial to interpretation. The *Comment* segment then follows the traditional structure of the commentary, offering exegesis of the various components of a passage. Finally, a brief comment is made on *Meaning*, by which is meant the message that the passage seeks to communicate within the book, highlighting its key theological themes. This section brings together the detail of the *Comment* to show how the passage under consideration seeks to communicate as a whole.

Our prayer is that these new volumes will continue the rich heritage of the Tyndale Old Testament Commentaries and that they will continue to witness to the God who is made known in the text.

David G. Firth, Series Editor
Tremper Longman III, Consulting Editor

AUTHOR'S PREFACE

Being immersed in the books of Judges and Ruth for the past months and years has been a huge privilege, and I'm very grateful to IVP for providing me with this opportunity. Given the nature of the material, it has not always been a joyful experience, but my own view of these books has been transformed and I have gained a real appreciation of their relevance in the murky world we live in today. God remains active and sovereign even when he insists that we notice the evil that surrounds us and acknowledge the failures as well as the successes, even, or perhaps especially, of those who claim to be his people.

I want to acknowledge here the great benefit I have received from interacting with, and bouncing ideas off, friends, students, colleagues, fellow church members and family. The support and encouragement of many people has been an important factor not only in my life but in the writing of this book. Nearly 150 years of good friendships are acknowledged in the dedication. I'm also grateful to those who have read and commented on sections of the manuscript, in particular Katharine McPhail, Amy Harper and the late Canon Godfrey Taylor. My gratitude is undoubtedly due and wholeheartedly given to Phil Duce at IVP for his patience when my manuscript has been delayed time and again, and to David Firth for his helpful and stimulating editorial comments.

My great hope is that any who dip into this book will themselves be stimulated to go back to the text of Judges and Ruth with the expectation that God will speak to them through it, and that they will be challenged again, as I have been, to live our lives as God's people in the way he intended. Judges might often be a negative example but it is a very good one!

Mary J. Evans
Warrington, 2017

CHIEF ABBREVIATIONS

AB	Anchor Bible
ABD	D. N. Freedman et al. (eds.), *The Anchor Bible Dictionary*, 6 vols. (New York: Doubleday, 1992)
AD	Anno Domini
BARev	*Biblical Archaeological Review*
BC	Before Christ
Bib	*Biblica*
BibInt	*Biblical Interpretation*
CBQ	*Catholic Biblical Quarterly*
ch(s).	chapter(s)
ed(s).	editor(s)
EvQ	*Evangelical Quarterly*
Hen	*Henoch Journal*
Int	*Interpretation*
JBL	*Journal of Biblical Literature*
JBQ	*Jewish Bible Quarterly*
JETS	*Journal of the Evangelical Theological Society*
JSOT	*Journal for the Study of the Old Testament*
JSS	*Journal of Semitic Studies*
lit.	literally
LXX	Septuagint (pre-Christian Greek version of the Old Testament)
MT	Masoretic Text (the standard Hebrew text of the Old Testament)
n.	note

NAC	New American Commentary
NCB	New Century Bible
NIBC	New International Bible Commentary
NICOT	New International Commentary on the Old Testament
NIVAC	NIV Application Commentary
OT	Old Testament
OTE	*Old Testament Essays*
OTG	Old Testament Guide
OTL	Old Testament Library
pl.	plural
sing.	singular
SJOT	*Scandinavian Journal of the Old Testament*
TOTC	Tyndale Old Testament Commentaries
VE	*Vox Evangelica*
VT	*Vetus Testamentum*
VTSup	Vetus Testamentum Supplement
ZAW	*Zeitschrift für die Alttestamentliche Wissenschaft*

Bible versions

ASV	American Standard Version, 1901
ESV	English Standard Version, published by HarperCollins Publishers © 2001 by Crossway Bibles, a division of Good News Publishers
JB	Jerusalem Bible, copyright © 1966 by Darton, Longman & Todd Ltd
KJV	King James Version
NASB	New American Standard Bible, copyright © 1960, 1962, 1963, 1968, 1971, 1972, 1973, 1975, 1977, 1995 by The Lockman Foundation
NEB	New English Bible, copyright © Oxford University Press and Cambridge University Press 1961, 1970
NET Bible	The NET Bible®, New English Translation, copyright © 1996 by Biblical Studies Press
NIV	New International Version, copyright © 1973, 1978, 1984

NIV 2011   New International Version 2011, copyright © 1973,
            1967, 1984, 2011 by Biblica, Inc.
NJB   New Jerusalem Bible, copyright © 1985 by Darton,
            Longman & Todd Ltd and Doubleday, a division
            of Bantam Doubleday Dell Publishing Group, Inc.
NKJV   New King James Version, copyright © 1982 by
            Thomas Nelson, Inc.
NLT   New Living Translation, copyright © 1996, 2004,
            2015 by Tyndale House Foundation
NRSV   New Revised Standard Version, Anglicized edition,
            copyright © 1989, 1995 by the Division of Christian
            Education of the National Council of the Churches
            of Christ in the USA
RV   Revised English Version, 1881
TNIV   Today's New International Version (Good News
            Translation), copyright © 2001 [2005] by
            International Bible Society

SELECT BIBLIOGRAPHIES

Judges

Amit, Y. (1990), 'Hidden Polemic in the Conquest of Dan: Judges 17–18', *VT* 40: 4–20.

Andersson, G. (2001), *The Book and Its Narratives: A Critical Examination of Some Synchronic Studies of the Book of Judges* (Örebro: Örebro University Press).

Bailey, K. (2008), *Jesus through Middle Eastern Eyes: Cultural Studies in the Gospels* (Downers Grove: IVP Academic).

Bauer, U. F. W. (2000), 'Judges 18 as an Anti-Spy Story in the Context of an Anti-Conquest Story: The Creative Usage of Literary Genres', *JSOT* 88: 37–47.

Beavis, M. A. (2010), 'The Resurrection of Jephthah's Daughter: Judges 11:34–40 and Mark 5:21–24, 35–43', *CBQ* 72: 46–62.

Blumenthal, F. (2005), 'Samson and Samuel: Two Styles of Leadership', *JBQ* 33: 108–112.

Boling, R. G. (1975), *Judges*, AB 6A (New York: Doubleday).

Butler, T. C. (2009), *Judges*, WBC 8 (Nashville: Thomas Nelson).

Cundall, A. E. and L. Morris (1968), *Judges and Ruth*, TOTC (London: IVP).

Curtis, A. H. W. (2005), 'Canaanite Gods and Religion', in B. T. Arnold and H. G. M. Williamson (eds.), *Dictionary of the Old Testament: Historical Books* (Leicester: IVP), pp. 132–142.

de Hoop, R. (2009), 'Judges 5 Reconsidered: Which Tribes? What Land?', in J. van Ruiten and J. C. de Vos (eds.), *The Land of Israel in Bible, History and Theology: Studies in Honour of Ed Noort*, VTSup 124 (Leiden/Boston: Brill).

Dumbrell, W. J. (1983), '"In those days there was no king in Israel; every man did that which was right in his own eyes": The Purpose of the Book of Judges Reconsidered', *JSOT* 25: 23–33.

Emmrich, M. (2001), 'The Symbolism of the Lion and the Bees: Another Ironic Twist in the Samson Cycle', *JETS* 44: 67–74.

Evans, M. J. (1994), '"A Plague on Both Your Houses"; Curses and Blessing Reviewed', *VE* 24.

—— (2000), *1 and 2 Samuel*, NIBC (Peabody, MA: Hendrickson).

—— (2004), *The Message of Samuel: Personalities, Potential, Politics and Power*, The Bible Speaks Today (Leicester: IVP).

Exum, J. C. (1980), 'Promise and Fulfillment: Narrative Art in Judges 13', *JBL* 99: 43–59.

—— (1981), 'Aspects of Symmetry and Balance in the Samson Saga', *JSOT* 19: 3–29.

Fleishman, J. (2006), 'A Daughter's Demand and a Father's Compliance: The Legal Background to Achsah's Claim and Caleb's Agreement (Joshua 15:16–19, Judges 5:12–15)', *ZAW* 118: 354–373.

Fokkelman, J. P. (1995), 'The Song of Deborah and Barak: Its Prosodic Levels and Structures', in D. P. Wright, D. N. Freedman and A. Hurvitz (eds.), *Pomegranates and Golden Bells* (Winona Lake: Eisenbrauns), pp. 595–628.

Gillmayr-Bucher, F. S. (2009), 'Framework and Discourse in the Book of Judges', *JBL* 128: 687–702.

Gray, J. (1967), *Joshua, Judges and Ruth* (London: Nelson).

Guillaume, P. (2001), 'Dating the Negatives Besitzverzeichnis (Judges 1:27–34): The Case of Sidon', *Hen* 23: 131–137.

Gunn, D. M. (2005), *Judges* (Oxford: Blackwell).

Hackett, J. A. (2004), 'Violence and Women's Lives in the Book of Judges', *Int* 58: 356–364.

Harris, J., C. Brown and M. Moore (2000), *Joshua, Judges, Ruth* (Peabody, MA: Hendrikson).

Herr, D. D. and M. P. Boyd (2002), 'A Watermelon Named Abimelech', *BARev* 28: 34–37.

Houtman, C. (2005), 'Rewriting a Dramatic Old Testament Story: The Story of Jephthah and His Daughter in Some Examples of Christian Devotional Literature', *BibInt* 13: 167–190.

Jost, R. (1996), 'Die Fluch der Mutter: Feministischsozialgeschichtliche Überlegungen zu Ri 17:1–6', in U. Bail and R. Jost (eds.), *Gott an den Rändern* (Gütersloh: Kaiser), pp. 17–23.

Lindars, B. (1995), *Judges 1–5* (Edinburgh: T. & T. Clark).

McCann, J. Clinton (2002), *Judges* (Louisville: John Knox Press).

Martin, L. R. (2007), 'The Intrusive Prophet: The Narrative Function of the Nameless Prophet', *JSS* 16: 113–140.

Miller, P. (2003), 'Moral Formation and the Book of Judges', *EQ* 75: 99–115.

Miller, R. D. (2002), 'Deuteronomistic Theology in the Book of Judges?', *OTE* 15: 411–416.

Na'aman, N. (2005), 'The Danite Campaign Northward (Judges 17–18) and the Migration of the Phocaeans to Massalia (Strabo IV 1–4)', *VT* 55: 47–60.

Olson, D. T. (2004), 'Buber, Kingship, and the Book of Judges: A Study of Judges 6 – 9 and 17 – 21', in B. F. Batto and K. L. Roberts (eds.), *David and Zion: Biblical Studies in Honor of J. J. M. Roberts* (Winona Lake: Eisenbrauns), pp. 199–218.

Robinson, B. P. (2004), 'The Story of Jephthah and His Daughter: Then and Now', *Bib* 85(3): 331–348.

Schneider, T. J. (2000), *Judges* (Collegeville, MN: Liturgical).

Smith, M. S. (2009), 'What Is Prologue Is Past: Composing Israelite Identity in Judges 5', in *Thus Says the Lord: Essays on the Former and Latter Prophets in Honor of Robert R. Wilson*, Library of Hebrew Bible/OT Studies 502 (New York/London: T. & T. Clark), pp. 43–58.

Soggin, J. A. (1981), *Judges*, OTL (London: SCM).

Stone, L. G. (2009), 'Eglon's Belly and Ehud's Blade: A Reconsideration', *JBL* 128: 649–663.

Trible, P. (1984), *Texts of Terror: Literary-Feminist Readings of Biblical Narratives* (Philadelphia: Fortress).

van der Kooij, A. (1995), '"And I also said": A New Interpretation of Judges ii 3', *VT* 45: 294–306.

Vincent, M. A (2000), 'The Song of Deborah: A Structural and Literary Consideration', *JSOT* 91: 61–82.

Webb, B. (1987), *The Book of Judges: An Integrated Reading* (Eugene: Wipf and Stock).

—— (2012), *The Book of Judges*, NICOT (Grand Rapids: Eerdmans).

Weitzman, S. (2002), 'The Samson Story as Border Fiction', *BibInt* 10: 158–174.

Wilcock, M. (1992), *The Message of Judges: Grace Abounding*, The Bible Speaks Today (Leicester: IVP).

Willis, T. M. (1996), 'The Nature of Jephthah's Authority', *CBQ* 59, 33–44.

Wong, G. T. K. (2005), 'Is There a Direct Pro-Judah Polemic in Judges?', *SJOT* 19: 84–110.

—— (2006), 'Ehud and Joab: Separated at Birth?', *VT* 56: 319–412.

—— (2007), 'Song of Deborah as Polemic', *Bib* 88: 1–22.

Yadin, A. (2002), 'Samson's *Ḥîdâ*', *VT* 52(3): 407–426.

Yee, G. (1993), 'By the Hand of a Woman: The Metaphor of the Woman Warrior in Judges 4', *Semeia* 61: 99–132.

Younger, K. L. (1995), 'The Configuring of Judicial Preliminaries: Judges 1:1 – 2:5 and Its Dependence on the Book of Joshua', *JSOT* 68: 75–92.

—— (2002), *Judges, Ruth*, NIV Application Bible (Grand Rapids: Zondervan).

Ruth

Atkinson, D. (1983), *The Message of Ruth: The Wings of Refuge*, The Bible Speaks Today (Leicester: IVP).

Bauckham, R. (1996), *Is the Bible Male? The Book of Ruth in Biblical Narrative* (Cambridge: Grove).

Block, D. I. (1999), *Judges, Ruth*, NAC 6 (Nashville: Broadman & Holman).

Carasik, M. (1995), 'Ruth 2:7: Why the Overseer Was Embarrassed', *ZAW* 107: 492–494.

Claassens, L. J. M. (2012), 'Resisting Dehumanization: Ruth, Tamar, and the Quest for Human Dignity', *CBQ* 74: 659–674.

Driesbach, J. (2012), in J. Coleson, L. Stone and J. Driesbach, *Joshua, Judges, Ruth*, Cornerstone Biblical Commentaries 3 (Carol Stream: Tyndale House).

Goswell, G. R. (2014), 'The Book of Ruth and the House of David', *EvQ* 86: 116–129.

Gray, J. (1977), *Joshua Judges and Ruth*, NCB (London: Oliphants).

Grossman, J. (2007), '"Gleaning among the Ears" – "Gathering among the Sheaves": Characterizing the Image of the Supervising Boy (Ruth 2)', *JBL* 126: 703–716.

Halton, C. (2012), 'An Indecent Proposal: The Theological Core of the Book of Ruth', *SJOT* 26: 30–43.

Harris, J., C. Brown and M. Moore (2000), *Joshua, Judges, Ruth*, NIBC (Peabody, MA: Hendrickson).

Hubbard, R. L. (1988), *The Book of Ruth*, NICOT (Grand Rapids: Eerdmans).

Jones, E. A. (2014), '"Who Are You, My Daughter?" A Reassessment of Ruth and Naomi in Ruth 3', *CBQ* 76: 653–664.

Larkin, K. J. A. (1996), *Ruth and Esther*, OTG (Sheffield: Sheffield Academic Press).

Levenson, A. T. (2010), 'The Mantle of the Matriarchs: Ruth 4:11–15', *JBQ* 38: 237–243.

Lim, T. H. (2011), 'How Good Was Ruth's Hebrew? Ethnic and Linguistic Otherness in the Book of Ruth', in D. C. Harlow, K. M. Hogan, M. Goff and J. S. Kaminsky (eds.), *The 'Other' in Second Temple Judaism: Essays in Honor of John J. Collins* (Grand Rapids: Eerdmans), pp. 101–115.

Luter, A. Boyd and R. O. Rigsby (1996), 'An Adjusted Symmetrical Structuring of Ruth', *JETS* 39: 15–31.

Roache, S. (2004), *Ruth and Naomi Find Joy after Tragedy* (Maitland, FL: Xulon Press).

Rowell, G, (2003), *The (Spiritual) Adventures of CyberCindy: Dialogues in Cyberspace* (Milton Keynes: Paternoster Press).

Schipper, J. (2012), 'The Syntax and Rhetoric of Ruth 1:9a', *VT* 62: 642–645.

—— (2013), 'Translating the Preposition *'m* in the Book of Ruth', *VT* 63: 663–669.

Shepherd, D. (2001), 'Violence in the Fields? Translating, Reading, and Revising in Ruth 2', *CBQ* 63: 444–463.

Siquans, A. (2009), 'Foreigners and Poverty in the Book of Ruth: A Legal Way for a Poor Foreign Woman to Be Integrated into Israel', *JBL* 128: 443–452.

Smith, M. S. (2007), '"Your People Shall Be My People": Family and Covenant in Ruth 1:16–17', *CBQ* 69: 242–258.

Stone, T. J. (2013), 'Six Measures of Barley Seed: Symbolism in Ruth', *JSOT* 38: 189–199.

Trible, P. (1992), 'Ruth', in *ABD* 5 (New Haven, CT: Yale University Press),

Younger, K. L. (2002), *Judges/Ruth*, NIVAC (Grand Rapids: Zondervan).

JUDGES

INTRODUCTION

Judges is not an easy book to read, although the effort it takes to do so will prove very worthwhile. It contains some difficult material from both a literary and a narrative point of view. Some of the stories can only be seen as extremely unpleasant, although there are some wonderful 'high spots'. Problems in understanding the book arise particularly when, as seems to have happened regularly in church contexts, the 'hard stories' are largely ignored and only the 'high spots' are known and talked about. However, problems also arise when narrative sections are viewed as intended to be determinative or exemplary, and readers therefore either try to find ways of defending what can only be seen as indefensible behaviour, or dismiss the book, and often the God of whom the book speaks, as intrinsically violent and indefensible. Recognizing that the book as we have it regularly uses humour, riddles and, in particular, irony to make its points provides a defence against both of the above approaches, although we should note here that Judges 'represents tragedy not comedy. Its irony leads to dark humour not vaudeville laughter' (Butler 2009: lxiii). If we are to take the text seriously in its

own right and understand it in its own context, then it is important
that we ask questions about structure, genre and context before we
attempt to interpret the text. Looking at these introductory questions
is therefore not simply an optional extra, secondary to the main
task of exegeting the text, but an essential prologue enabling that
exegetical process to take place. Of course, we have something of
a 'chicken-and-egg' situation. Some of the sections in this Introduction will clearly be grasped more fully after the text itself has
been read and considered. Nevertheless, readers of the commentary
are strongly encouraged to attempt to interact with these introductory questions at some stage, preferably before undertaking any
detailed reading of the text.

1. Literary issues

a. Overall structure

There is little dispute about the fact that the book of Judges is
composed of three more or less separate sections: 1:1 – 3:6; 3:7 –
16:31; 17:1 – 21:25. There is less agreement about the relationship
between those sections or indeed between the different passages
within those sections. Some would argue that what we have here is
a collection of different narratives with no inherent cohesion –
intended or otherwise. Others take the view that although Judges
can certainly be described as a collection of narratives from different
sources, nevertheless there is deliberate purpose and an intended
structure to the document as a whole. One representative of the
first group is Greger Andersson, who argues,

> If several independent narratives are put together, they are not thereby
> transformed into a larger single narrative even though they may contain
> common patterns and motifs. Hence, the individual story represents the
> primary level of meaning and discrete elements are understood as motifs
> within a literary construction. The stories of the book of Judges are
> therefore texts within a text. This explains why the book lacks a coherent
> ideology or morality.

He further argues that the tensions and ambiguities within the book,
which undoubtedly exist, 'cannot be resolved by classifying it as a

literary construction ... on the contrary, doing this confirms and explains the difficulties in the book – that is, the inconsistent character of both the book and its narratives' (Andersson 2001: 11). On the other hand, Barry Webb, building on the work of Boling and others, argues that 'certain exploratory synchronic studies have suggested that an integrated reading of the text is possible and that the book possesses a deeper coherence than has been recognized by most historical-critical scholars' (Webb 1987: 208; 2012: 8–9).

Andersson's insistence that each story should be looked at in its own right needs to be taken seriously, but that does not mean that the search for a 'deeper coherence' will automatically prove unfruitful. It is possible to argue that one can indeed find coherence in both the structure and the ideology and morality of the book as a whole.

It is clear that the three sections of the book of Judges are different in both style and content, and that even within those sections the different stories have different approaches. Section 1 (1:1 – 3:6) deals with the attempt by, and failure of, the Israelite tribes to take over the land and establish a functioning community distinct from the surrounding tribes and the previous occupants of the land in terms of governance, societal structure and religion. Section 2 (3:7 – 16:31) contains a series of accounts of varying length describing the life and times of twelve deliverers (traditionally known as 'judges') of Israel. It is true that both from a military and a spiritual point of view there are some successes described. Nevertheless, it is made very apparent that if there was an aim to establish a functioning community that could realistically be described as living in covenant relationship with Yahweh, then again the keynote is failure. Section 3 (17:1 – 21:25) includes two series of narratives focusing on the stories of individual Israelites and the ripple effects stemming from their actions. If the intention of the occupation of the land was to set up a community of people living in obedience to, and relationship with, God in line with the requirements of the covenant, then yet again it seems that the writers are presenting us with a story of failure. If this is so, then even at the basic level we see that there is at least some coherence between the three separate sections of the book. For this reason my sympathies are certainly more with Webb's position on the existence of an imposed overall structure than with Andersson's.

b. Dating and authorship

As already noted, Judges is a compilation of narratives from a number of different sources. Therefore, it needs to be made clear, when we are talking about both dating and authorship, whether we are referring to the book as a whole or to a particular individual narrative. In both cases it has to be said that actual information is scanty. At no stage is any author named or identified. There is a Jewish tradition that assigns authorship to Samuel but there is no real evidence to support this. There is a widespread conviction, based on both verbal and theological links, that Judges, in a similar way to Joshua, Samuel and Kings, is closely tied to Deuteronomy. The appropriateness of describing this broader section of the Old Testament as the 'Deuteronomic History' is widely accepted, and the links between some of these books will be discussed further in section 2 of the Introduction. However, even given these links, the identity of any and each individual author or editor is unknown, and any discussion of these identities can only be speculative. Again, even for those of us who are convinced that there is an intentional structure and coherent purpose within Judges as a whole, it is not clear whether this editorial structure was imposed by an individual or a group, or whether particular emphases are imposed by the editors or originate with an earlier source. For these reasons this commentary, when referring to authorship in general, refers to 'the writers'. In this context it needs to be stressed that the acknowledgment of several participants in the production of the final text of Judges does not mean that the text itself or the events described should automatically be seen as incoherent or untrustworthy. It is possible that later editors may have brought out specific perspectives or added more material. However, there is no reason not to assume that they did so in a way that took the original material very seriously so that the opinions, insights and information provided by earlier writers was not lost. In other words, acknowledgment of the existence of later editors does not in any way require the conclusion that the text and/or its stories must automatically be seen as inauthentic. Most modern readers, who are not approaching the text from the context of an academic background, may have many problems of different kinds with the material in Judges, but in general they would acknowledge that, at least in terms of the three sections, the material reads smoothly and makes sense as it now stands.

As far as dating is concerned, the period of the Judges lasts from the death of Joshua until the appointment of Saul as king, that is, from approximately 1200 to 1020 BC. However, there is no way of placing any of the individual stories found in Judges at a specific point within that timescale. Judges 18:29–31 makes it clear that the final compilation cannot have taken place until at least after the monarchy was settled in Jerusalem. If, as seems likely, the reference to the captivity of the land is to the mass deportations of later times, then the earliest it could be is after the first exile of the northern kingdom to Assyria around 734 BC, but it could be as late as 586 BC, after the exile of Judah to Babylon. However, again it is impossible to know whether the book was fairly well formed rather earlier than that and the final editing process simply 'tidied it up'. The suggestion that the compilation occurred at or soon after Jeroboam's involvement in the division of the kingdom is worth noting. In terms of the dating of the individual sources, there is often little agreement, and it does depend on whether one is referring to the earliest written form of an account or to the origin of oral accounts. The song of Deborah is often considered to be particularly early, nearest to the timing of any events described. Some scholars are sceptical about the historical authenticity of many of the other narratives within the book. However, it is worth pointing out that in oral societies where the retelling of ancient stories is part of the fabric of society, the level of accuracy in the retelling of those stories is remarkable (see Bailey 2008). No documents have been discovered which contain any of the individual narratives within the book of Judges (apart from those passages that are parallel to the accounts in the book of Joshua). This means that any discussion of the origin of these accounts can only ever be speculative. Where it is relevant, the dating of these individual sections is considered within the commentary.

c. The nature of narrative

There is some poetry in Judges and the occasional military list, but the vast majority of the material is narrative, that is, description of events. There is editorial comment where the writers insert some reflection on the events they are describing, but this is relatively rare, and in many instances readers are left to draw their own conclusions about the meaning and significance of the events described. However, this does not mean that the writers are simply objective recorders. Events are things that happen; accounts are records of those events that always present them from a particular point of view and with particular emphases and interests. Written narratives are always accounts. Sometimes the editorial insertions make the position of the writers very clear; at other times, although there is no explicit comment, the way the story is told directs the reader very clearly towards a particular perspective. On other occasions such direction is harder to identify, and readers have to determine for themselves – perhaps governed in part by the material that is clearer – whether the events being described should be seen as good or bad, in accordance with God's purposes for Israel or not. In the light of the book as a whole, and indeed of Scripture as a whole, an assumption that where there is no comment, any event described must automatically be seen as the thing that God wanted to happen is manifestly nonsense.

Stories are told not just to enable readers to know what happened in a particular situation, but also to help them think, assess, analyse and learn. We are told how people behave, the results of that behaviour, and how and when God does or does not respond to what is done. Narratives can be used to describe both historical and fictional events, and it is often suggested that some, or even many, of the stories of Judges have been produced, or at least substantially modified, in order to make some particular point or to serve the needs of a later community. However, it is rarely disputed that the writers themselves intended the events they record to be seen as historical and almost certainly assumed that they were. The question of historical validity is important and needs to be – and at times within the commentary will be – considered, but this is certainly not the only question that interpreters need to ask. Just as important is the question of why these particular stories are being told, and told in this particular way. The book of Judges, along with Joshua, Samuel and Kings, forms part of the section of the Jewish canon known as the 'Former Prophets'. This is a recognition that what we have here may be history, but it is always preached history.

It is important that readers are looking out for the message of the preaching as much as the information about events.[1]

d. Recurring motifs

The boundary between recurring motifs and theological themes is not always a clear one, but it is worth noting at this point the existence of one or two such motifs. First, the sense of repeated patterns that is emphasized by the use of the term *again*: *Again the Israelites did evil* (3:12; 4:1; 10:6; 13:1); *Again the Israelites cried out* (3:15); *Shall we go up again . . . ?* (20:28). The commonality between the different narratives in section 2 reinforces this concept that history repeats itself. Second, given the patriarchal nature of the times and the amount of material dealing with military campaigns, there is an interest in the lives and concerns of women within the book of Judges that could be described as unexpected. We have stories of Caleb's daughter, Jael, the woman from Thebes who killed Abimelek, Jephthah's daughter, Ibzan's daughters, Samson's mother, the various Philistine women involved with Samson, Micah's mother, the mistreated women of chapters 19 – 21 and of course Deborah. Women are described as significant players, capable of independent thought and action and deserving of respect – as well as on the receiving end of what is clearly viewed as dreadful treatment.[2] One cannot necessarily determine an intention on the part of the writers to change society, but their observation of society is certainly worth noting. A third thing to note is the attention paid to promises or vows. The overall interest in the covenant promises made by Yahweh to Israel and Israel to Yahweh is most obvious here. However, we also have Caleb's oath concerning his daughter (1:12), Jephthah's oath which led to the sacrifice of his daughter (11:31), the Nazirite vow made

---

1. A more comprehensive survey of the nature of narrative, and in particular the relevance for preachers of the prevalence of narrative within Scripture, can be found in my volume on 1 and 2 Samuel in The Bible Speaks Today series (Evans 2004).
2. Jo Ann Hackett's article (2004) provides a fascinating discussion of the way in which stories of women and stories of violence interweave in Judges.

by Samson and his mother (13:5, 14), Samson's promise to harm the
Philistines (15:3), Micah's mother's oath (17:3) and the Israelites'
oaths concerning Benjamin (21:1, 5). A further suggested recurring
motif is the failure of the family. Smith examines the theme of
marriage and family and argues that the failure of families is
presented as having a significant negative effect on the life of the
nation (2009). The stories of Gideon, Jephthah, Samson and the
Levite from the hill country of Ephraim could certainly be seen as
supporting this view.

e. Author's intention

When we have no external knowledge relating to the author or
authors of any book, then the only way we can determine the
author's purpose in writing that book is to examine the text as we
have it. Can we identify a consistent purpose by looking at both what
the writers say and sometimes what they don't say? For example,
there are several accounts where God is not mentioned at all, or only
in a very incidental way, and we can perhaps draw almost as many
conclusions from that lack of mention as we can from the specific
discussions of God's purposes. One of the factors we need to take
into account in this discussion is the part played in the narrative by
the narrator. The narrator's main contribution is in the various introductions found within the book, but can also occasionally be found
within the dialogue. As Gillmayr-Bucher puts it, 'The perspective of
the introductions adds a grain of doubt to the reading of every
hero-story' (2009: 701–702), and this perspective certainly challenges
readers to question the acceptability of the events being described.

There is no doubt that there are many motifs within Judges, that
is, many ideas that recur at various stages within the different
accounts found in the book and many commonalities in approach.
We shall examine some of these below in section 5. The question
is whether these commonalities and motifs can legitimately be
brought together into something that could be described as a theme
for the book as a whole. Of course, in very broad terms we can see
and say that the book is concerned with the life of the Israelite tribes
as the people of Yahweh in the land given to them by Yahweh. The
relationship between those people – as a whole, as tribes and as
individuals – and Yahweh is as central to the book of Judges as it is

to Deuteronomy and the other books seen as part of the Deuteronomic History. There seems no doubt that the writers, across the board, are interested in when, whether and how far the people are living in a way that would make them able to be described with any real accuracy as the 'people of Yahweh'.

We have already noted (see 1a above) that there seems to be a deliberate intention within the three main sections of Judges to present failure. In section 1 Israel as a whole failed to occupy the land. In section 2 not even the national redeemers sent by Yahweh were able to ensure long-lasting allegiance to the covenant and its requirements. Any positive influence they had never lasted beyond their death when Israel is pictured as immediately reverting to a state of rebellion against God. In section 3 we see both Levites and ordinary Israelites from various tribes behaving in ways that can only be seen as completely unacceptable in covenant terms. I would suggest therefore that one of the writers' main concerns, if not the main concern, is to present this period of Israel's history before the institution of the monarchy as 'This is not how it was meant to be'. Of course, that is not the whole picture. We do have stories of times and individuals when it was working, when people did obey, did follow, did relate properly to Yahweh. In other words, there are enough 'high spots' to show that God was not demanding something impossible. It would have been possible for Israel to live as God's people, to live in the way that it 'was meant to be', but in fact they did not. Thus, Judges becomes a picture not of a positive example to be followed, but of failure to be avoided.

Because Judah is the tribe mentioned most often and arguably most positively within the book, it is often supposed that the writers of Judges had a pro-Judah bias. However, this perspective is somewhat subjective and is strongly disputed by Wong (2005), who thinks that the positive view of Judah has been exaggerated and in any case can be explained by factors other than a pro-Judah bias. Because of the interest in leadership, also seen throughout the three main sections, and in particular because of the repeated phrase in section 3 that *In those days Israel had no king*, it is sometimes assumed that Judges was written primarily to show that kingship was an essential prerequisite of covenant living. It is seen, in essence, as an apology for the monarchy. This is certainly a possible conclusion.

However, there is another possibility. I have argued elsewhere that the books of Samuel in fact provide a critique of leadership, and in particular of kingship; examining and reflecting on the nature, accession, use and abuse of power (Evans 2000: 1–10; 2004: 14–22). If this is correct, and if, as I have argued, the overall view of kingship in Samuel and Kings is in fact more negative than positive, then it is possible that the references to kingship and its absence at the time of the events described in Judges are not implying that the lack of a king is the primary reason why Israel was 'not how it was meant to be'. Rather, it may be saying that while later kingship might be blamed for many things, it could not in fact be blamed for the situation that existed in the times described by the writers of Judges, because *in those days Israel had no king.*

f. Judges as 'Scripture'

This is not, strictly speaking, a literary issue, but it is of concern to all those who understand the whole of the Bible to be the inspired and authoritative Word of God. What does it mean to understand a book like Judges, which contains so many moral and spiritual negatives, as 'Scripture'? All the factors mentioned above, in particular our understanding of the nature of narrative, our assessment of the recurring motifs and themes within Judges and our conclusions concerning the intention of the writers, will influence the way in which we understand God speaking to us in and through the book of Judges. Paul Miller (2003) recognizes Judges as Scripture and helpfully argues that although Judges cannot be seen as 'prescriptively ethical in the sense that it presents explicit norms and rules of conduct', nevertheless 'it deals with an equally important matter: the community of faith as the context for moral formation' (2003: 99). We should not necessarily expect a book dealing with the community of God's people 3,000 years ago directly to answer our questions relating to issues emerging in the twenty-first century. Miller concludes, 'The main ethical thrust of Judges could be summarised as follows: The very capacity to make moral judgements itself arises from the desire to obey God. The community of faith is the context in which this capacity of obedience is learned and practised' (2003: 103). Miller goes on to argue that an awareness of the presence of 'irony' in Judges, which he sees as deliberately introduced by the writers, will give readers a much better understanding of both what is going on and how we should interpret it. The book in fact shows 'the horror of life without God' (2003: 115), or as we have argued above, presents us with a picture of 'life as it was not meant to be'.

2. Canonical context

The book of Judges does not exist in isolation. Historically, the events are pictured as part of a much longer story. They are presented by the writers as coming between the entry of the tribes of Israel into the Promised Land as described in Joshua, and the accounts of the life of Samuel and the beginning of the monarchy as described in the books of Samuel. From a wider perspective they play their part in the whole Old Testament picture which describes the history of Israel in such a way as to show that the possibilities presented in the promises made to Abraham and through Moses were never going to be worked out without some further direct action by God. In that sense there is also even a historical link with the New Testament, which presents Jesus as bringing into reality the kingdom of God in a way that the writers of Judges saw little or nothing of. From a literary perspective, Judges is linked with Joshua, 1 and 2 Samuel and 1 and 2 Kings. These books are, in Hebrew tradition, jointly described as the 'Former Prophets', a title that both emphasizes the link between them and indicates an awareness that all of them are as much concerned with theological teaching as they are with providing a historical account. Theologically, there are also strong links with Deuteronomy – indicated by the fact that in modern scholarship the books of the 'Former Prophets' are often referred to as the 'Deuteronomic History'.[3] All of these books share

---

3. The theory that the books of Joshua – 2 Kings can be linked together and seen as the work of Deuteronomic editors is set out in Martin Noth's book *The Deuteronomistic History* (JSOT Press, 1981). Noth argues for a single final editor, which explains the underlying commonalities that can be found in the material which is otherwise hugely diverse and clearly comes from several sources. Further helpful discussion is

a common understanding of just what it is that God requires of his people and a common commitment to the building up of the covenant community. One could say that there are also strong theological links with the New Testament presentations of what it does, could or should mean to live as the people of God.

a. Relationship to Deuteronomy

The relationship between the books of Judges and Deuteronomy is not quite as clear or well defined as that between 1 and 2 Samuel, or in particular 1 and 2 Kings, and Deuteronomy. However, although the level of common phrasing does not seem to be quite so high or quite so clear, nevertheless it does exist. The first two sections of Judges contain more examples of this but it is not entirely absent even in the third section. Some examples of the linguistic relationship are Judges 2:1–3/Deuteronomy 7:9, 12, 16; Judges 2:12–14/Deuteronomy 31:16–17; Judges 3:4/Deuteronomy 8:2; Judges 4:14/Deuteronomy 9:3; Judges 6:25/Deuteronomy 7:5; Judges 7:2–3/Deuteronomy 8:17; 20:8; Judges 10:14–16/Deuteronomy 32:36–37; Judges 11:20–22/Deuteronomy 2:32–36; Judges 13:22/Deuteronomy 5:26; Judges 20:13/Deuteronomy 17:12; Judges 21:25/Deuteronomy 12:8. It seems clear that the writers of Judges, at least those who were responsible for the final compilation, were well aware of the content of Deuteronomy. We have already noted the shared commitment to the development of Israel as a covenant community, which reflects a shared commitment to Yahweh and his kingdom and a shared understanding of what it is that Yahweh requires of his people.

b. Relationship to Joshua

The closest and most obvious link between Judges and the rest of the Bible is with the book of Joshua. Judges 1:1 refers to the death

---

(note 3 *cont.*) provided by D. A. Knight, in J. L. Mays, D. L. Petersen and K. H. Richards (eds.), *Old Testament Interpretation: Past, Present, and Future* (Abingdon, 1993), pp. 518–655. A different perspective is provided by R. D. Miller (2002), who argues for a unique theology in Judges that cannot be identified with the general Deuteronomic pattern.

of Joshua, which has been described in Joshua 24:29, so at first glance it appears that the events described in Judges come after those described in Joshua. In general, that is correct, but there is also some overlap and it is not easy to determine exact chronology. The closest parallels are in section 1 of Judges, and we will consider these in some detail. Within sections 2 and 3 (Judges 3:7 – 21:25) there are many references to places, individuals and groups previously mentioned in Joshua (e.g. places: Judg. 3:28; 4:11; 5:17; 8:18; 18:31; 20:45 / Josh. 2:7; 19:33; 19:29; 19:22; 18:1; 15:32; and people: Judg. 4:2; 6:11; 11:25; 19:11; 20:28 / Josh. 11:1; 17:2; 24:9; 3:10; 24:33). There are also a few accounts which show some commonality, that is, different events working out in similar ways, as the references to the use of trumpets (Judg. 7:18 and Josh. 6:4–5, 9, 20), or ambushes (Judg. 9:32; 20:29–38 and Josh. 8:2–20). Perhaps more significant are a number of passages which show theological similarities. One such example can be found in Judges 6:16 and Joshua 1:5, referring to Yahweh's promise that he *will be with you*. Judges 7:9 and Joshua 2:24 both refer to Yahweh delivering land and enemies *into your hands*, and Judges 10:16 and Joshua 24:23 refer to the importance of getting rid of foreign gods (cf. Judg. 14:4/Josh. 11:20; Judg. 16:20/Josh. 7:12; Judg. 20:23/Josh. 7:6 which make other parallel points). There are few signs in Joshua of awareness of events described in these sections of Judges, but Joshua 19:47 makes it clear that at least the final editors of Joshua were aware of the migration of the tribe of Dan described in Judges 18.

The chronological and literary relationship between Judges section 1 (1:1 – 3:6) and Joshua is not easy to determine. There are clear indications that the Judges material originated at a later time, as when Joshua talks about land assigned to various tribes and Judges notes that the people in that area were not 'driven out', for example with Manasseh and Naphtali (Josh. 17:11; 19:38; Judg. 1:27, 33). However, for Ephraim and Dan both books inform readers that the territory was not able to be taken (Josh. 16:10; 19:42, 47; Judg. 1:29, 35). On a number of occasions Joshua makes a statement that 'if' the people behave in a certain way, 'then' Yahweh will take action against them; Judges picks up the same ideas with a 'because' they have behaved that way, Yahweh is now going to act (Josh. 23:12–13, 16; Judg. 2:3, 18–21). Similarly, Joshua 3:10 predicts that Yahweh 'will drive out' the Perizzites, and Judges 1:4 says that he did so. The fact that the Jebusites were not able to be ousted at this time is clear in both Joshua (15:63) and Judges (1:21), but how this relates to the statement in Judges 1:8 that Jerusalem was taken and set on fire is hard to determine (see p. 42). The relationship between the references to Caleb and his family in the two books is also a little confusing. Joshua 14:13–15 tells us that Hebron was given to Caleb and the land has 'belonged to [him] . . . ever since', and that 'Then the land had rest from war', and Joshua 15:13–14 repeats the information that Hebron was given to Caleb 'according to Yahweh's command' and also mentions Caleb defeating the three sons of Anak who are named as Sheshai, Ahiman and Talmai. Judges 1:20 repeats the information that Hebron was given to Caleb, although here it was *as Moses had promised*. It also repeats the information that Caleb drove out the three sons of Anak who are not named at this point. However, Judges 1:10 describes the defeat of these three, who are named at that point, not specifically to Caleb, but to the tribal forces of Judah. The story of Caleb's daughter and her marriage to Othniel is told in Joshua 15:14–18 and in Judges 1:10–14. Judges 1:12–15 is a word-for-word copy of the text in Joshua 15:16–18, but although Judges 1:10–11 repeats the content of Joshua 15:14–15, it changes the subject from Caleb to the tribe of Judah. None of these differences is particularly significant, but they do make it difficult to determine whether the writers of Judges were using Joshua as a source, and if so, why they made changes, or whether both books were using a separate source.

c. Relationship to 1 and 2 Samuel

There is little in either the books of Judges or Samuel that shows a direct relationship or even awareness of the other, although the books of Samuel do know of places, people and even events mentioned in Judges. For example, place names like Bezek, Gibeah and Jabesh Gilead occur (Judg. 1:4; 19:14; 21:8; 1 Sam. 11:8; 10:26; 11:1). Samuel's farewell speech in 1 Samuel 12 gives a brief outline of the events described in Judges, mentioning Sisera, Jerub-Baal, Barak and Jephthah, but whether this implies that he was aware of the book of Judges is a matter of debate. The main link between Judges and the books of Samuel is that both refer to Deuteronomic ideas, such as the Spirit of the Lord coming on people (Judg. 3:10; 11:29; 14:19; 1 Sam. 11:6) or leaving them (Judg. 16:20; 1 Sam. 16:14), God having the freedom to decide or to do what he wants (Judg. 10:15; 11:27; 1 Sam. 3:18; 24:12), awarding victory to Israel (Judg. 12:3; 1 Sam. 19:5) or delivering them up to enemies (Judg. 13:1; 1 Sam. 12:9). One could argue that a further link is found in the refrain found in section 3 of Judges that *in those days Israel had no king*, but rather that *everyone did as they saw fit*. Thus, Judges is seen as preparing for the account of the monarchy that begins in the books of Samuel. Whether the statement in Judges is positive or negative towards the monarchy is also a matter for debate. The positive view suggests that the writers are describing a fairly awful situation but are assuming that when a king comes it will be better. The more negative view recognizes that the kings described in the books of Samuel and Kings were rarely effective and can be seen in some sense as responsible for Israel's failures during the monarchy; however, in spite of that, one cannot blame kings for what happened in Judges (see pp. 181–182, 185–186, 188–189, 195–196, 215–216).

3. Historical and political background

a. Summary of events
The writers of Judges take for granted the historical background presented in the first five books of the Old Testament. There is not a great deal of discussion of previous times, but the clear assumption is that the tribal groups descending from the sons of Jacob developed during the many years in Egypt. They all left Egypt during the exodus and lived for forty years in the wilderness as a semi-nomadic desert community. Under Joshua's leadership they entered the land that God had promised to them, established bridgeheads and gradually began to take over the different tribal lands. The book of Judges begins at this point. It is abundantly clear that the takeover of the land still had a long way to go. Section 1 (chs. 1 – 3:6) starts from a position where no tribe has yet fulfilled its commission, and a description is given of a series of campaigns by the tribes, beginning with Judah. Some of these campaigns are pictured as reasonably successful, others as notably unsuccessful, but across the board the previous inhabitants were never fully ousted and are seen as remaining as both snares and

threats to the long-term existence of Israel as Yahweh's covenant people. This picture is replicated in sections 2 and 3, although there are some passages where the Israelite people are described as having hardly a foothold in the land and others where there seem to be fairly large areas that are exclusively Israelite.

The land and the surrounding territories were occupied by a variety of ethnic groups and a large number of kingdoms and fiefdoms of various sizes, some not much more than a small city-state, others extending over quite large territories and functioning as what might be described as nations. Some of these groups were linked together in more or less collaborative ways, but these associations were often flexible and not necessarily very long-lasting. Judges gives the strong impression that events did not happen as they were supposed to and the Israelites did not live as they were supposed to live. However, in spite of this, there is also an impression that the military successes gradually exceeded the failures, and that after all the events described there was enough settlement and enough unity to make the possibility of a single nation under a single king a foreseeable reality.

Working out the timing in Judges is not always easy. The use of symbolic numbers in the Old Testament is common, and the frequency with which round numbers are used is perhaps an indication that the writers of Judges made use of this technique. (Forty years occurs four times, twenty years twice and eighty years once.) However, not all the numbers fit this pattern, so we cannot be sure exactly how the numbers are to be understood.

b. Surrounding tribes and nations
At least fourteen different people groups are mentioned in Judges, almost always in the context either of groups that Israel should be displacing in the land or as enemies seeking to destroy Israel or prevent them from ever becoming a viable community. There is overlap between some of the groups so that clear descriptions of exactly where they were based and who they were cannot always be determined with precision. Nevertheless, it is helpful at this stage to consider what we do know about the various groups:

1. Canaanites: This appears to be a general term used to describe many or all of the different groups living in the area. There is no clear evidence of a specific group who were known as the Canaanite

nation. Judges refers to Canaanites fifteen times in chapter 1 and twice in chapter 2. However, in the rest of the book they are scarcely mentioned, although there are three references to Jabin king of Canaan in chapter 4 and a further mention of kings of Canaan in 5:19. The existence of a named king could imply a specific group, but this could simply be a reference to one of the kings in Canaan. Whether Hazor, described in Joshua 11:10 as a central city, should be seen as a distinct group separate from Canaanites in general is a moot point. The relationship between events in Joshua, where Hazor was razed to the ground and king Jabin was killed (Josh. 11:10), and Judges, where a king Jabin was still an active force against Israel is not clear (see pp. 73–74).

2. Amalekites: The Amalekites are mentioned six times in Judges (3:13; 6:3, 33; 7:12; 10:12; 12:15), and almost always described as in alliance with others, notably the Midianites or the Ammonites. They were much more of a problem to Israel in the time of David, and it appears that the defeats he imposed upon them were such that even if they still existed after this time, their influence was no longer of any significance. Judges describes them as part of the 'Eastern peoples', and it seems clear that their territory was south of the lands assigned to Israel. Again we can't be sure of the exact boundaries of their influence, and in any case these probably changed even over the time under consideration in Judges.

3. Ammonites: Ammon, like Moab, is recorded as a descendant of Lot, and so the Ammonites do have ethnic links to the Israelites. Hence the instruction in Deuteronomy 2:19 that Israel should not attempt to take over Ammonite territory or to 'harass them or provoke them to war'. However, for almost all of the centuries when the two nations existed together, they related only as enemies. Ammon's refusal to assist Israel during the exodus period may have been the start of that enmity (Deut. 23:4). Ammonite territory is to the east of the Jordan, further east than the territory assigned to Gad and half of Manasseh, and north of Moab. Judges 3:13 tells us that they were allies of Moab when Moab is portrayed as the main oppressor. However, Ammon itself becomes the 'lead enemy' in the stories around Jephthah (10:6 – 12:7).

4. Amorites: This group is referred to in 1:34–36; 3:5; 6:10; 10:8, 11; 11:19, 21, 23. Chapter 1 tells us that they were active in the areas

assigned to the tribes of Dan, Manasseh and Ephraim (the *tribes of Joseph*) and describes their land as *from Scorpion Pass to Sela and beyond* (1:36). There are several suggestions regarding the identity of these places, but no real evidence to back them up. Scorpion Pass is mentioned in Numbers 34:4 as on the border of the land assigned to Israel (cf. Josh. 15:3), and it may be that 1:36 is describing the border of the Amorite land that they should not have crossed. All other references to the Amorites are very general apart from those in Jephthah's speech to the king of the Ammonites (11:19–23), where he tells of Israel being refused peaceful passage through Amorite land and then being attacked by the Amorite army. The Amorites suffered a heavy defeat, and it is possible that at this point groups of Amorites fled from their original territory on the East of the Jordan River and set up in new territory within the western parts of Canaan.

5. Aram Naharaim: Aram is mentioned only in 3:8–10, although 10:6 also tells us that Israel served the gods of Aram. Aram, in north-west Mesopotamia, mostly between the Tigris and Euphrates rivers, that is, north-east of Israel largely in land covered by modern Syria, became a much more significant enemy in the later years of Israel's history. In Judges they, under the king Cushan-Rishathaim, were used by Yahweh to punish Israel for idolatry, but 'on appeal' they were then defeated by Othniel. Naharaim, not present in 3:10, is, like the Rishathaim part of the Aramite king's name, almost certainly added to 'convey upon the enemy a dimension of fearfulness, strangeness and distance' (Butler 2009: 65).

6. Hittites: The Hittites came from the area north-west of Israelite territory covering some of what is now north-west Syria and much of modern Turkey. The Hittite kingdom was at times apparently quite significant, probably even deserving its description as an empire. However, its major times of strength seem to have been both before and after the time covered by the Judges accounts. In Judges the Hittites are mentioned only in passing, as the final destination of the man who betrayed Bethel to the Joseph tribes (1:26), and in the list describing some of the former inhabitants of the land (3:5) that the Israelites *lived among*.

7. Hivites: We know virtually nothing about the Hivites other than what we find in the Bible. It is possible that they were a branch

of the Hittites but we can't be sure. Shechem, who wanted to marry Jacob's daughter Dinah, was a Hivite (Gen. 34:2ff.), as were the inhabitants of Gibeon, who deceived Joshua into making a treaty with them (Joshua 9:1–27), so the city was not attacked at that stage although the inhabitants were enslaved. Joshua 11:3 suggests that the Hivites held significant territory in the area below Mount Hermon. In Judges we read of them only in 3:3–5 as those left in the land to *test the Israelites*.

8. Jebusites: Jebus was the old name for Jerusalem. Although apparently several attempts were made, 'Judah could not dislodge the Jebusites' (Josh. 15:63) and the city remained independent. It was not taken over by Israel until the time of David (2 Sam. 5:6–10). Judges 1:21 confirms the fact that the Jebusites remained in Jerusalem, and the suggestion is of a reasonably peaceful coexistence with Israelite neighbours from the tribe of Benjamin. They are also named in the list in Judges 3:5 of the peoples *the Israelites lived among*. In 19:11 the Levite refused to stop overnight in Jebus because he did not want to *go into any city whose people are not Israelites*.

9. Kenites: The Kenites were the family of Moses' father-in-law. A group of these had clearly continued to travel with the Israelite tribes and are described in Judges as having a distinct identity and apparently a distinct area allotted to them (1:16). All the other references to them relate to Jael and her husband Heber. It seems that Heber had branched out from the rest of the Kenites (4:11) and that the alliance with Jabin, king of Hazor (4:17), was a personal one not involving the Kenites in general. Jael clearly prioritized the wider family alliance with Israel, rather than her husband's new commitment to Jabin (1:16).

10. Midianites: Midian was one of the sons of Abraham through his second wife Keturah. He, along with his brothers, was given gifts and sent away from Isaac to 'the land of the east'. Midianites were not Canaanites but, like the Moabites and Ammonites, invaded from their territory outside Canaan. It is difficult to be precise about the boundaries of their own territory, but it was apparently to the south of Moab and Ammon. In Judges they are mentioned only in connection with the stories of Gideon and his family. At this time they are clearly perceived as both powerful and oppressive. It is again possible that Midianite was a general term used for the southern

and south-eastern nations and that they were also influential during the times of the other leaders but under different, more specific names.

11. Moabites: Moab is situated on the south-east side of the Dead Sea, above Edom and below the land on the east of the Jordan allocated to Reuben. The Moabites existed alongside Israel for many centuries, sometimes in a tense peace, but often in a state of enmity or war. Moab regularly allied itself with Ammon or Edom against Israel. At times within that history, Moab was the dominant player; at other times, Israel was in control. It was the king of Moab who was so unceremoniously killed by Ehud (3:21–22). At that time we are told that Israel had been under Moab's thumb for eighteen years, but after the resulting fighting when a large section of Moab's army were killed, *Moab was made subject to Israel, and the land had peace for eighty years* (3:30).

12. Perizzites: The Perizzites are again virtually unknown outside of the Bible, although they are named in a large majority of the lists of those occupying the land before Israel. On a number of occasions, including the two in Judges 1:4–5 (cf. Gen. 13:7), they are placed in a twosome with the Canaanites, and it is possible that this term is also used as an umbrella for different groups. The only other mention in Judges is in the list in 3:5. Any attempt to assign a specific territory to the Perizzites or identify them more closely can only be speculative.

13. Philistines: Philistine territory bordering the Mediterranean Sea was to the west of the southern part of Israelite land, including the area today known as the Gaza Strip. They were themselves immigrants from Caphtor (Deut. 2:23; Jer. 47:4), which was somewhere in the west and possibly refers to Crete. However, the borders fluctuated and there were clearly often incursions into the land assigned by Yahweh to Israel. Philistia was in reality a collection of city-states, with a strong allegiance between them. Hence, Judges 3:3 speaks of the *five rulers of the Philistines*. The five main cities were Gaza, Ashkelon, Ashdod, Gath and Ekron. In Judges the Philistines were opposed by Shamgar (3:31) and referred to as a secondary enemy allied to the Ammonites in chapter 10 (vv. 6–14). Otherwise, we read of them only in the Samson stories where they are pictured as the main oppressors of Israel.

14. Sidonians: Sidon was a coastal town that still exists in modern-day Lebanon. It is north of the territory assigned to Israel and it is not clear why 1:31 tells us that Asher did not drive out those living in Sidon. Chapter 10 puts the *gods of Sidon* among those that Israel served (v. 6) and lists the Sidonians as among those who *oppressed* Israel (v. 12). The only other mention of Sidon is in 19:28, where it is suggested that they might have opposed the Danites' takeover of Laish if only they had lived a little bit nearer.

c. 'Other gods'

Several times in each of the three sections of the book of Judges the accusation is made that Israel turned away from Yahweh and worshipped other gods. Given the seriousness of the accusation and how much their behaviour influenced the failure of Israel to develop as a nation, it is perhaps surprising that so little information is given about the gods that they decided to worship. It is interesting to speculate as to whether the writers made a deliberate decision to limit what they said about these gods in order to de-emphasize their significance. In general they are simply described as 'other gods', 'their gods', 'various gods', 'foreign gods' or 'household gods'. The most detail is given in 10:6 where we learn that *they* [Israel] *served the Baals and the Ashtoreths, and the gods of Aram, the gods of Sidon, the gods of Moab, the gods of the Ammonites and the gods of the Philistines*, and *the gods of the Amorites* are also mentioned specifically in 6:10.

Baal is a general term, meaning 'lord', which apparently came to be used for a range of Canaanite gods, hence the appropriate use on a number of occasions (e.g. 2:11; 3:7; 10:10) of the plural 'the Baals'. There is specific mention of *Baal-Berith* in 8:33, probably popular with the Israelites because of syncretistic confusion given the meaning of the name as 'Lord of the Covenant', but the writers very clearly distinguish this god from Yahweh. Much of what we know about Baal comes from the discovery of the ancient city of Ugarit, at Ras Shamra in Syria in 1929. Texts found there speak of Baal in the singular. Because of its more northerly position, we can't be certain of whether this was representative of the whole Canaanite pantheon. However, if it was, then it seems that in the area that Israel was seeking to take over, either the Baals were local ways of speaking of the same deity or the Baal cult had itself become corrupted in that area. From Judges we might gather that the Baals were fertility gods, but the key issue for the writers seems to have been that they were not Yahweh and did not have the power of Yahweh.

The Baals are closely associated with two goddesses; Judges 6 25–30 speaks several times of Asherah poles, and the Ashtoreths (interestingly again in Judges referred to only in the plural) are mentioned in 2:13 and 10:6. Asherah is known elsewhere as Athirat, and it is generally assumed that Ashtoreth is the Hebrew way of referring to Astarte or Athtart. As Curtis puts it, 'The form of the name doubtless being a deliberate distortion of the name of the Canaanite goddess by the substitution of the latter part of the name of the vowels of the Hebrew word *bōšet* (shameful thing), thereby not simply naming her, but making a judgement on her' (Curtis 2005: 141). It is possible that the use of the plural is referring in a general way to all female deities. The writers were not sexist in their condemnation of 'other gods'! It would be impossible to tell from Judges just how Asherah poles functioned or indeed what form the worship of any of these deities took, although temples of Baal-Berith and Dagon are mentioned.

4. Geographical background

All the activity within Judges takes place within a fairly small area of the Middle East. Most of this is centred on areas within modern-day Israel but occasionally moves out into the northern area of what is now Lebanon and possibly also the south-western side of modern Syria, the eastern area across the Jordan into what is now the nation of Jordan and to some areas, in the west, now largely inhabited by Palestinians. The area consists of the two major ranges of hill country, in the east of Israel running right down the southern half of the country, and in the central northern area between the Lebanese coastal plain and the northern part of the fairly wide Jordan valley. That valley runs in the east of Israel from north of Dan right down to the Dead Sea. Between the northern and southern mountains is the valley of the River Kishon crossing the country from east to west.

Some of the towns mentioned still exist today using names already known and mentioned in Judges (e.g. Jerusalem and Hebron).

Others exist today with a different name, or are clearly known from literary or archaeological evidence (e.g. Dan and Shiloh). However, the identity of many of the place names mentioned cannot be identified with any certainty. There may be several possibilities that could be investigated, but the only real conclusion can be that we are not sure. Often we know the general area but not necessarily the precise place. In a commentary of this size there is not sufficient space to discuss all the possibilities. Where the exact location seems important to the meaning or significance of the story, there will be discussion within the commentary. However, for wider discussion of the identity of the places named, larger commentaries or Bible atlases will need to be consulted.

5. Theological themes

Any examination of books in the Bible demands some recognition of what is sometimes called the 'interpretative spiral'. Our understanding of the Bible as a whole depends on a preliminary understanding of the individual books. Our understanding of books or sections of books depends on a preliminary understanding of the individual accounts of which they are comprised. Our understanding of accounts depends on a preliminary understanding of the individual paragraphs and verses. However, it is also true to say that our understanding of individual verses and paragraphs depends on a preliminary understanding of the accounts that they make up. Our understanding of identifiable accounts depends on a preliminary understanding of the books and sections of books in which they are found. And our understanding of those books depends in some way on a preliminary understanding of the nature, purpose and meaning of the Bible as a whole. Thus, any growth in understanding involves a constant moving from the individual verse or passage to its wider context. As we look at the book of Judges, for example, our appreciation of any broad theme or motif can only be grasped from an examination of the smaller sections. But with that appreciation we can then re-examine the smaller sections with new eyes and may then gain fresh insights which in turn may influence our view of the book as a whole. This means that consideration of theological themes is always to some extent tentative. Looking at some of these themes before a close examination of the individual passages may be helpful in the interpretation of those passages. However, it is clear that our assessment of the validity of the themes must also be reassessed after the passages have been considered in their own right. Having said that, one has to start somewhere, and as there is widespread agreement that the writers of Judges have a major concern for the relationship between Yahweh and his covenant people, we will consider here some of the ideas that convey the portrayal found in the book concerning the nature of God, the people, and the relationship between them.

a. The nature of God

It is clear from the very first verse that Judges shares the presuppositions about Yahweh that are found throughout Scripture. First, God is: the existence of God is taken for granted throughout the book. There is no hint of questioning regarding this. Second, God reveals himself: he is, in some sense, knowable. It is possible to discover something of who God is and to know what he requires. Third, God is transcendent: he is, in some sense, unknowable. It is certainly not possible to control or manipulate Yahweh and not even to fully understand his nature or actions. Fourth, God relates: Yahweh is not just looking for mindless obedience; he is looking for relationship. He wants Israel and Israelites to follow his purposes so that they can relate to him, can indeed be his covenant people.

Expanding on these presuppositions, we see in Judges that God communicates. He will respond to questions asked of him, although the nature of his response to such questions is seen as depending on the reason for the request and the attitude and behaviour of those asking. God does have a special relationship with Israel – they are *his people* in a way that other peoples are not. God has given *the land* to Israel and will, given the proviso above relating to their attitude and behaviour, assist and support them in the securing of that land. God is powerful and able to influence events both within and outside the land that he has given to Israel. However, Israel's cooperation with God is presented as essential if the promise of land being given to them is to be fulfilled. It is clearly not just an unconditional promise. God has purposes for, and makes demands on, Israel and on the tribes, families and individuals that make up the nation. God holds Israel and Israelites accountable for their behaviour and will allow the consequences of that behaviour to stand. Being in covenant relationship with Yahweh is never seen as an automatic ticket to prosperity and success. It is in a very real sense a relationship that involves responsibilities on both sides. Having said that, Yahweh is clearly presented as desiring good for his people and as being ready to respond not only to repentance and faith, but also to expressed and acknowledged need. God's communication with Israel involves calling. He calls all Israelites to love and serve him. He also calls individual Israelites to fulfil particular responsibilities on his behalf, acting as 'redeemers' to reflect his nature as a redeeming God. God's concern for righteousness and covenant obedience is clear. However, certain events described in Judges clearly do not evidence the concerns for community loyalty, justice or for the weak that we see reflected in other parts of Scripture. However, on some of these instances God seems to be absent. He is not described as intervening, or even mentioned at all. So much so that one is reminded of Isaiah's cry: 'Truly you are a God who has been hiding himself, the God and Saviour of Israel' (Isa. 45:15). Perhaps on these occasions the writers of Judges are making a deliberate point in not mentioning God, saying, by implication at least, that God has nothing to do with this.

b. The nature and responsibilities of the nation

In fact, to speak of a 'nation' during the period covered in the book of Judges is somewhat problematic. In modern times, for a nation to be fully recognized as such, there needs to be clear and acknowledged geographical boundaries, an effective national government and a leadership system that is acknowledged and accepted throughout the land and also recognized outside the land. In this instance none of these things applies. There was no nationally recognized leadership and indeed no form of national governance. The boundaries, where they could be identified, were still very fluid. At one point it was popular to describe Israel as an amphictyony, or tribal league, but there is no evidence of any official or contracted agreement between the different tribes. It is clear that the writers of Judges were well aware of all these things. They may be looking back from a later time, but there is no anachronistic presentation of a united nation under a united, or indeed any form of, national government or even truly national leader. Having said that, the writers of Judges were convinced that Israel was an identifiable unit consisting of the descendants of Jacob. There is no doubt that a clear distinction is made between those who belonged to Israel and *the people of this land* (2:2) or the *nations* (2:21; 3:1) who lived alongside them but were not part of them. The terms *Israel* and *Israelites* are used almost 150 times across the different sections of the book. The whole people are seen as coming together on a number of occasions. God addresses Israel, and speaks of the fact that although he would never break his covenant with them (2:1), they were under judgment because they, corporately (i.e. as a nation), had *violated the covenant I ordained for their ancestors and* [had] *not listened to me* (2:20). The term *covenant* occurs only in chapter 2 and in 20:27 where the presence of the *ark of the covenant* is noted. However, covenant language, for example, references to Israel as Yahweh's people and Yahweh as Israel's God and to Israel's responsibilities before God, occur throughout the book. It is clear that the writers saw Israel's nature as a covenant people as very significant. With or without a national government Israel were seen as corporately relating to God as his people and corporately held responsible for living in a way that reflected their identity as the people of Yahweh, worshipping only him and obeying his commands. They are corporately held accountable for their failure to do any of those things. Because at this stage taking over the land was crucial to the ongoing existence of the people of Israel, the main functions of the nation are presented in military terms, particularly but not exclusively in section 1 (1:1 – 3:6) of the book. However, the requirements for the people as a whole to give exclusive allegiance to Yahweh, to avoid making covenants with other peoples and to live in a way that demonstrates justice and loyalty, are also clearly presented.

c. The nature and responsibilities of the tribes

We have seen that the writers of Judges are concerned to present the responsibilities of Israel as a whole, but there is also evidence throughout the book of their interest in the different tribes. Over the years, questions have been raised about the historicity of the accounts of Israel's entry into the Promised Land and about whether or how far we can be sure about the origin of the different tribes. However, this is not the place to deal with those questions.[4] As far as the writers of Judges are concerned, the tribes consist of the descendants of the twelve sons of Jacob. Ephraim and Manasseh are usually pictured as separate tribes, although there are two references to the 'house of Joseph' in chapter 1. All of the tribes except for Simeon and Gad are specifically mentioned, although in some cases there are a lot more references than in others. Only Judah and Ephraim are named in all three sections. Asher, Manasseh, Naphtali and Zebulun are referred to in sections 1 and 2, Benjamin and Dan in sections 2 and 3, Reuben and Issachar come only in section 2, and Levi only in section 3 and then only in relation to individual Levites. The reason for the omission of Simeon and Gad is not clear (see p. 61).

Unlike Israel as a whole, the individual tribes are pictured as having an organizational and even governmental structure based on the family system. It is recognized that there are tribal leaders or elders who are apparently able to make decisions on behalf of that tribe. Having said that, the tribe as a whole is seen as having responsibility for occupying the land given to that tribe by God and for living in the land in accordance with the pattern given to them in the covenant commands. The tribe as a whole is held accountable for any failure to do what is required of them. Although the primary responsibility of each tribe is for life in its own area, there is clearly an expectation of loyalty to, and support for, the other tribes. The various discussions of, and questions to, God as to which tribe should *go first* indicates the need for, and existence of, intertribal cooperation. If one tribe is struggling, there is an expectation that they can send for others to back them up, and that failure to provide such support is unacceptable. The final set of narratives concerning the actions of the tribe of Benjamin shows that there is a supposition that tribes will be held responsible for unacceptable behaviour within their ranks. But they also show that where a tribe fails to take action against individual 'criminals' or where a tribe steps out of line

---

4. Larger commentaries, such as Butler 2009 and Webb 2012, do provide details of such arguments.

and acts in ways that are condemned by the rest, then the gathered tribes are, in a way similar to that of the modern United Nations, clearly expected to take disciplinary action. Failure to ensure justice, worship God exclusively and complete tasks assigned by God are instances of such unacceptable behaviour.

d. The nature and responsibilities of individuals

Section 1 of Judges is concerned primarily with the people as a whole and with the tribal responsibility to take over the land. However, even here there is clear recognition that the people and tribes of Israel do consist of individuals. The inclusion of the story of Caleb, Achsah and Othniel reminds us that the lives of individual Israelites are noteworthy and that how individuals behave does count. Section 2 concentrates on leaders and the influence and effect those leaders have on the nation, but again there are many references to individuals who are not necessarily involved in leadership. Section 3 concentrates on the influence and effect that specific individuals can have on the life of the nation. From all three sections we learn that individuals, as part of the covenant community, are also held responsible for living out their lives in line with covenant requirements. They are assumed to have responsibilities towards God and towards fellow Israelites. Each person is expected to give God obedience and exclusive worship. It seems to be taken for granted, for example in the story of Samson's parents in Judges 13, that all people have the ability to hear from God and the responsibility to listen to his word, whether it comes via an angelic messenger or through knowledge of covenant law. Each person is required to act towards others, both within and outside their own tribes and families, with justice and loyalty. The book recognizes that this does not always, and maybe does not often, happen. Sometimes there is explicit comment on this, but the structure of the narratives also provides evidence of the writers' concern to show that the way they were living was not how life in Israel was supposed to be lived.

e. The nature and responsibilities of leadership

One could argue that leadership is a central motif within the book of Judges. The main second section focuses almost completely on the life and work of a range of leaders, although these have varying

roles and spheres of influence. Neither the first nor the third section
mentions any individual leader apart from the deceased Joshua, but
they both take for granted the existence of tribal *elders* (Judg.
2:7) who are able to make both military and political decisions for their
tribes. Section 1 prepares for the central section by setting out the
pattern of Yahweh-appointed 'judges' who served for their lifetime
but had very little lasting influence on the life, behaviour and attitudes
of the people as a whole. It thus creates questions in the mind of
readers so that in the second section they are looking out for whether
any particular judge can be seen to have a lasting effect on the nation.

The method of appointing tribal leaders is not discussed. One
can assume that this is because it is determined solely on lineage,
but the writers of Judges are clearly more interested in the general
approach of the tribes as a whole than in the way in which any
'power' within the tribe is exercised. Whatever the leaders did and
how they did it is apparently significant only insofar as it helped or
caused each tribe to fulfil its responsibilities. These are presented as,
first, military responsibilities in the taking over of the land assigned
to that tribe and, second, religious and social responsibilities in
the living within that land in accordance with their covenant with
Yahweh.

The term 'judge' has been traditionally used to translate the
Hebrew word (*šōpĕṭîm*), used in Judges 2:16–19 and 3:10. In the light
of this, all the leaders described in section 2 have been known as
judges, hence the name of the book! However, particularly in recent
years the appropriateness of that term has been questioned. Only
Deborah is pictured as functioning as judge in the way one might
normally understand it, that is, as giving judgment in a court situation
or mediating in disputes. Various terms have been suggested as
an alternative, such as 'deliverer' or 'saviour'. It is interesting that
the writers themselves use different terms in different parts of the
narrative, and therefore perhaps it is best to use the general term
'leader'. There seems little doubt that the writers see all of the twelve
leaders as having been sent by Yahweh. Although none of the
accounts of the minor 'judges' gives any indication of how they
were called, both Shamgar and Tola are said to have *saved* Israel. Of
the six major 'judges', Othniel, Ehud and Gideon are explicitly sent
by Yahweh, and this is also strongly implied in the accounts of

Deborah and Samson. Jephthah is pictured as appointed by local 'elders', but the account is clear about God's involvement in Israel's victories at this point. The major area of responsibility for these leaders was military; they brought 'deliverance' from foreign powers who sought either to take the land that Israel already possessed or to prevent them taking over the land God had given them. However, the background narratives constantly make clear that the way in which the various leaders behaved was important and that justice, loyalty and worship of Yahweh, and Yahweh alone, were responsibilities for the leader to observe and to inculcate among those they led. The writers were well aware that this did not always happen, but that does not change the fact that this was their expectation, or at least hope, of how leadership in Israel ought to have been. There is no doubt that one can find both positive and negative instances of leadership in Judges, and it may be that the authors are intending to show how God can carry out his work and accomplish his purposes by using human people and structures that are fundamentally flawed (cf. Olson: 2004).

6. Ethical issues facing twenty-first-century readers

Cultural assumptions
There is no doubt that our ethics are influenced by many factors. Christians in general like to feel that the Bible is the primary influence on their ethics. Undoubtedly, it is a very important influence, but the different approaches taken by different churches in different countries and at different times is evidence of other factors at work. Economic, social and philosophical assumptions stemming from the attitudes of our individual cultures make a huge difference to our ability to hear what the Bible is actually saying: hence the possibility of apparently sincere Christians fundamentally disagreeing over whether the Bible as a whole supports or condemns apartheid, slavery, capital punishment, smoking, homosexual practice, the involvement of women in leadership, and so on. It is important for us all to seek to identify and assess our own cultural assumptions about class, race, money and values in general. However, it is also important when reading biblical narratives that we take time to consider the cultural assumptions of the writers and the society of

which they write before we make judgments about what is being said. It is vital not to assume that Judges, for example, will have any answers to questions that we might be asking but that neither the characters in the narratives nor the writers had ever considered. The reaction of many modern readers when approaching Judges for the first time is shock. It describes dreadful behaviour, dreadful attitudes and dreadful relationships. How can such a book be included in the Bible? Is this really telling us what God is like? Does he really approve of this kind of violence, rape and murder? Often the solution is either not to read Judges at all or only ever to concentrate on the 'nice bits'! However, it is important that we face up to these difficulties in a way that acknowledges the issues honestly and also takes seriously the context of the material. Of course, our questions are often anachronistic and would not have occurred to early readers, but they do occur to modern readers and are therefore worth consideration even though we must take care not to push the text into saying things that the writers had no intention of putting across. There are many questions that we could look at, but here we will consider just six. Further comments will be made in the commentary section when these issues arise within the text, but it may be helpful to consider some of the implications at this stage. Accepting the position that Judges was written not to describe a God-approved way of life, but was intended in fact to show that how Israel were living life at that time was not how it was supposed to be, does make a difference to our understanding of what Judges might be implying about the issues raised here.

a. The takeover of previously occupied land
Disputes over land are complex. How far back does one go? Should land that has been lived in by one tribe or family for many generations be given back to the tribe or family from whom it was taken many years or even centuries earlier? Should compensation be paid? Had the previous 'owners' taken the land from someone else in the first place? What does it mean to 'own' land anyway? Whose laws should be applied? The questions that might be important in one time and culture may seem irrelevant or unimportant to another. In the time of the book of Judges it was taken for granted that land was something to be fought for, and it was obvious to them that the

conqueror would take possession. Jephthah's message to the Ammonite king (11:14–27) sets out the agreed understanding clearly: 'Whatever your god enables you to conquer is yours, and whatever our God enables us to conquer is ours' – end of story. As far as the writers were concerned, their God, Yahweh, was powerful in all lands and had the right to give whatever land he wanted to his people Israel. The question that disturbs modern readers – 'Is that fair?' – was not of great importance to them. The question for them was rather: 'If we have not conquered the land, does that mean that Yahweh is not as powerful as we have been taught?' The writers go out of their way to show that Israel were unsuccessful in their task of taking over the land because of their own rebellion against Yahweh and their failure to carry out the responsibilities that he had given them to live as his covenant people.

Nevertheless, there is an understanding that Israel did not have the right to take over whatever land they wanted. Some land had been given to other peoples, and no attempt was to be made to conquer those lands. It is interesting that although Jephthah states that the Ammonites will take *what your god Chemosh gives you*, the rest of his argument strongly implies that it is Yahweh who decides who will have a particular area of land, both within and outside Israel. The story of the Danites' takeover of land in the north (18:27ff.) makes no explicit statement, but it is told in such a way that the implication that the writers did not approve of what had gone on cannot be avoided. Elsewhere it is made clear that the gifting of the land of Canaan to the Israelites was not an arbitrary choice that ignored the rights of the original inhabitants. Deuteronomy 9:4–6, for example, makes it very clear that the reason why the Canaanites were to be driven from the land was not because of any right or righteousness on Israel's part but as a punishment for 'the wickedness of these nations'. The gift to Israel and the punishment of the nations were integrally connected. So although Judges itself has little to say about the question of 'fairness', the issue is addressed elsewhere.

b. The mistreatment of women

There are several accounts in Judges that indicate that in the society at that time women's rights, opinions and welfare were, in general, seen as of very little account. In chapter 11 Jephthah's love for his daughter is clear, but there is no question in his mind that the fulfilling of his own vow overrode any possible rights that she might have. Chapter 13 demonstrates the attitude that the testimony of women could not be trusted. Samson's father prayed that the angel would come again so that he, and not just his wife, could hear the message. In chapter 14 it is taken for granted that it will be the male members of the family who make decisions about the various women who were involved with Samson. Chapter 19 shows the way in which the Levite's concubine was treated as an object, and any offence is presumed to be against him rather than against her; and chapter 21 describes what in effect was the rape and kidnap of various women being sanctioned by the authorities in order to satisfy the perceived needs of men.

If readers take the view that the society described is an ideal, God-ordered and God-sanctioned society, then the implication that Judges, and by inference God himself, sanctions the abuse of women cannot be avoided. However, there is little doubt that the writers, while clearly aware of, and realistic about, the attitude to women prevalent at that time, on several occasions provide a critique of that attitude. On some of these occasions it is possible that this critique is made incidentally rather than by conscious decision, but at other times it is very hard to see it as anything other than deliberate. The angel's refusal to accept Manoah's attempt to ignore the testimony of his wife clearly falsifies that particular attitude. The way in which the stories of the concubine's rape and the search for Benjaminite wives are told clearly indicates the writers' view that what happened was not acceptable. Indeed, one could argue (see p. 203) that if the primary intention of Judges is to describe Israel as living in a way that was 'not how it was meant to be', then the epitome of that unacceptable behaviour is the mistreatment of women as depicted in the final chapters. Judges describes unacceptable behaviour and unacceptable cultural attitudes. Moreover, given the descriptions of the leadership skills and initiatives taken by women such as Achsah, Deborah, Jael and Manoah's wife, it is very apparent that the book of Judges cannot be viewed as justifying the violence against women or even the negative attitude towards women that is seen so clearly in the events described.

c. Forced labour
Another problem for modern readers is the issue of forced labour, or slavery. It is taken for granted in Judges that any outsiders who remained in a land taken over by another group would expect to be used in forced labour. Those involved might not like it very much, but it is apparent that no-one in the whole region at that time would have questioned the ethics of the practice. To introduce our questions into the text here is clearly anachronistic. Unlike the previous two issues we have looked at, there is no indication that the writers ever critiqued this attitude. We know that Deuteronomy introduces questions regarding the treatment of foreigners where both positive and negative approaches are mentioned. On the one hand, foreigners are to be destroyed and no alliances made with them. On the other hand, foreigners living in the land are to be treated well. If the writers were part of, or influenced by, the Deuteronomic School, then they must have been aware of the tensions between these approaches. However, Judges is concerned with the setting up of the original covenant community and not with how an already well-established community should function. The emphasis is therefore on how 'foreigners' can be prevented from undermining the setting up of the community rather than on how they can be utilized in the ongoing running of the community. One certainly cannot use Judges to support the abolition of slavery, but neither would it be appropriate to use it to support the use of forced labour in other contexts.

d. The excessive use of violence
Throughout history there have been disagreements about what level of violence is appropriate in a situation of war. Are there ever circumstances when civilians can be legitimate targets? Can torture ever be justified? Does the end justify the means, even if the means is clearly not acceptable? Having said that, most modern readers of Judges would agree that the level of violence, both that perpetrated on and by Israel and Israelites, is excessive. Again one could argue that the writers tell the stories in a way that encourages readers to ask questions about whether or not this level of violence is acceptable, with the strong implication being that it is not – particularly in the Samson narratives. However, no explicit answers are provided

for modern questions. The nature of biblical narratives is such that readers are often left with the responsibility of assessing whether or not the actions and events described are in accord with the revealed will of God. On this particular issue one needs to look elsewhere in Scripture to determine what that revealed will is – of the God who is both a mighty warrior and the God of peace.

e. Diplomatic deceit

Another problem raised by modern readers in regard to the Judges narratives is the acceptability or otherwise of diplomatic deceit, that is, the telling of lies to an enemy in order to achieve victory. Again, there is no indication that the writers even saw this as an issue. For them, as for Ehud and other participants in such deceits, there was apparently no problem. Enemies, those seeking to prevent God's purposes from being achieved – in this case the full possession by Israel of the land given to them by God – do not deserve truth. With regard to this particular dilemma, it is not clear that any detailed answer can be found elsewhere in Scripture. The importance of truth is abundantly clear, but it is harder to be certain whether this means that any lie is automatically outside of God's will. Certainly, as far as Judges is concerned, the problem lies on the table!

f. The priority of vows over righteousness

Does the importance of keeping vows take priority over any evil consequence that the vow might initiate? There is nothing wrong with making vows! Leviticus (22:18–25; 27:1–33) and Numbers (6:1–21; 30:1–16) explain clearly that although vows are voluntary – that is, there is in general no obligation to make them – once made, it is very important that they are fulfilled. Making a vow is a serious thing. Having said that, it is also made clear that where a vow is over-ridden by someone perceived as having authority over the vower – for example, a father or a husband – then the one making the vow is not to be blamed. And if an inappropriate vow is made, for example, to bring into the temple money gained in prostitution (Deut. 23:18) or to offer a defective animal to be sacrificed (Lev. 22:21), then it is not to be fulfilled. In the Ancient Near East in general, vows were commonly used as a way of bribing the deity – in effect, the vower is saying, 'If you give me this, I will do that for

you.' The way in which vows are spoken of throughout the Penta-
teuch shows clearly that such an approach is completely inappropriate
in relation to Yahweh: vows are freewill offerings, not bribes!
Yahweh's actions will not be determined by presents offered to him.
However, it is apparent that in the common life of Israel vows were
sometimes used in this way. Certainly, the cultural assumptions of
the local society, that to fail to keep a vow brought shame upon the
vower, were fully accepted. So what should happen when a vow is
made that has unforeseen consequences – for example, Jephthah's
vow (11:31) or the vow of the Israelite tribes concerning Benjamin
(21:1, 5)? The writers again do not explicitly discuss the issue, but it
is arguable that the stories are told in a way that encourages the
readers to ask the questions. There is a strong implication that
the actions taken in order to fulfil the vows were in themselves
wrong. Interestingly, in 1 Samuel 14:24ff. when Saul makes a foolish
vow, it is overridden by his army and there are apparently no negative
consequences to this overriding. One is tempted to argue that the
writers of Judges would have approved of the army's approach!

It is worth restating at this point that the concerns which so
challenge us today are different from those of both the writers and
the early readers of Judges. It would be wrong simply to take the
stories of Judges and assume that the huge cultural gaps between
the situations they describe and our own world can be ignored. The
text does not always say the things we would like it to say, or directly
answer the questions we would like it to, and it would also be wrong
to make it do so. However, that does not mean that Judges has
nothing to teach us, even on these issues, and the fact that the stories
do raise such issues for modern readers adds to the challenge
of how we should react to the text and whether and how far our
understanding should be influenced by what we find in the rest of
Scripture.

ANALYSIS

1. INTRODUCTION (1:1 – 3:6)
A. Introductory overview/setting the scene (1:1 – 3:6)
  i. Initial military overview (1:1–36)
    a. The southern campaign (1:1–21)
    b. The northern campaigns (1:22–36)
  ii. Initial spiritual overview (2:1 – 3:6)
    a. The angel's rebuke (2:1–5)
    b. The first generation (2:6–9)
    c. The downward spiral (2:10 – 3:6)

2. THE JUDGES (3:7 – 16:31)
A. Introductory comments
B. Othniel (3:7–11)
C. Ehud (3:12–30)
D. Shamgar (3:31)
E. Deborah (4:1 – 5:31)
  i. The story (4:1–23)
  ii. The song (5:1–31)
F. Gideon and Abimelek (6:1 – 9:57)
  i. Gideon: his achievements and his failures (6:1 – 8:35)
    a. The start of a new era (6:1–40)
    b. Gideon's campaign (7:1–25)
    c. Emerging problems (8:1–35)
  ii. Abimelek (9:1–56)

G. Two 'minor' leaders (10:1–5)
      i. Tola (10:1–2)
     ii. Jair (10:3–5)
H. Jephthah (10:6 – 12:7)
      i. Preface (10:6–18)
     ii. Jephthah is appointed (11:1–11)
    iii. An attempt to find a solution through diplomacy
         (11:12–28)
     iv. Victory and vow (11:29–40)
      v. Problems with Ephraim (12:1–7)
I. Three more 'minor' leaders (12:8–15)
      i. Ibzan (12:8–10)
     ii. Elon (12:11–12)
    iii. Abdon (12 13–15)
J. Samson (13:1 – 16:31)
      i. Annunciation and birth of Samson (13:1–24)
     ii. Samson's marriage (14:1–20)
    iii. Samson's revenge (15:1–20)
     iv. Samson's downfall and final feat (16:1–31)

3. STORIES OF INDIVIDUALS: EXEMPLIFYING
THE TIMES (17:1 – 21:25)
A. Introductory comments
B. Stories related to Micah (17:1 – 18:31)
      i. Micah's idols and priests (17:1–13)
     ii. The Danites take Micah's priest (18:1–31)
C. Stories related to the Levite from Ephraim (19:1 – 21:25)
      i. The Levite's concubine (19:1–28)
     ii. A search for justice (19:29 – 20:48)
    iii. The salvaging of the tribe of Benjamin (21:1–25)

COMMENTARY

I. INTRODUCTION

A. Introductory overview/setting the scene (1:1 – 3:6)

This is the first of the three major sections which form the book of Judges. The central section of the book describes the lives of, and activities related to, specific leaders, and the third section looks at cycles of stories set in motion by ordinary Israelites. This first section provides an introduction to what is to come by painting the big picture. We are given a broad idea of what was going on for the nation as a whole during this period between the death of Joshua and the introduction of the monarchy. In one sense we see a story of failure. It begins by describing the failure of the various armed forces to complete the occupation of the land that Joshua had initiated, and continues by describing the nation's moral failures. Right from the beginning the writers want us to understand that what they are describing was not how it was supposed to have been. This is not how God intended life in the land to be for his chosen covenant people. However, at the same time we are given room for hope and encouragement. There are individuals who are living in the way that they were meant to, and there are signs that, in spite of their failures, God was still active among them. The writers are more interested in providing an overall impression than in the precise details of chronology, geography or the terminology relating to people groups. Perhaps because of this, some elements, for example the mention of the death of Joshua, are repeated because of their relevance to both parts of this introductory section.

i. Initial military overview (1:1–36)
a. *The southern campaign (1:1–21)*

Context
The book of Joshua gave details of the first stage of the conquest of the land and the assigning of the various regions to different tribes within Israel. However, it is clear that the land was still populated by earlier inhabitants and that each tribe was responsible for completing the conquest of their own particular areas. The account relating to the southern tribes of Simeon (whose territory was contained within that of Judah), Benjamin and in particular of Judah occupies twenty-one verses and is much more detailed than the rest. This might indicate that the writers came from the south and had access to more detailed documentation relating to, and perhaps more interest in, that area. The reference in verse 1 to Joshua's death serves two purposes. It asserts that Joshua is not to be held responsible for what is to come and emphasizes that there was now no central government or armed forces leadership. Each tribe had to take responsibility for their own fate. However, as we see on a number of occasions throughout the book, the tribes were sometimes called to assemble together for a variety of purposes, usually military (see the discussion of national identity on pp. 25–28), and it seems that is what happened here. The theme of this introductory chapter has sometimes been seen as Israel's early battles. However, as Butler (2009: 17) points out, the story of Achsah and the information given in verses 16 and 26 do not fit that theme. On the other hand, they do add to our understanding of the big picture and the impression of interrupted failure that the writers seem to want to leave with us.

Comment

1:1–7. It would have been disadvantageous to all parties if too many campaigns were being undertaken at the same time, so, as their question in verse 1 indicates, they decided to take it in turns. Boling (1975: 53) suggests that they asked the wrong question,¹ as they should have recognized that it was God himself who went *up first to fight*, but God's response in verse 2 gives no indication that their question was unacceptable. The initial distribution of the land had been determined by lot, 'as the LORD had commanded through Moses' (Josh. 14:2; cf. Num. 34:13ff.). It is possible that the same method was used to determine Yahweh's answer in this instance as well, although the additional information that God has *given the land into* Judah's hands may imply that a different method, yielding more information than a simple yes or no, was used. The means of determining God's response to their request is not specified here.² Whatever the method, Judah was given the first chance, the assurance of victory not only bolstering their confidence but also providing a reminder that the land had been given by God in the first place and that he was involved in the process.

The Judeans sought the cooperation of the Simeonites to take their combined territories. For the most part, the account of the Judean campaign gives basic details of a number of attacks, with extra information provided in one or two cases. The first attack on

---

1. He points out that the same question was asked in 10:18 but in the wrong place (i.e. not where the ark was), but 20:28 shows the right question in the right place with the right attitude.

2. Other known methods of determining God's will involve the Urim and Thummim (Lev. 8:8; Ezra 2:63; Neh. 7:65) or the ephod (1 Sam. 21:9; 23:9; 30:7). We don't really know how either of these worked or even exactly what they were, but we do know that the Urim and Thummim were incorporated into the garments of the high priest and the ephod seems to have been kept within a priestly context. It is worth noting that although the ephod seems to have been in common use for consulting God in the time of David, the only references to an ephod in Judges are to the idols made by Gideon (Judg. 8:27) and Micah (Judg. 17:5 –18:20).

Bezek[3] was clearly successful. 'Canaanite' is a general term including a range of groups, but the reference to Perizzites (v. 4) and later to Jebusites (v. 21) and Amorites (v. 35) helps to create a picture of a land that was occupied by a number of different ethnic groups in a collection of fairly loose alliances. The treatment of Adoni-Bezek (vv. 5–6; his name means 'the lord of Bezek') seems strange. To cut off the thumbs and big toes would render the person completely incapable of using weapons or of being involved in any kind of fight or battle, but although this was common in the Ancient Near East generally, there is no mention of this kind of punishment being used elsewhere in Israel. Perhaps the record of Adoni-Bezek's own reaction is provided in order to explain that this was simply a matter of applying his own system to himself. He sees his defeat as being brought about by *God*, but whether he means the God of Israel, or a deity of the seventy kings he had disabled, cannot be determined. It is also unclear why he was not actually killed, but maybe a humiliated leader was seen as a more effective way to subdue the rest of his people than a dead leader (cf. the discussion of the Philistines' treatment of the captured Samson, p. 174). Whether he died from his wounds or at a much later stage is not clarified.

8. The references to Jerusalem create some difficulty. Joshua 15:63 states that the Jebusites could not be dislodged from there, and 1:21 confirms that their expulsion was not achieved at this time either. Jerusalem is in the territory of Benjamin but fairly close to the Judean border. It may be that the name was applied to a wider area than the actual town, and part of this area was taken by the Judeans at this time and used as a base for their wider campaigns. It is also possible that a reference to the Judean headquarters was anachronistically described as Jerusalem by some later editor or copyist. The suggestion that the city was taken and burned by the Judeans, but later reclaimed by the Jebusites, is difficult to reconcile with verse 21, although the lack of chronological clues does make it hard to estimate any potential time gaps.

---

3. See discussion on geographical names and places in Introduction, pp. 16–23.

9–15. These verses are repeated from the account in Joshua 15:13–19. Part of the repetition is word for word, although the Joshua account tells us that it was Caleb himself who took Hebron and defeated Sheshai, Ahiman and Talmai, whereas here, although Caleb's leadership of the attacking force seems clear, the victory is ascribed to Judah as a whole, rather than personally to Caleb.[4] The change of name of Debir illustrates the writers' interest in such changes (e.g. 1:23; 10:4; 18:12). The point here is perhaps to emphasize the transfer of power within the land: new names indicate new ownership. The account of military campaigns is interrupted by the reference to Caleb's daughter. It is possible that this reference to Achsah is incidental, included here simply because the writers wanted to incorporate the description of the conquest of the Hebron area, and this story was in the earlier account that they were using. However, given the structure of Judges as a whole, it seems much more likely that this story is deliberately placed here to stand as a contrast to the treatment of Jephthah's daughter in chapter 11 and in particular to the treatment of women in the final chapter of the book. In chapter 21, after a range of accounts showing just how low Israel had sunk, the climax – the lowest of the lows, as it were – was the appalling mistreatment of daughters from Jabesh Gilead and Shiloh. Judges constantly provides us with an overall picture of complete failure alongside a few highlights, showing by examples that it was possible for people to live in a good way and that there were some who took the opportunity to do just that. Because of Achsah's story we know from the beginning that in spite of the later horrific examples, some daughters did receive good treatment. Of course, it would be possible to argue that a culture that encourages the giving of daughters as a reward for service is, in itself, somewhat twisted. However, we cannot tell what lies behind this particular instance, nor whether Othniel undertook the task of capturing Kiriath Sepher because a relationship between himself and Achsah

---

4. Caleb's father is described as a Kenizzite (Num. 32:12; Josh. 14:6), which would imply an origin among the Canaanite peoples (cf. Gen. 15:19), but there is never any question about Caleb's identity as a member of the tribe of Judah (cf. Num. 13:6).

was already developing. In either case, although the book shows
both awareness and strong criticism of what is presented as mistreatment of daughters, there is no hint that Achsah's marriage is
seen as deserving criticism. The writers here clearly did not share
today's cultural sensitivities, which perhaps makes the critique of
the cultural assumptions of their own time even more forceful. The
wording of the phrase usually translated as *when she got off her donkey*
is unclear,[5] as is the reason for including such specific information.
Again this may be simply a repetition from the material used in
Joshua 15. However, it is interesting to note that the other reference
to a donkey in Judges[6] is in 19:28 when one is used to transport the
body of the mistreated woman.[7] The suggestion that Caleb's original
gift of land to Achsah was 'inadequate' and her resulting 'disappoint-
ment' led to her 'cunning' response (Fleishman 2006: 354–373) is
clearly negated by Caleb's swift and apparently affectionate further
response. This incidence of Caleb giving land to his daughter (it is
possible, of course, that the legal title for the land passed to Othniel,
but the text states that it was given to Achsah herself) provides
further background to the discussion in Numbers 27 and 36 about
the legality of the giving of land to daughters – although, unlike
Zelophehad, Caleb's children were not all girls (1 Chr. 4:15).

There is a textual issue here relating to who initiated the request
and why. Some Septuagintal versions have 'he urged her' as opposed
to the MT's 'she urged him'. It does not make a lot of difference to
the overall meaning. It seems clear that the one who actually made

---

5. The word for 'getting down' is only found elsewhere in Judg. 4:21,
   apart from the parallel passage in Josh. 15, so the meaning is difficult
   to determine. Having said that, it is worth noting that the translation
   chosen in the NEB, 'she broke wind', has 'not found wide acceptance'
   (Boling 1975: 57).

6. Other than Samson's use of the jawbone of a donkey (15:15).

7. It is worth noting the number of instances like this where links can be
   seen between section 1 and section 3 of the book of Judges. This does
   provide support to the view that the different sections were intended,
   whether by authors or editors, to be seen as a whole (see Introduction,
   pp. 2–3).

the request was Achsah. There may be significance in that the original suggestion was to ask *for a field*, but she eventually asks for *springs of water*, presumably located within a field. In either event, Achsah emerges as a competent and confident woman, the first of several such depicted within the book of Judges.

16–21. The reference in verse 16 to the Kenites, the family of Moses' father-in-law, may similarly be included here to provide a context for Jael (see 4:17–22), an example of another competent woman who was married to Heber the Kenite. The area inhabited by the Kenites, in the Negev region near Arad, is in the territory assigned to Simeon, and that leads neatly on to the reference in verse 17 to the taking of the Simeonite town which became known as Hormah. It is being made clear that the Judeans fulfilled their obligations to the Simeonites by continuing to work together in the conquest of their joint territories. As it later becomes apparent that Gaza, Ashkelon and Ekron remained Philistine cities well into the time of David, it seems that the Septuagintal reading of 'did not take' is more likely to be accurate than the MT's 'took'. However, it is possible that the writers, wanting to emphasize the big picture and to stress the successes of Judah, are at this point conflating time and including territories that were eventually, although not immediately, taken by Judah. There is no doubt that early readers would have been well aware that even for Judah success was neither immediate nor complete, hence perhaps the reference to their failure to take full control of *the plains*. On one level the book of Judges is constantly wrestling with the paradox of Yahweh's presence with, and promises to, Israel, standing alongside Israel's failure in almost every area. Verse 19 sets out that paradox in that we are told in successive sentences that *The LORD was with the men of Judah* and that *they were unable to drive the people from the plains.* There may be deliberate irony in the addition of the opinion that it was because the plains people were equipped with the latest weapons that any failure took place. Perhaps that was the excuse the Judeans gave to themselves, and the writers here are encouraging reflection on the issue. Certainly, the book goes on to place the responsibility for their failure squarely on the shoulders of the Israelites themselves, their lack of trust and their *evil* behaviour (e.g. 2:11–13, 19–21). The repetition of Caleb's success, providing the extra information (already found in Josh. 15) that the three men named in verse 10 were indeed Anakites, stands alongside the failure of the Benjaminites and reinforces the overall picture of constant failure punctuated by occasional successes.

Meaning
This first section is presented without any editorial comment. It simply describes events without assessing the rights and wrongs of what is happening. However, the initial reference to Joshua indicates that a knowledge of how Israel were expected to proceed is presupposed, and there is a strong implication that they had not lived up to those expectations and that such failure was blameworthy. In other words, there is an implicit assumption that the inability to expel the original inhabitants from the land was at least as much, and probably more, 'would not' than 'could not'.

The rest of the book provides many examples not only of the political and military oppression that came from their fellow residents but also of the spiritual and moral influences that turned Israel away from loyalty to Yahweh and to the covenant that he had made with them. The consequences of the failure of the tribes of Israel to obey God at this point are clearly revealed in later sections of the book, but even here the possibility of individuals – like Caleb – not being caught up in the failures of the whole nation is made apparent. What happened to Israel was not, and never had been, inevitable.

b. The northern campaigns (1:22–36)

Context
The final fifteen verses of chapter 1 begin and end with a reference to the house of Joseph, which technically refers only to Ephraim and Manasseh but, as the reference in verse 35 relates to the territory of Dan, appears to be used here as a generic term for all the northern tribes. No reference is made to Gad or Reuben who had been permitted to take territory east of the Jordan and who appear to have met with little resistance, or to Issachar, but all the other northern tribes are mentioned. The level of negativity in this section of the account is even higher, perhaps again indicating that the writers have a stronger interest in, and support for, the south. The only victory described is the conquest of Bethel in Ephraim, perhaps singled out

because of its significance both before and after this time. However, the statement that *the LORD was with* the house of Joseph in this venture makes it clear that the writers are not suggesting that God's interest and support were in any way restricted to the south. Indeed, although a cursory reading might make it appear as if the writers want to present the successes of the south and the failures of the north (see Younger 1995: 75–92), a closer look indicates their clear awareness both that the south failed and the north had successes. It is possible that the intended readers of the final compilation were from the south, and the writers are actually deliberately undermining presuppositions relating to southern superiority that they initially appear to be confirming.

Comment

22–26. Bethel's conquest was made possible by the capture of a local man who betrayed the city in order to save his own family. There are echoes here of the part played by Rahab in the defeat of Jericho, but unlike Rahab who accepted the sovereignty of Yahweh and became a part of the Israelite community (Josh. 2:8–11; 6:25), this man left the area and rebuilt his life well away from any possible retribution. His decision to name his new town after the one he had left was perhaps an attempt to blot out the fact that he was responsible for the destruction of the first Luz.

27–36. For Manasseh (vv. 27–28), Ephraim (v. 29), Zebulun (v. 30), Asher (vv. 31–32),[8] Naphtali (v. 33) and Dan (vv. 34–36), the information given is largely limited to the determination of the original inhabitants to survive and the names of a range of cities and towns that the various tribes were not able to conquer and areas that they were not able to occupy. The location of some of these towns is known, others are harder or impossible to

---

8. P. Guillaume (2001: 131–137) suggests that the mention of Sidon and omission of Tyre in v. 31 indicates that the material must have been produced during the relatively short time (709–677 BC) when Sidon was dominant. However, this depends on the assumption that Tyre must also have been undefeated. The later ascendancy of Tyre makes this a real possibility but by no means a certainty.

identify,[9] but the extensive list helps the writers to convey a sense of frustration and failure. Apart from Bethel, no towns that were conquered are listed, but it is clear that such towns must have existed. We are informed that Manasseh, Zebulun, Naphthali and Dan did become strong enough to subject the remaining locals to *forced labour*, which means they must have eventually developed fairly strong centres of their own. There is no real reason to suppose that the same thing did not happen in Ephraim, Asher or indeed the unmentioned Issachar. But the point is clearly made that Israel was not alone in the land. It is difficult to see why, if Israel was strong enough to subject other local inhabitants to *forced labour*, she was not also able to drive them out. The question certainly arises, as it does with Judah's reference to the difficulty of overcoming chariots, as to whether these are merely excuses. Was the imposition of *forced labour* because they could not drive them out of the land, or a deliberate strategy to take the easy route in maintaining the upkeep of the land? Was the situation that the original inhabitants wanted (*were determined*, v. 35) to stay and it was easier to negotiate and let them stay than it was to fulfil the letter of the instructions Israel had been given by God?

Meaning
Again there is no editorial comment, but the sense that the failure of the northern tribes to occupy the lands assigned to them is even stronger than in the section speaking of the attempts of the southern tribes. It is clear both that God is concerned for all the tribes, northern as well as southern, and will hold all the tribes accountable for their actions. The more negative presentation in this section may indicate that the writers have a bias towards the southern tribes, but it cannot be seen as evidence that God shared that bias.

ii. Initial spiritual overview (2:1 – 3:6)
Context
Whereas chapter 1 concentrates on military issues, this second overview contains a summary of the overall 'state of the nation' in

---

9. See discussion on geographical names and places in Introduction, p. 22.

the period between Joshua and the start of the monarchy, and prepares us for the specific issues and problems described in the second and third major sections. Unlike chapter 1, the editorial perspective here is explicit. The reader is left in no doubt about God's condemnation of Israel and the reasons for it. However, it begins with a specific incident where the time and the place are probably deliberately obscure. This brief passage provides a key to understanding the whole of Judges, as it sets out a rationale for both their successes and their failures. It also helps both ancient and modern readers to understand something of the relationship between God's promises and human response and responsibility in the ongoing life of this people with whom God had made his covenant. There is some question as to whether 2:1–5 belongs to this section or looks back to chapter 1, and there is no scholarly consensus on this point. Judges 2:1–5 certainly provides a context for assessing the information set out in chapter 1 and can therefore perhaps legitimately be seen as an editorial comment on that chapter, but the specific reference to *covenant* in 2:20 also indicates a primary link with the verses that follow.[10] The language of verses 1–5 is sometimes perceived as legal, with the angel bringing a case against Israel. The 'crime' stressed here is not so much that they failed to drive out the occupying peoples, but that they made a covenant with them and in that way betrayed their covenant with Yahweh (see Wilcock 1992: 26). Verses 6–19 provide evidence of that betrayal throughout the entire Judges period. The fact that 2:1–5 are set at the beginning and 2:6–19 cover the whole period indicates the difficulty of working out the timings of both the events themselves and the bringing together of the various elements within the book.[11] Because of the close links between 2:6ff. and the last chapter of Joshua, and because the style here changes to include much more flowing narrative and more critical analysis, this is sometimes seen as the beginning of the book, with the preceding material as 'obviously an interpolation' (Soggin 1981: 31). However, although it seems likely that the two

---

10. There are only three references to *covenant* in Judges, all found in ch. 2, vv. 1, 2 and 20.

11. See Introduction, pp. 2–4, 15–16.

sections were originally different documents, with 2:1–5 perhaps
coming from a third source, there seems little reason to assume that
the final writers did not deliberately place them together in this
particular way to serve their own purposes.

a. The angel's rebuke (2:1–5)
2:1–3. The angel had come up to Bokim from Gilgal. The site of
Bokim is unknown, although it is apparently a place where the Israelite
tribes assembled together. It has been associated with Bethel, partly
because of the naming of the burial place of Rebekah's nurse,
Deborah, near Bethel, as 'the oak of weeping' or *'allôn bakût* (Gen.
35:8). However, although the name Bokim could be related to *bakût*,
there is no real evidence for a link between these places. Gilgal is the
site not far from Jericho where Joshua had made his camp and which
apparently remained his headquarters for all of the early campaigns
at the beginning of the conquest of Canaan. Although the word
'angel' does not occur in Joshua, Joshua 5:13–15 makes reference to
a presumably angelic visitor who reveals himself to be 'the commander
of Yahweh's army', and makes it clear that this does not necessarily
imply that he will automatically be on the side of Israel. The concept
of the angel of Yahweh is often used in the Old Testament to describe
a theophany, or visible experience when God himself visits his people.
Some reject that interpretation here because they find problems with
the concept of the angel of Yahweh travelling from one place to
another – in this case, from Gilgal to Bokim – but that kind of meta-
phorical language is common throughout the Bible and neither
confirms nor refutes the identification of a theophany in this instance.
The implication of the reference to Gilgal is that the writers want
their readers to think back first to Exodus 23:23ff., where the promise
from God is clear: 'My angel will go ahead of you and bring you into
the land of the Amorites, Hittites, Perizzites, Canaanites, Hivites and
Jebusites, and I will wipe them out', but also to the ambiguity of
Joshua 5:14. The mention of the angel's journey emphasizes that God
was with them at that point (i.e. in Gilgal), but also that they could
not take his continuing presence and support for granted.

Judges 1 has specifically mentioned the failure of Israel to wipe
out Amorites, Perizzites, Canaanites and Jebusites. This appearance
of the angel of Yahweh answers the unspoken question: 'Why then

has God failed to deliver on his promises?' The angel's words emphasize that the promise to bring them out of Egypt and into the new land had been kept – they had been brought to Gilgal. He also confirms that God had promised never to be the one who broke the covenant between himself and Israel. However, part of the covenant was that they should give him exclusive allegiance. There were to be no alliances with the people already occupying the land and certainly no tolerance of their religions. This had simply not happened. Almost from the beginning they had been paying at least lip service to the local gods as a perceived necessary means of ensuring survival, and had cooperated with the local population in this. There had also clearly been a level of intermarriage (3:6), which, aside from the fact that this in itself was a betrayal of the covenant, almost certainly exacerbated the situation of increasing idolatry. The Torah does stress God's promises and his permanent commitment to Israel, but it also stresses their responsibility and the fact that failure to fulfil that responsibility will bring serious consequences (see Exod. 33:1–3; Num. 14:23; 32:11; Deut. 1:34–35; 31:19–22). In Exodus 23:29 where the words *I will not drive them out* are originally found, it explains that the promised driving out would take time, the reason for this being to ensure that the development of the new nation could be sustained. Joshua's farewell speech to Israel makes clear his understanding that the occupation of the land was dependent on their obedience to the covenant demands and fulfilment of their own obligations to keep themselves separate from the current inhabitants. He knew that without this the Canaanite survivors would become *snares* and *traps*, and it would eventually be Israel that was driven out (Josh. 23:12–13). The angel's use of Joshua's terminology undercuts any theological understanding that assumed God's promises were unrelated to any responsibility on their part and that they could demand from God a right to success. That was not, and had never been, the picture that they had been given. The words of God here are not new statements[12]

---

12. See van der Kooij (1995: 294–306). Boling (1975: 66) concludes that the angel was there to 'communicate a change in heaven's strategy', but it is hard to see how repetition of what God has already said can be seen as indicating a change of approach.

but, as in Micah 6:8, a reminder of what they should already have known and heeded. The question they should be asking themselves is not 'Why has God failed Israel?' but 'Why has Israel failed God?' God acted as he had said he would, but Israel did not, so it is they, not God, who need to explain – hence we have the *Why have you done this?* of verse 2.[13]

4–5. Israel heard, understood, wept and brought sacrifices. Whether they wept because they were genuinely repentant or only because they had begun to understand the consequences of their own actions is not clear. The bringing of sacrifices may or may not indicate that they were genuinely sorry, and this was a kind of covenant renewal ceremony. But the ongoing narrative reminds us of the short-term nature of any repentance. However, it also reminds us that God, in his grace, had not deserted Israel. He did provide them, in the midst of constant disobedience and failure, with constant opportunities to get it right, to start again and live in the way he had intended and which would bring them, even now, great blessing.

b. The first generation (2:6–9)

6–9. These verses again bring us back to Joshua, *the servant of the* LORD. It is interesting that although Samson refers to himself as God's servant (15:18), as does his father Manoah (13:8), the writers only give this title to Joshua. Joshua replaced Moses, who is described as 'the servant of the LORD' fourteen times in the book of Joshua before Joshua himself was awarded the title; but as far as the writers here are concerned, no-one, not even the leaders sent by God, replaced Joshua. Joshua's task as God's servant was to send the tribes out to take up their responsibilities and fulfil their own calling. The implication that the people did do everything right during the lifetime of Joshua and all his contemporaries may reflect a somewhat optimistic view of events. However, in this context it is designed to show that it was possible to live in the way God intended and that

---

13. The NRSV puts this as a statement: 'See what you have done', but the majority of translations leave it in question form, which does seem to fit better with the overall flow of the verse.

for a while they did, on the whole, manage to do so. The reference to Joshua's death and burial at Timnath Heres[14] serves to distance the accounts to come from the leadership of Joshua. What came next was not the responsibility of Joshua and his generation but lay entirely on the shoulders of the generation experiencing these events. In the chapters that lie ahead we will see on several occasions the writers both presenting and subtly critiquing the cultural and theological assumptions of the Israelites. There was clearly a constant tendency to try to offload blame for their troubles onto someone else, whether God or their forebears, but the writers of Judges are having none of it.

The wording of these verses is almost identical to that of Joshua 24:28–31 and is clearly taken from that source. But the order and therefore the emphasis is different.[15] In Joshua the section ends with the statement that Israel served Yahweh throughout Joshua's lifetime – and the hope there is that this will continue. In Judges that statement is moved to before the description of Joshua's death and burial, and there is therefore no expectation that their service will outlive Joshua. The addition of *great* in verse 7 to the description of the things Joshua and his contemporaries had seen God do perhaps adds further emphasis to the criticism of the next generation.

c. The downward spiral (2:10 – 3:6)

10–13. Of course one could say that the fact that the second generation *knew neither the LORD nor what he had done for Israel* does show that the first generation failed in at least one of their responsibilities, that of passing on the faith and instilling covenant loyalty in their children, but that is not the point being made here. We will read shortly of faithful exceptions, but it is clearly important to the writers that the broad picture of Israel's betrayal of their covenant with Yahweh is understood first. Verses 10–23 contain four strands.

---

14. Timnath Heres is referred to elsewhere as Timnath Serah (Josh. 19:50; 24:30). The reversal of consonants in the latter reflects either an alternative name or a scribal error.

15. Butler (2009: 38–39) provides a detailed and helpful analysis of the differences between the two passages.

The main thrust is a devastating appraisal of Israel's shortcomings. But this is intertwined with, first, a picture of God's increasing anger, second, his judgment, coming in the form of the continued presence of other nations and, third, a cycle of his repeated provision of chances for them to change and their repeated failure to take advantage of these chances. The wording in verse 10 contains echoes of Exodus 1:8 where the new Egyptian king 'did not know Joseph' (ESV). As the writers here had clearly been looking at Joshua 24, it is possible that the reference to Joseph there, which follows the section quoted, stimulated further reflection and influenced the terminology here.

The statement that the *Israelites did evil in the eyes of the LORD*, which recurs six times in the central section of the book, is elucidated here in shocking detail. They *forsook the LORD, followed and worshipped various gods, served Baal and the Ashtoreths, prostituted themselves to other gods*, turned from following *the ways of their ancestors who had been obedient to the LORD's commands*. There is no doubt that in the mind of the writers God's anger, which is described in repetitive detail (vv. 12, 14, 20), was fully deserved and his action in judgment fully justified. It may be correct to suggest that *the Baals* (2:11) are not necessarily different gods, but 'the various local manifestations of the same deity'.[16] However, it is likely that many Israelites and many of their original adherents saw them as distinct gods, and the plurals in verses 11 and 12 recognize this. Baal's consort is variously called Astarte (2:13; 10:6) and Asherah (3:7). Again the plural form is used (Ashtoreths represents the plural form of Astarte), but whether this implies that Baal had several consorts or that these were the consorts of several Baals is unclear and, as far as the writers of Judges are concerned, not really relevant.[17]

---

16. Soggin (1981: 43). There are several specific names given to Baals in the OT as well as the regular use of the general term. We have Baal of Peor (Num. 25:3, 5), Baal-Berith (Judg. 9:4) and Baal-Zebub (2 Kgs 1:2), and it is possible that the many place names incorporating Baal (e.g. Baal Zephon in Exod. 14:2; Baal Meon in Num. 32:38 and Baal Gad in Josh. 11:17) also indicate the local names for their deity.

17. See Introduction, pp. 21–22, for further discussion on the gods of Canaan.

14–23. The cycle is clear. Israel failed to keep their covenant promises (i.e. 'did evil'); because of their disobedience God was angry; he therefore allowed raiders to defeat and oppress them; the people were distressed; God sent leaders (i.e. judges)[18] to deliver them; they did not respond to this; the judge died; Israel's behaviour got worse; the oppression came back; the people were distressed; another leader was sent and the cycle continued. There are eighteen references to Yahweh in chapter 2 (as opposed to four in ch. 1), and he is very much a primary actor within the narrative. The writers are concerned that their readers should understand the character of this God with whom they were in covenant relationship. God's anger towards, and punishment of, Israel did not mean that he had rejected them completely. He was still showing his grace, still providing opportunities for the covenant to be worked out. Indeed, the anger described so clearly in this chapter can be understood as stemming from a deep sorrow that this people, whom he longed to bless, were destroying themselves by not responding to his overtures. Rather than following the example of their ancestors (vv. 12, 20, 22), almost certainly referring to Joshua and his generation rather than to the earlier patriarchs,[19] they have followed the example of those from whom they were called to separate themselves (see Butler 2009: 42).

3:1–6. There is a paradox in the way that the existence of the remaining nations within Israel is portrayed. In the first place they are there because Israel failed to fulfil their obligation to drive them out. The reason for this failure was primarily Israel's increasing involvement with the gods of these nations. This idolatry is also presented as the reason why God allowed the nations to remain. Thus again God's sovereignty sits alongside human responsibility. However, two further reasons for God's allowing the nations to remain are provided. First, it was to test Israel's loyalty (2:22; 3:4). Judges 2:20–21 shows that the testing is the reason why this

---

18. See Introduction, pp. 28–30, for further discussion on the nature of the leadership of the 'judges'.

19. See v. 19, which clearly refers to the immediately preceding generation.

particular punishment was chosen and does not negate the disobedience of Israel as the primary cause. It meant that Israel had
an opportunity as it were to test their spiritual mettle. But sandwiched in the middle of these two statements about testing their
loyalty is the comment in 3:2: *he did this*, that is, left the nations to
live in the midst of them, *only to teach warfare to the descendants of the
Israelites who had not had previous battle experience*. The writers, or at
least the final compilers of the text, must have been aware of the
apparent contradiction here, and it seems clear that they have deliberately allowed it to remain. The NIV and some other versions
indicate the problem by placing verse 2 in brackets, indicating that
this is an editorial comment. However, given the critiquing of the
Israelite understanding that we see elsewhere in Judges, it seems
possible that the writers are presenting this as the excuse used by
Israel to prevent any blame being ascribed either to themselves or
to Yahweh. The nations are there to give battle experience, so we
don't need to see it as failure on anybody's part! The repetition in
3:4 that the testing was *to see whether they would obey the LORD's commands*
forces readers to examine the issues and to question at least the
validity of the *only* in verse 2. What is very clear, however, is the pre-
diction of Joshua 23:13 that 'if' they turned away and violated the
covenant, then 'the LORD your God will no longer drive out these
nations', has now become a reality. In 2:1–5 God's words indicated
what could happen; by verse 21 the 'could' has very definitely
become a 'would'. There is a huge irony here, of which the writers
must have been aware, that Yahweh is using the armies of the lands
and peoples who see themselves as empowered by other gods to
punish Israel for betraying their relationship with him and following
those other gods!

As 2:1–5 stands both as an assessment of chapter 1 and an introduction to 2:6–23, so 3:1–6 stands both as a conclusion to the whole
of the first section of Judges and also as an introduction to section
2. However, the discussion of testing makes its primary link with
the preceding verses. The close connections seen throughout Judges
with the work of the Deuteronomist are particularly evident in these
few verses. The list of nations in verse 5 closely parallels the list in
Deuteronomy 7:1, although the Girgashites are not included here
and the Canaanites have been brought to the beginning of the

list.[20] The fact that the list in verse 3 is different probably indicates
that the writers had a number of different sources available to them.

Meaning
There are a number of theological themes introduced in this section
which are developed and referred to in the rest of the book. The
question of God changing his mind is an ongoing theme. The writers
are investigating how this can occur without its affecting the
unchanging promises of God. Certain things about the character of
God are highlighted: readers need to know first that God cares
deeply about how his people behave; evil does make him angry.
Second, God also cares deeply about his people and longs for them
to be in a good relationship with him. The importance of the land
is also emphasized. The question as to whether Israel will accept or
reject God's good gift to them remains in the air, although there are
strong indications that it will eventually be answered in the negative.
Will Israel be able to remain separate from the other nations, whether
or not they eventually expel them, or will they take the easy route of
compromise and assimilation?

This passage certainly makes clear to later generations why God's
people got into so much trouble, why the monarchy failed and why
the two kingdoms of Israel and Judah both suffered collapse.
However, in its own context, the whole of this introductory summary
is in preparation for the central section of Judges, which comes next
and includes the stories of specific instances of the leaders God
sent. The description of the cycle here and the concerns and
questions already raised mean that readers know what is happening
and what to look for in the individual stories and can understand
how these stories relate to the big picture. They are going to be
looking out for the ways in which Israel failed but also for the,
perhaps rare, examples of those who were still seeking to follow
Yahweh and the requirements of his covenant. They will notice
instances of both God's anger and his grace.

----

20. See Introduction, p. 12, for discussion of links with the Deuteronomist,
    and pp. 16–21 for a more extensive discussion of the tribes and peoples
    of the region.

2. THE JUDGES (3:7 – 16:31)

A. Introductory comments

This main central section of the book of Judges provides twelve accounts of varying length (thirteen if the story of Abimelek is not seen as a subsection of the Gideon narrative). Each account centres on the role of particular leaders. Six of these accounts, relating to Shamgar, Tola, Jair, Ibzan, Elon and Abdon, are brief and contain very little narrative material. The others, relating to Othniel, Ehud, Deborah, Gideon, Abimelek, Jephthah and Samson, are more extensive. All, apart from the story of Abimelek, begin with the phrase: *The Israelites did evil in the eyes of the LORD.* Thus, we have an initial clue to the writers' major concerns – to demonstrate Israel's failure to keep the promises that were made in the covenant renewal ceremony at Shechem (Josh. 24), to show that God will not tolerate this failure and to illustrate their ongoing lack of response to the many advances made by God towards them.

During the whole of the period described in the book of Judges it seems that the method God chose to use to communicate his feelings to Israel was to subject them to a time of oppression and servitude. It is not always clear whether this action should be seen primarily as a punishment or as a means of teaching the Israelites a lesson, that is, in order to bring them to their senses. It serves both of these purposes. But it is evident that their behaviour is both unacceptable to God and damaging to themselves. These two factors are not unrelated. One reason why it is unacceptable to God is because it is damaging to themselves, and one reason why it is damaging to themselves is because it is unacceptable to God. The identity of their oppressor constantly changes. Sometimes the focus is on an individual king and sometimes a whole people group, but although the Philistines do come more to the fore in the second half of the book, there is no one overarching or unassailable world or regional power, such as we see later in the books of Kings when the Assyrians, Babylonians and Persians arrive on the scene. In the Judges period powers constantly came and went, and the numbers given in the first half of this section indicate that the times of peace and independence for Israel in the early stages were far longer than the times of oppression. Israel had no evidence to support the view that any of the gods of the surrounding nations could claim supremacy or were worth serving in a way that their own God, Yahweh, was not. Even from their own selfish perspective, there was no adequate rationale for their failure to keep their covenant with Yahweh.

There seems to be a standard pattern, and every one of the accounts, again apart from that concerning Abimelek, contains some – although not all and not necessarily in exactly the same order – of the elements listed below:

1. The statement that Israel did evil
2. Description of that evil
3. God's anger towards them
4. God gives/sells them to oppressive enemies
5. Oppression takes place for a specified number of years
6. Israel cries out to God.
7. God responds negatively
8. Israel shows some kind of repentance
9. a) A leader emerges, b) sent by God
10. The leader takes action

11. There is peace for a specified number of years
12. The leader a) dies, and b) is buried.

It is also clear that there is a strong link between the six major narratives, particularly the Othniel account, and the overall description of the pattern of life seen in 2:11–19, which also reflects the fact that this is a repeating pattern. It is often assumed therefore that the accounts were formulated in the light of 2:11–19. However, the stress in that section that the Israelites did not listen to their judges is not a major emphasis in the narrative accounts, where the 'evil' seems to be at its height between judges. Also elements 5–8 of the list given above are not found in 2:11–19. Thus the evident links, both thematic and linguistic, with the earlier passage do not automatically imply that it was used as a structural paradigm.

The Abimelek story does not seem to fit this pattern. It tells of an internal power struggle within Israel rather than giving any details of Abimelek saving Israel from outside enemies. Furthermore, although there is significant narrative, it contains none of the elements identified above except that it describes Abimelek's death. It does therefore seem probable that we should include the story of Abimelek in Judges 9 within the cycle of stories about Gideon (chs. 6 – 9). This leaves us with twelve leaders – a number often chosen to represent the twelve tribes (see Table 1). The writers do not explicitly draw our attention to this, but it is perhaps significant that although the pattern is not complete unless one accepts the rather speculative suggestions made below, even without these suggestions the representation of the tribes across these twelve narratives is remarkable. It seems likely that these twelve judges are chosen to represent the whole of Israel. It shows both that God is concerned for all the tribes and that he can use people from any tribe – including those who, because they are left-handed, women, come from insignificant clans or are prone to irrational behaviour, might not normally be seen as good leadership material – to carry out his purposes and to be involved in his attempts to save Israel. The geographical spread of the home base of these leaders also makes it clear that the evil activity within Israel and their need for both punishment and redemption was not restricted to one area of the country or one section of the community.

Table 1 The leaders of the twelve tribes

LEADER	TRIBE
Othniel	Judah
Ehud	Benjamin
Shamgar	Naphtali?
Deborah	? Lived in Ephraim
Gideon	Manasseh
Tola	Issachar
Jair	Gad or Reuben
Jephthah	Gad or Reuben
Ibzan	(from Bethlehem)
Elon	Zebulun
Abdon	Ephraim
Samson	Dan

Notes on table

1. See the comments on Judges 3:21 in support of Shamgar's identification with Naphtali.

2. Gilead, the home area of both Jair and Jephthah, was assigned to the tribes of Gad, Reuben and half the tribe of Manasseh. As Gideon belonged to Manasseh, it is not unreasonable to suggest that Jair and Jephthah came from Gad and Reuben. Although Numbers 32:41 does speak of a Jair who was 'a descendant of Manasseh', names were not always used in only one tribe.

3. Counting Ephraim and Manasseh as two separate tribes means that the omission of Levi still leaves us with twelve tribes. The two tribes not then directly linked to any of the leaders are Simeon and Asher. Simeon was apparently absorbed into the southern tribes fairly quickly, and it is again not unreasonable to suggest that Ibzan from Bethlehem could have belonged to Simeon. Deborah lived, presumably with her husband Lappidoth, in the territory of Ephraim. Is it possible that she, like old Anna the prophet (Luke 2:36), originated from the tribe of Asher? Of course, this is speculation, but if so, it would complete the pattern and leave us with a remarkable situation where a woman counted as a tribal representative. Even if this is not so, Deborah remains as one of the twelve leaders chosen to represent Israel.

B. Othniel (3:7–11)

1, 2, 3, 4, 5, 6, 9, 10, 11, 12a[1]

Context
The story of Othniel as the first of the identified leaders provides
a strong link, both in content and structure, with the introductory
overview. This account provides very little specific narrative detail,
and we are told nothing about Othniel other than his identity. For
this reason and because a significant number of phrases are repeated
word for word from 2:11–19, some commentators assume that
this is here not as the inclusion of a previously existent story but
especially composed to set the pattern for the rest (Butler 2009: 62;
Lindars 1995: 100–101, 129; McCann 2002: 41). Othniel is chosen
as the first leader to be described, apparently in order to provide a
link with Joshua (Josh. 15:17–18) and possibly to ensure that the
first leader mentioned came from Judah. The fact that in 1:11–15
Othniel is identified as having conquered a town within Israel,
whereas here his role is to fight external enemies, is seen as supporting the view that this is a paradigmatic rather than historical narrative.
However, although it seems likely that this particular account has
been formulated to match 2:11–19, it does contain differences, such
as the specific reference to eight years, the fact that the people cried
out and the reference to them 'forgetting' God (incidentally, a term
used only here within Judges). There is no reason to suppose that
in his later years Othniel's activities did not go beyond those
described in the short reference in chapter 1. This section is clearly
evidence that it did.

The links with the earlier narrative, and with Joshua, are surely
intended to remind us that these are not just isolated 'hero' tales,
but are presented as stories of real people in real historical situations,
providing part of the history of the nation of Israel, part of the
heritage of the intended later readers of the book. It also gives us

---

1. The list of numbers at the start of each of the twelve accounts shows
which of the elements listed above on pp. 59–60 is found within that
particular account.

at least a hint of a sense of timing. Othniel was Caleb's younger brother. Presumably, he was a child at the time of Caleb and Joshua's first visit to Canaan, not held responsible for Israel's refusal to enter the land at that time and therefore not caused to perish in the wilderness (Num. 13 – 14). However, he was clearly part of the first generation who entered the land, and this story shows just how fast and how far Israel had fallen from their first calling and commitment.

Comment

7–11. Even at this early stage when many, if not most, of those who had made the commitment at Shechem to serve and obey Yahweh (Josh. 24:22–24) were still alive, *they forgot the LORD their God and served the Baals and the Asherahs* (v. 7).[2] Already the influence of the local people and the belief that local gods were more likely to bring them benefit was clearly stronger than the influence of their past knowledge of, and commitment to, Yahweh the God of Israel. No wonder God was angry (v. 8)! As we will come to see as the norm, God's reaction is to give the Israelites what they seem to be asking for: that is, he allows them to come under the domination of a nation that purports to follow the gods that Israel wishes to serve. In this case an individual oppressor is named: Cushan-Rishathaim[3] from Aram Naharaim. His name is unknown outside Judges, and he cannot be identified with any known figure, but his kingdom (lit.

---

2. Asherah (the pl. of *asherah* is *asheroth* and some translations prefer that term) refers to a female goddess, usually viewed as the wife or consort of the Canaanite god Baal. However, the term is also used for the wooden pole that is strongly associated with Asherah and often used to represent her.

3. The LXX calls him *Chousarsathaim*, and we cannot be sure if the name should be seen in two parts, as in the NIV, or as one. The first half of the name has sometimes been related to the area of Cush in North Africa, but this connection seems unlikely. There is nothing here to point to it, and Aram is north, not south, of Israelite territory. The second half of his name can be interpreted as 'especially' or 'doubly' wicked and is therefore sometimes seen as a semi-humorous nickname.

'Aram of the two rivers') is identified with (and in several biblical
versions including the NKJV and ASV translated as) Mesopotamia, in
the region north-west of Israelite territory lying between the Tigris
and Euphrates rivers. It took eight years of servitude before Israel
thought to cry out to Yahweh, but when they did, he is presented
as acting immediately by particularly empowering Othniel. This
empowering is indicated by the *Spirit of the LORD* coming upon him,
as we are later told also happened to Gideon (6:34), Jephthah (11:29)
and Samson (four times: 13:25; 14:6; 14:19; 15:14). In Judges this
seems to refer to an infusion of energy improving military prowess
rather than an increase in spirituality. But it ensures that readers
understand that Yahweh was involved in the appointment of this
particular leader. There is no evidence to indicate that Othniel's
leadership went beyond military command, but although no details
are given, he was enabled to defeat Cushan-Rishathaim, and for the
forty years of his lifetime *the land had peace*. This presumably means
that he spent five times longer (although the forty years may of
course be symbolic) as a peacetime leader than as an army
commander. As Butler puts it, 'The judge as leader is not called to
devote his life to battle and violence . . . The judge is to be used of
God to lead God's people in war; but the judge's ultimate goal is to
lead them to and in peace' (Butler 2009: 68).

Of course, there are several unanswered questions here. What
was Othniel doing during the eight years of subjection? How does
this relate to the events concerning Othniel in chapter 1, or to 3:10?
Was the army of Aram simply driven away, or was Aram itself made
subject? But the pattern for this central section of Judges is set and
it has been made very clear that God will react both to Israel's
betrayal and to their heartfelt cries.

Meaning
Whether or not Othniel's story was found in the sources used by
the final compilers of Judges or was deliberately formulated by them
to match 2:11–19, it is clear that it does stand in some senses as a
pattern for the rest of the Judges accounts. There is less narrative
than in the other major accounts, and the style is more formal, but
the message is apparent. Disobeying God and forgetting God have
serious consequences for a community theoretically committed to

serving him. But God is merciful, and crying out to him also has consequences – much more positive ones. It is interesting that there is no mention of the people repenting. Of course, one can assume that this is implied by, or included in, their 'crying out', and in other instances the need for repentance is clear. However, God's action on their behalf seems in this case to be inspired primarily by their willingness to admit their need. Without a change of behaviour the cycle will restart and problems will re-emerge, but God's default procedure seems to be to send help as soon as he sees even the slightest acknowledgment on their part that he might be the one who can help them.

C. Ehud (3:12–30)

1, 4, 5, 9, 10, 11[4]

Context
Whereas the account of Othniel is formal and with little personal information, the story of Ehud is told in an almost comedic style giving many small details, perhaps designed to amuse as well as encourage the Israelites who heard it. Lindars (1995: 135) is convinced that the style implies lack of historicity, but others disagree, for example Butler, who concludes that 'the story is almost a farce but that does not deny its historical base' (2009: 57). Certainly, there is no indication of symbolic numbering, as the eighteen years of their subjection to Moab has not been rounded. Often humour is the only way that oppressed peoples can 'fight back' against their enemies, and such stories are certainly not unknown throughout the Ancient Near East.[5] As in Othniel's case, the enemy during Ehud's time is personalized as an individual king, this time Eglon, king of Moab, Israel's neighbour on the eastern side. However, the Ammonites

---

4. The list of numbers at the start of each of the twelve accounts shows which of the elements listed above on pp. 59–60 is found within that particular account.

5. McCann (2002: 45) provides interesting discussion of the use of humour in this passage.

from the north-east and the Amalekites, who were influential in the
southern area, were allied with Moab and made Israel's problem
worse. Eglon and his forces were able to overrun and control the
eastern side of Israel, including not only the area east of the Jordan
but also some sections on the west of the Jordan, including Jericho
(the City of Palms).

Comment

12–14. This time we are not given details of the particular evil
behaviour involved. Presumably, the repeated *in the eyes of the LORD*
is enough to bring to mind both the covenant requirement to serve
God wholeheartedly and the idolatry outlined in 3:7. With the *again*
of verse 12 the writers begin to emphasize both the repeating pattern
and Israel's refusal to learn from history. There is no doubt in the
minds of the writers that Moab's dominance over Israel at this time
was allowed by Yahweh because of Israel's continuing evil behaviour.
For a long eighteen years Israel could find no strength to deal
with the problem of Moab. *Again the Israelites cried out to the LORD* –
note the repeated *again*, and that their cry generates the same
response. Yahweh again sends them a *deliverer*. The tables were
turned, Moab became a subject nation and Israel had peace for
eighty years.[6] The incident that initiated that delivery and led to *eighty
years* of peace is described in fascinating and darkly amusing detail.
Clearly, although the repeated pattern is constantly emphasized, this
does not imply in any sense that the pattern controls events or that
there is no validity in the individual stories. The detailed accounts
of specific incidents rather illustrate the fact that although there is
huge variety in the ways people act and in the things they do, nevertheless there remains an underlying similarity. People keep turning
away from God's path for them and then keep objecting to the
consequences of their actions. God keeps giving them another
chance, sending yet another individual to act on his behalf and
deliver them – and at the same time providing evidence that it is

---

6. See the comment on times and dates in the Introduction, p. 16. It is
worth noting that the time of peace after Ehud's actions is recorded
as double that during Othniel's life.

possible for human beings to act in ways that are not contrary to
God's purposes. They cannot excuse themselves by asserting that
their behaviour, and therefore its consequences, is inevitable and
thus cannot be seen as blameworthy.

15–18. The Israelites sent Ehud to carry their tribute – that is, as
representing their acceptance of their subjection to Moab. But Ehud
clearly has another task in mind! The main incident in the account
centres on Ehud's left-handedness.[7] Most ancient cultures were wary
of left-handedness. Perhaps simply because it was unusual, it was
often viewed in a negative way or with suspicion. In fact, there is no
evidence of this perception in Scripture itself, although
there is perhaps surprise expressed in Judges 20:16 at the skill of the
left-handed soldiers. Ehud's father's name Gera is unknown outside Benjamin, but seems to have been fairly common within that
tribe.[8] However, we know virtually nothing, apart from the name,
about any of the Geras mentioned. Ehud was clearly an accepted
member of the community, trusted to carry the Israelites' tribute to
Moab. Was he a civil servant given a quasi-military role or a soldier
given a quasi-diplomatic role? Was he already a leader at this point
or someone who was trusted but also considered dispensable?
What was the selection process for this kind of job? The text does
not provide answers to any of these questions. The only question
that interested the writers was: 'How is this apparently unalterable
situation going to be changed?' Although there is no evidence that
the rest of the community knew this until later, readers have been
told at the start that Ehud was going to be a deliverer, so the
question of how and how soon he was going to deliver hangs in
the air.

---

7. Soggin (1981: 50) suggests that the word describing Ehud's left-
handedness (lit. 'bound in his right hand') is more likely to indicate
some kind of deformity, perhaps rendering his right arm useless. There
is not much support for this view, probably because the same idiom
when used in 20:16 cannot have that implication. However, if Ehud's
left-handedness was of necessity, it would provide further explanation
for the reason why he was not seen as any kind of threat.

8. Cf. Gen. 46:21; 2 Sam. 16:5; 19:16; 1 Kgs 2:8; 1 Chr. 8:3, 5, 7.

Ehud had gone to Moab with an escort, but they were sent away as soon as the tribute was delivered, and the strong implication is that in his later exploit he acted alone and without the knowledge of those who sent him. It is possible that he wanted to make sure that he had fulfilled the task assigned to him by Israel before he moved on to his personal mission. He was clearly a man of intelligence, imagination and courage, who had a very good understanding of how people, both Moabites and Israelites, were likely to act in particular circumstances. This was no spur-of-the-moment seizing of an opportunity. It seems as if everything was planned to the last detail. He had with him a short[9] double-edged sword: double-edged perhaps because this made it easier for a left-handed man to handle, or possibly because it could also be used as a dagger. It was long enough to be a very effective weapon, but short enough to be inconspicuous, not hindering his movement when strapped to his thigh underneath his garments. The discovery of such a hidden weapon would have led immediately to Ehud's death, but a sword was normally placed on the left side so that it could easily be pulled out and used in the right hand. Even if an ancient system of 'frisking' were in place, it would have concentrated only on the left side. Ehud was taking full advantage of what others might just have seen as his misfortune, that is, being left-handed (or, if Soggin is right, deformed; see n. 7 above). He also made full use of what must have been a well-known physical characteristic of Eglon. The Moabite king was very fat.[10] This would not necessarily have been

---

9. The word giving the length of Ehud's sword (v. 16) is a *hapax* – i.e. a word found nowhere else in the OT – and the exact length is impossible to determine. Although the standard translation as a cubit (around 45 cm) is unlikely to be too far out, the sword may have been as short as 30 cm.

10. Stone 2009: 649–663 argues that the word normally translated as 'fat' is more likely to imply fitness, and Eglon should rather be seen as 'a splendid strapping specimen' (651). But the deliberately humorous way in which the story is recorded and develops probably works better if we accept the normal translation. There seems no particular reason to refer to the fitness of a military opponent.

regarded as a negative characteristic; it could rather be an indication of prosperity. But in this instance it was seen by Ehud as an opportunity.

19–22. Ehud's plan was not initiated immediately. He left, maybe with the escorting company, and travelled as far as the stone images at Gilgal. This reference is somewhat obscure. It appears to be far enough away from Moab's camp to lessen the impact of Moabite influence and to give the Israelites a sense of safety. It may have been some kind of boundary marker, but it could possibly refer to the twelve stones set up by Joshua (Josh. 4:19–24) which are very likely to have become a notable local landmark. However, these could have been Moabite images, and in that case, the information that he had received a message from God – or a god – at this place would make sense to Eglon. It seems likely that a Moabite cohort travelled with the Israelite company to this point. Ehud then turns back alone purportedly with a *secret message*. The word translated as 'message' could have been translated as 'thing', which might indicate deliberate ambiguity. The king is expecting a message, but what he is going to get is a sword! Having received a visit from a larger group where there were no signs of trouble, any suspicions that the Moabites might have had were allayed and the return of the unaccompanied Ehud seems to have been accepted without question.

Ehud's plan depended on being able to arrange a private meeting with the king. Perhaps the king was known to have an interest in omens and portents, and Ehud expected him to be easily persuaded to listen when he came back with his *message from God*. Note the use of the general term for God, Elohim, which was used throughout the region, rather than Yahweh, the specific name for the God of Israel, which is widely used elsewhere in this section of Judges. The secret meeting was arranged. What danger could there have been from an apparently unarmed, unaccompanied diplomat who had visited previously with no signs of ill intent? The meeting took place in the roof chamber,[11] apparently a substantial room with a

---

11. Wong (2006: 319–412) points out that there are apparent allusions
    to the Ehud narrative in the stories of Joab. Joab takes Abner into

lockable door and what would today be described as having en suite
facilities. The king rose as Ehud approached, perhaps as a mark of
respect because the message was coming from God. With his exceptional bulk it is unlikely that he could have moved fast enough to
avoid trouble anyway, but this certainly made it easier for Ehud. He
acted swiftly and thrust the sword into the king's abdomen. One
wonders if what happened next was as much a shock to Ehud
as the attack would have been to Eglon! The sword disappeared
into the king's vast belly. Did Ehud leave the sword there because
there was no time to secrete it again and carrying a bloody sword
through the outer court would have aroused instant suspicion, or
because he simply could not bear to pull it out? Certainly, these
details, including the fact that the king's bowels discharged and
the description of the reaction of his retinue, do seem to add
authenticity to the account.

23–26. Taking Eglon's key and locking the door as he left was a
masterstroke. Eglon's servants simply assumed that Eglon had
locked it himself. It may be that his weight had caused major bowel
problems on a regular basis and they were used to him spending
long periods in the toilet room. It would be interesting to know
how long it was before *the point of embarrassment* arrived. It was
certainly long enough for Ehud to get well away before they discovered the king's death. Again, given the king's bulk, it may have
been even longer before they realized that Eglon had actually been
assassinated.

27–30. Verses 27–29 return to the more normal 'battle-story'
form but do not detract from the fact that Ehud's real victory was
won by cunning subterfuge rather than in war. However, this next
stage of Ehud's campaign seems to have been equally well planned.

(note 11 *cont.*) an inner chamber to stab him in the stomach (2 Sam.
3:27) and also stabs Amasa in the belly so that his intestines spill out
(2 Sam. 20:8–10). The link is interesting and may be deliberate, but
as Wong recognizes the priority of the Ehud account, his conclusion
that the negative presentation of Joab's behaviour should lead us to
rethink the generally positive evaluation of Ehud's behaviour remains
unconvincing.

The death of Eglon would have left a power vacuum in Moab. The Israelites would have known this and thus had the confidence to respond to Ehud's call to battle. They retook all the Israelite territory on the west side of the Jordan and apparently crossed over into Moab's own territory. If the Moabite army was temporarily without clear direction and control, then such a devastating destruction of troops is not impossible to conceive. Whether the Moabite army had a major base west of the Jordan and the occupation of the river crossing prevented this force from returning home, or whether the Moabite army was killed trying to cross into Israelite territory to reinforce their sovereignty, is not clear. Apparently, the unchangeable situation had been transformed. Although we don't know anything of Ehud after this, 4:1 does indicate that he himself did become Israel's leader and took control until his death. We are told that Israel *had peace*, indicating that they were not subjected to any outside powers, for eighty years. Ehud, like Othniel, was a leader for far longer in peacetime than in war.

Meaning
As in the story of Othniel, there is no mention of the people repenting. Here, as throughout Judges, they seem to be much happier to assimilate to Canaanite ways than to follow God's ways. The emphasis in this account is not on anything the people might deserve, but again on Yahweh responding to their acknowledgment of need and of the possibility that Yahweh might, or would, meet that need. We are not told of Ehud's being provided with 'the Spirit of the LORD', which may be because his main role in deliverance was not primarily a military one, and possession of the 'Spirit of the LORD' was usually evidenced by military prowess. Indeed, there is no mention of Yahweh in the body of the story. But he is clearly there at the beginning, strengthening Eglon in his overlordship of Israel, and then providing Ehud as a 'deliverer'. This description of Ehud as a Yahweh-sent deliverer is presumably intended to imply Yahweh's involvement in the whole process. He is not restricted in the people or the methods he can use to fulfil his purposes. Left-handed men are as usable as right-handed men. Subterfuge can be used as forcefully as military might.

D. Shamgar (3:31)

9a, 10[12]

This is the shortest of the accounts and the detail is very limited. We are told only of one incident: the 600 Philistines killed by an ox-goad, which was a pointed, spear-like probe normally used to control the domestic beasts. There is no corroborating evidence relating to this event. It is reminiscent of Samson's activity with a donkey's jawbone (15:15), but in spite of the similarities there is not really any reason to suspect any dependence on that story. Shamgar is mentioned in the song of Judges 5 (5:6) as an apparently notable figure. This account may be included in order to provide background to that reference. However, it could also support the theory that the writers want to show that leaders emerged from all the tribes; and possibly also that not only can God use all kinds of people, he can make use of all kinds of weapons. We are not told Shamgar's tribe, but his father's name Anath may be linked to the town of Beth Anath in the region assigned to Naphtali, a tribe that is not referred to in relation to any of the other judges.[13] The next account, telling of Deborah's time in office, begins with a reference to Ehud, not to Shamgar (4:1), and this may indicate that his activities took place during the time when Ehud was still in control. This again could support the argument that the story of Shamgar was included to widen the tribal representation. It is likely that there were many incidents and stories circulating about the activities of various 'hero-type' figures, and the reason for including one like this where the detail is so sparse is otherwise unclear.

---

12. The list of numbers at the start of each of the twelve accounts shows which of the elements listed above on pp. 59–60 is found within that particular account.

13. Shamgar's name is possibly of Hurrian origin, and it has been suggested that the reference to Anath is to the Canaanite goddess of that name and could infer that he was a follower of that goddess. However, there is no indication in the text that Shamgar was not another Israelite listed among the collection of deliverers.

E. Deborah (4:1 – 5:31)

i. The story (4:1–23)

1, 4, 5, 6, 9a, 10, 11[14]

Context

The chronology of the composition of this section has been debated. There is general acceptance of the ancient origin of chapter 5 with some (e.g. de Hoop 2009) suggesting that the story in chapter 4 was formed to elucidate the song. Others are sceptical of the use of the material as evidence for the early history of Israel (e.g. Smith 2009: 27–42). There has also been debate about how this section relates to the rest of Judges with regard to the perceived anti-northern bias there, which is missing here. However, the compilers of Judges as a whole are clearly presenting the material in a historical context and wanting readers to accept the concept of the God of Israel at work in the whole nation. The oppressive overlord here is Jabin king of Canaan, who reigned in Hazor. Although the unusual ascription 'Canaanite king' is in the grammatical construction of a proper name, Canaan did not exist as a united nation and Jabin would have been 'a' rather than 'the' Canaanite king. Hazor was a major city situated in Israelite territory about 30 miles (50 km) north of the Sea of Galilee. Today it is a significant archaeological site known as Tell el-Qedah. Joshua 11 speaks of Jabin king of Canaan summoning a large army from the surrounding states and attacking Joshua. We are told that Joshua soundly defeated this army, killed the king and burned Hazor. Naturally, there has been debate as to how this relates to the story of Jabin here in Judges. Some suggest that the two accounts have been confused or that two separate events, involving first Jabin and second Sisera, have been conflated; others suggest that Hazor was rebuilt and this Jabin is a descendant of the earlier one. Jabin is notably absent from the main section of

---

14. The list of numbers at the start of each of the twelve accounts shows which of the elements listed above on pp. 59–60 is found within that particular account.

the story in Judges, and it is possible that the name of Jabin was added here later. However, Psalm 83:9 does associate Jabin with Sisera, so others prefer to think that the name Jabin was added later into the Joshua account. In fact, there is no real evidence to help us solve this puzzle, so perhaps it is better simply to leave it as a puzzle.

Comment

4:1–3. Once more the emerging pattern is stressed, as this account also begins with *again*. As with the Ehud narrative, the nature of the evil is not described. It seems that the description of idolatry given in the Othniel account carries through into all the other stories, although when we get to Jephthah in chapter 11, the further expansion given there repeats the same charge. Israel's enemy is once more personalized, and this time the aggressor is Jabin of Hazor. The main contender in this chapter is Sisera, described as the head of Jabin's armed forces. Sisera's possession of *nine hundred chariots fitted with iron*[15] is probably specifically mentioned because this kind of chariot was one of the most advanced military resources of the time. His ownership of so many is seen as the reason why Sisera was able to control the areas occupied by Israelites. His cruel treatment is particularly stressed, but this time it was twenty years before Israel was ready to turn to Yahweh for help. Sisera's base at Harosheth Haggoyim has not been definitively established, but the discovery of a tablet identified as part of the linchpin of a chariot wheel has led to the suggestion that the El-Ahwat site where it was found may be the location of Sisera's town – although this can of course only be speculative.

4–5. The statement that God responded to their cry by sending a named leader is omitted in the story of Deborah, but the text is clear that she spoke for God (vv. 6, 9) and that it was God who brought salvation (v. 23). We have much more background information about Deborah than we were given for either Othniel or Ehud, and it may be that her role as a prophet, not given to any of

---

15. The NIV translation brings out the fact that these 'chariots of iron' were not built entirely from iron but had iron coverings and possibly iron weapons (spikes) attached. The point is (as in 1:19) that they were the most advanced equipment of that time.

the other judges, was seen as making redundant any further statement
that she was sent by God. It is not unknown for married women to
be identified in terms of parents as well as husband (e.g. 2 Sam. 11:3;
17:25), but in this case Deborah's parentage is unknown. She was
married to a man called Lappidoth, although his profession is not
mentioned and it is possible that she was widowed. She had clearly
been functioning as a judge, that is, one who makes judgments in
the case of disputes, for some time before overseeing the military
endeavours that led to Israel once more becoming free. Deborah,
unlike most of the other judges, is not actively involved as a warrior,[16]
and the story could have been told simply in relation to Barak as the
military commander, but the writers thought it was important to
recognize and include the role of Deborah, perhaps in the overall
account making sure that it was understood that women, as well as
left-handed men and those from any of the tribes of Israel, could
be used by God as national leaders! In this particular account she
parallels the Canaanite king, Jabin, whereas Barak parallels the army
commander, Sisera. It may be significant that the place where she
held court is described as being between Bethel, one of Israel's most
important shrines, and Ramah, later to be the birthplace of Samuel.
This was in Ephraimite territory, but there is no direct mention of
the birthplace or tribal identity of either Deborah or Lappidoth.[17]

6–10. Deborah's authority is underlined by the fact that when she
sent for Barak, himself a man with the authority to summon the
armed forces to come together,[18] there was no question that he saw
her as having the right to call him, nor that he accepted the accuracy
of her claim to be speaking for *The LORD, the God of Israel*. This title
has been used regularly in Joshua, emphasizing that Yahweh was

---

16. Gale Yee (1993: 99–132) assumes that the writers here are using and
    exploring the metaphor of 'woman warrior', but if so, then they are
    presenting an unusual picture of what a warrior would normally be
    considered to be.

17. See p. 61 above.

18. Not until the time of Saul did Israel have any kind of standing army.
    Each time action was considered necessary, the irregular forces from
    different tribes were called together to oppose the current enemy.

indeed Israel's God, to be distinguished clearly from the gods of the other inhabitants of the region. However, this is the first time it is used in Judges, perhaps particularly relevant here because Israel's forces are to be sent to fight against the forces of those who, rather than attacking from outside places like Aram and Moab, actually laid claim to the territory given to Israel by God. Barak is to call up the men of Naphtali and Zebulun, tribes closest to Jabin and Sisera's headquarters and presumably most affected by their control. Barak himself came from Naphtali (v. 6) and was probably chosen for that reason. They are to take action against Sisera, but they go with the assurance that the result of that action is predetermined. The God of Israel, their God, will give them success. The mention of *ten thousand men* is sometimes seen as 'evidently an exaggeration' (Soggin 1981: 65), but although numbers are sometimes rounded up or used symbolically, it does not seem impossible for that number of men to be raised from two tribes if it is assumed that the large majority of able-bodied men are expected to take part.

Barak's response underlines the sense of charisma that is linked to Deborah but does seem to indicate that his trust is in her and maybe her connection to God, rather than in God himself. It seems very likely that Deborah had every intention of going with him to the north anyway. But Barak's apparent refusal to understand and accept the power of Yahweh as his own God would mean that he would not be the one to deliver the final blow against Sisera; that privilege instead would go to a woman. Readers might expect here that this woman would be Deborah, but in fact it was not Deborah who would take up this role but, as the account shortly reveals, another woman, Jael, who was probably not even an Israelite.[19] Deborah and Barak went together to Barak's home town Kedesh, south-west of Lake Galilee, and there Barak, this time fulfilling the role that had been assigned to him, summoned his forces.

11. Before we find out what happens in the ensuing battle, we are given, in brackets as it were, information about the family of Heber the Kenite, which is necessary to the ongoing story. The

---

19. Of course, Heber could have had an Israelite wife, but it seems more likely that she also was a Kenite.

Kenites had been allied with Israel since the time of Jethro, Moses' father-in-law.[20] The specific mention of Heber's separation from the rest of his clan seems to indicate that, unlike Heber, they had remained loyal to Israel. But Heber, perhaps understandably as he lived within the territory controlled by Jabin's forces, had made his own alliance with Jabin (v. 17). The great tree of Zaanannim was certainly a landmark forming part of the boundary of the territory assigned to the tribe of Naphtali (Josh. 19:33). However, many such notable trees also became shrines, and it is possible that Heber deliberately settled nearby in order to associate himself with local gods.

12–15. In response to the movement of the 10,000 Israelite troops, Sisera summoned an unknown number of his own forces, including those who manned the famed 900 chariots. It is possible that the mention of the chariots is significant. As is normal in Judges, identifying precise locations, even when sites are mentioned, is not easy. The fighting apparently took place not too far from the Jordan plain – the Kishon River flows north-west across Israel, entering the Mediterranean Sea near the modern city of Haifa – but seems to have been centred on the hill country near Mount Tabor, somewhat north-east of the Kishon. As many well-equipped forces over the centuries have discovered to their cost, right equipment in the wrong area can end up being a hindrance rather than a help. It is possible that it was Sisera's trust in his powerful chariots that led to his downfall. Deborah in verse 14 makes it clear that although Barak and his forces are called to *go* and do their job, it is Yahweh and trust in Yahweh that will actually make all the difference. The awareness seen throughout the Old Testament of the relationship between God's sovereignty and human responsibility is evidenced here. God is an active partner: it is he who goes ahead of them and routs Sisera *and all his chariots*. However, he does it *by the sword*, that is, by the sword of Barak and his army. As far as Deborah and the writers of

---

20. Exod. 18:27 tells us that Moses' father-in-law returned to his own land, whereas in Num. 10:29–36 he appears to have remained with the travelling community. In either case, it seems clear that a significant number of his family remained as a distinctive group within Israel.

Judges are concerned, as long as God is involved, sword will defeat chariot any day of the week! Perhaps, however, the fact that minimal details are given of the battle itself is a deliberate ploy to emphasize the key significance of God's actions. Again, significantly, we read that Sisera had to leave his chariot behind and flee on foot (v. 15). Sisera's chariot-supported army was wiped out, in spite of making it back as far as their own base at Harosheth Haggoyim.

16–22. The section telling of the death of Sisera might be seen as something of an aside, but it serves two purposes apart from the obvious one of restressing God's use of women and fulfilling Deborah's prophecy that the ultimate credit for the defeat of Sisera would go to a woman. The first of these is to show that the victory was complete and that there would be no possibility of Sisera returning to raise another army. The second demonstrates, as Judges does many times over, that the big picture is always made up of small incidents, and that the actions of individuals do make a difference to that big picture.

The details of what happened in Sisera's final hours are told briefly and clearly; the background and the motivations involved are less clear. He went to Heber's camp, to Jael's tent. She welcomes him, reassures him, covers him, gives him a nourishing drink, providing much more than the water he requested, and then when he sleeps, she kills him. There may be some significance in the overall interests of the writers of Judges in God's use of many different people to carry out his purposes, that a female foreigner is presented as achieving a result that was not, with the implication that it should have been, obtained by male Israelites. The reason for Sisera's seeking refuge in Heber's compound is given. Heber had declared loyalty to Jabin. But how did Sisera know of this? Was there some kind of flag or visible symbol indicating that loyalty? Was Heber particularly wealthy and significant and that was why Sisera knew of him? Did Sisera have a personal knowledge of the family? And given the fact that he did know of Sisera's loyalty to Jabin, why does the text mention that he went directly to Jael's tent rather than simply to Heber's compound? The way the story is told has led to the suggestion that Sisera had had a previous sexual relationship with Jael, perhaps against her will – the possibility of violent rape is raised. The impossibility of resisting a powerful – both physically and

politically – commander is obvious, and it is apparently not unusual
in such situations for the arrogance of the aggressor to lead him to
suppose that his advances would not be unwelcome. This would
explain both his approach to Jael's tent and the nature of her
welcome. It is not unlikely that she would have heard of the success
of Israel's forces, and therefore was half expecting that if Sisera did
escape, he might come to her for shelter. This is her opportunity.
She ushers him in, allays any suspicions, allows him to sleep and
murders him. The force involved in crushing a man's skull with a
tent peg – presumably pointed but not really sharp – must have been
tremendous, even with the help of the hammer normally used
to force tent pegs into the ground. This would be so particularly if
the peg was wooden, but would apply even if we assume that a metal
peg was being used – possible, if the tradition that the Kenites were
metalworkers is correct. Even for a strong woman this must have
been an act motivated by great passion, backed up by huge amounts
of adrenalin. If the motivation was simply political, there do seem
to be simpler ways of assassinating a sleeping man.

Of course, this, as any other suggestion, is only speculative. It
may be that, unknown to Sisera and perhaps even to Heber, the wife
of Sisera's friend had a personal loyalty to Israel and to Yahweh, and
totally rejected her husband's alliance with Jabin. Perhaps, like Rahab
(Josh. 2:9–13), she believed that as Yahweh had spoken, there was
no doubt that Israel would be successful and she wanted to protect
her family by ending up on the right side. Perhaps memory of Moses'
promise to their forebear Hobab had been retained and Jael took it
seriously. It is also possible that the news of Deborah's prophecies
had spread even among the immigrant communities. But even if
Jael had not actually heard about God's message, her knowledge of
Yahweh and the reason for her people's presence in this land would
have been part of her heritage. This latter conclusion could be
supported by Jael's action in approaching Barak to tell him of her
actions, but the text actually gives no real indication of the reasons
why she chose to kill Sisera. The fact of his death is enough.

23–24. The final mention of Jabin acts as an inclusio, bringing
the narrative to an end. The defeat of Sisera was a major step in the
defeat of the kingdom of Hazor, but it was not the whole story.
Jabin had been declared as the enemy, and it was Jabin who had to

be defeated, which he was. Deborah's trust in Yahweh had been amply repaid and Israel was once more free.

Meaning

The story of Deborah has often been seen as particularly significant for women, or affirming women. It certainly does affirm that women are capable and called to fulfil God's purposes in different ways. The focus on Jael indicates that Deborah was not to be seen as unique in that respect. However, although clearly both Deborah and Jael are significant characters, within the text there is little discussion of their gender or its relevance. Within the narrative itself it seems clear that for a woman to take a specifically military role was seen as unusual, and Barak's desire for her to be present is commented on. However, there is no indication in the text that her roles as prophet, able to speak for God, as judge, able to oversee the community, or as a national leader, initiating the campaign to oust the oppressive Canaanite forces, were to be seen as surprising or worth comment. Given that women leaders were in fact quite rare, the lack of any note of surprise is in itself perhaps surprising!

In the context of Judges as a whole, this section confirms the pattern that sees life in the Promised Land far from being lived in the way that God had ordained. Alongside this we have another indication that there were those around who did speak for God and live according to covenant principles. God had not given up on Israel and was still sending help to deliver them from enemies with the aim of bringing them back to himself and their own calling.

ii. The song (5:1–31)

Context

The song of chapter 5 is an anomaly in this largely narrative-based book. Its deliberate placing within the narrative is indicated by the fact that the final section of the narrative, the statement that *the land had peace for forty years*, is situated at the end of the song. This makes it clear that the writers intend the two sections to be viewed in some sense as a whole. It is known as the song of Deborah, but Barak is also mentioned as a singer, and no priority is given to Deborah other than the fact that she is mentioned first. The song itself is generally recognized to be early,[21] possibly contemporaneous with the events and probably included in a collection of triumph songs such as that referred to in Numbers 21:14 as the 'Book of the Wars of the LORD'. Wong's argument that its main focus is a challenge to encourage wide military participation of all the tribes and a rebuke to those who do not participate, rather than simply a celebration of victory, is also worth consideration (Wong 2007: 1–22).

In translation, this song does not come across as either great poetry or great history, and is more an impressionistic collection of ideas intended to evoke patriotic emotion perhaps when sung as soldiers or even the whole community gathered in the evening around the campfire. Nevertheless, although it does raise some questions, the passage backs up the basic historical analysis of the supposedly later narrative account and also supports its theological stance. It provides a resource for the people of Israel to do as they are often commanded: to 'remember' their history, their own failures and successes and the ways in which God rescued and blessed them. As is not unusual in ancient poetry, we see constant changes of speaker and addressee and also in the form between first, second and third person.

The poem can be analysed in the following way:[22]

1. General statement linked to a call to praise: 'When leaders lead and people serve, praise God!' (v. 2).
2. Personal statement: 'Listen, neighbouring powers! I will praise God!' (v. 3).
3. Statement to God: 'When you act, things happen, the earth responds!' (vv. 4–5).
4. Historical statement to the people from Deborah: 'Israel had given up when I Deborah came on the scene, but they did respond – praise the LORD!' (vv. 6–9).
5. Call to everyone to revel in the victory that belongs to God and people (vv. 10–11a).

---

21. Although Lindars (1995: 165) does question this assumption.
22. Alternative and more detailed structural studies can be found in Vincent (2000: 61–82) and Fokkelman (1995: 595–662).

6. Call from the people for Deborah to sing and Barak to act (vv. 11b–12).
7. Record of those who did and did not participate in the battle (vv. 13–18).
8. Poetic record of the battle itself (vv. 19–23).
9. Poetic record of Jael's killing of Sisera (vv. 24–27).
10. Poetic record of the fears and hopes of Sisera's family (vv. 28–30).
11. Final acknowledgment that it was God's victory, and prayer that all his enemies would fail in the same way and all his followers succeed (v. 31a).

Comment

5:1–2. There is something profoundly satisfying about a society that functions as it is supposed to function. It is possible that the writers have Israel's allegiance to the covenant in mind here, although the stress is on glad acceptance of given responsibilities. In this context the satisfaction is amplified because for many years Israel had been cowering rather than standing tall. Now at last she is behaving with confidence. Praise God indeed.

3. The confidence of Israel (or perhaps of Deborah) is justified because it is confidence in Yahweh himself. When God's people confidently and openly – in song – give praise to God, then it really is time for the surrounding rulers to take note and tremble. It was when Israel was afraid to speak and sing out her faith that the faith itself withered and the nation lost its identity as a covenant people.

4–5. Yahweh is proclaimed as the Lord of creation. The earth itself responds to his voice; how much more should the people he created bow before him. Deuteronomy 33:2 also associates Seir with Sinai. The particular point here may be that God gave this land to Israel; in reaching it, they too marched through Edom, and no local nation is going to be able to stand against Israel's great God. It seems likely that the language of theophany here was also intended to point the readers back to God's presence and activity at Sinai.

6–9. Why Shamgar and Jael are chosen for particular mention here is not apparent; what is abundantly clear is that Israel really had given up. They had forgotten that with their God behind and before them they were unstoppable, and had therefore hidden away as if they were people with no hope. The leaders didn't lead and the people didn't *willingly offer themselves*. This was the situation until Deborah came onto the scene, and as *a mother in Israel* – that is, one who will teach her children who God is and what it means to follow him – she brings new hope. Verse 9 returns to the satisfaction seen in verse 2. It is not actually Deborah herself who is the focus, but her joy in the possibility of leaders and people functioning properly together. Again, praise the LORD indeed.

10–11a. The uncertainty of the Hebrew in this little section does not detract from its force. Both riders and walkers, the rich, owning the rare and very valuable white donkeys, and the poor, with no donkey at all to ride, must take heed of the songs telling of God's victories. These are also the victories of the ordinary Israelite villagers. Without God these villagers will be left to hide in the countryside (vv. 6–7), but with God they will share in his triumphs.

11b–12. The central portion of the song is the call for Deborah and Barak to step up to the mark. Reflecting the repeated call to princes and people, they too must do what God has called them to do: for Deborah to sing – that is, to speak out, to prophesy, to proclaim God's plans and purposes for Israel and to call the people, including Barak, to action – and for Barak to act in his military capacity, to deal with those who have kept Israel in captivity and turn them into captives. When they do this, then through them God will be able to transform the situation and the whole of the rest of the song will become a reality.

13–18. In chapter 4 only Zebulun and Naphtali are mentioned, but here Ephraim, Benjamin, Makir (of Manasseh) and Issachar are also involved in the fighting. This has led to the suggestion that there were separate battles, one in the north perhaps directly involving Jabin and restricted to the armies from the two northern tribes, and another in the central region of Issachar, which includes Mount Tabor (cf. 4:12–15), and the northern section of the west-bank half of Manasseh where the others also came to join the fighting. Reuben, Asher and Dan are seen as blameworthy for not taking part, whereas in chapter 4 they were not called upon to do so. Whatever the relationship between the two texts, this section of the poem reminds Israel of the interdependence of the tribes. It is important for each one to come to the aid of the others, even when the particular problem to be dealt with is remote from their own territory. The singling out of Zebulun and Naphtali for special praise does tie in with the chapter 4 account.

19–23. It is not easy, either here or in chapter 4, to trace the exact course of the battle or battles. The River Kishon forms the southern border of the territory of Asher and Zebulun, quite a way west of Mount Tabor. Taanach and Megiddo were south of that, down in Manasseh territory. Whether it was Israel or the Canaanite forces who drew the battle in that direction is also not clear. But the stars, perhaps indicating a major rainstorm as the stars were sometimes pictured as the breaks in the heavens where the rain came through, and the river itself are seen as fighting on Israel's behalf. Mud caused by rain and marshy river land would, like the hill country, make chariots more of a disadvantage than an advantage. Meroz is unknown elsewhere, and we cannot be sure if it refers to an individual city, a region or a clan within Israel: there is no evidence to support the suggestion that Meroz involved non-Israelites. What is clear is that this was Yahweh's battle: even the forces of nature fought on God's behalf, and any human group who made a specific decision not to help would come under God's curse. In general, the curse of God exiles people from his presence (see Evans 1994), and the point here probably signifies that those who do not support God's actions will not be seen as part of God's people. This seems a stronger condemnation that that of Reuben, Dan and Asher in verses 15–17 and may indicate that Meroz was in the region where the fighting took place and their lack of involvement resulted from some deliberate decision rather than simply inaction.

24–27. The poetic account of Sisera's killing exactly reflects the narrative of 4:17–21, except that verse 27 could indicate that he was standing or sitting rather than lying asleep when Jael struck. However, it would be extremely difficult to get the force required from that kind of hammer blow against a target that was not stabilized. In fact, the falling at Jael's feet could equally easily be from off the bed. Early readers may have questioned Jael's breach of hospitality – by feeding him she had become his host and, as such, to harm him would be wrong – although if the suggestion that he had previously assaulted her is accepted, then he would himself have forfeited the right to hospitality. In modern society Jael's action could be seen as excessively violent, and inappropriate behaviour, particularly for a woman. However, we must beware of introducing questions that would not have been understood in their original context. In general, to kill an enemy in the course of a war would never have been seen as inappropriate. Also in this case as in many others, Scripture does not stereotype roles in the way that both ancient and modern cultures tend to do. The text has no hint of condemnation of Jael for any reason; in fact, quite the reverse. In a phrase reminiscent of Elizabeth's Spirit-inspired greeting to Mary (Luke 1:42) Jael is considered to be worthy of particular praise.

28–30. For the original hearers of this song the reference to the misperceptions of Sisera's mother and her household would probably have been seen as a matter for rejoicing: 'They assumed his success and thought he was delayed by collecting plunder from Israel, but they couldn't have been more wrong!' The reference to their revelling in the thought of that plunder does perhaps indicate that Sisera's family were not just innocent victims, but this section comes across to modern readers, and possibly this is also intended by the text, as very sad. All wars do have wide-reaching consequences. But the unquestioning acceptance of the Canaanite women that other women, one or two for each of their soldiers, would automatically be seen as an appropriate part of the spoils of war is also very sad.

31a. The song ends by coming back to the heart of the matter. This victory is Yahweh's and means disaster for those who oppose him and the warmth of sunshine for those who love him. Both of these are seen as very appropriate aspirations for the people of Israel.

31b. The song is over, the war is at an end and Israel again *had peace for forty years.*

Meaning

The song ensures that this narrative, and indeed all the other narratives in this section of Judges, is understood in the context of theological reflection, and in this instance also of worship. It is who God is, what he asks of them and the praise he deserves from them that make sense of the events and the way in which those events are

recorded. The difficulty of identifying the precise historical details
reminds us that this chapter was not intended to stand as a historical
record but as a poetic inspiration and encouragement

F. Gideon and Abimelek (6:1 – 9:57)

i. Gideon: his achievements and his failures (6:1 – 8:35)

1, 4, 5, 6, 7, 9, 10, 11, 12²³

a. The start of a new era (6:1–40)

Context
The extended account of Gideon's leadership follows the regular
pattern but in addition includes more detail concerning the extent
of, and results stemming from, the Midianite oppression, Gideon's
calling, his eventual idolatry and the disastrous disputes between his
sons after his death. Othniel, Ehud and Deborah are all portrayed
more or less positively; Gideon, on the other hand, is specifically
described as weak and fallible right from the beginning. He has his
heroic moments, but that he was, at best, a flawed hero is clearly
being deliberately emphasized. In addition, this section provides
much more detail about God's personal dealings with both Gideon
and the people. It is probably significant that Yahweh is a major
character in the first half of the narrative, constantly dialoguing with
Gideon in both chapter 6 and chapter 7, whereas in chapters 8 and
9 he is rarely mentioned and then only indirectly.

Comment
6:1–6. These verses act as a kind of preface to the long account
of the life and times of Gideon and his family. The narrative, as
with all the main accounts so far, begins with Israel's evil behaviour,
which resulted in Yahweh's initiating their subjection to an alien

---

23. The list of numbers at the start of each of the twelve accounts shows
which of the elements listed above on pp. 59–60 is found within that
particular account.

power. Nevertheless, it is significant that again a different enemy comes to the fore. The constant underlying implication is that if only Israel could have pulled together and behaved as the covenant people of Yahweh that they were supposed to be, all these different enemies coming from different directions into different areas could have been dealt with one at a time. Midian's control over Israel apparently lasted only seven years, but it seems to have had drastic effects. The picture is very far from the vision given in Joshua of Israel taking over the land and expelling, or at the very least absorbing, its inhabitants. At this point the Israelites had been reduced to small groups huddled away in remote areas or in fortified townships. Any attempt made to settle even small sections of the land was crushed. *Whenever* (v. 3) implies a constant onslaught of small attacks eating away at the confidence and security of the Israelites. The writers emphasize the extent of the oppression in order to bring out once more how bad it had to get before Israel *cried out to the LORD*. But the unfolding story shows just how strongly Baalism had influenced them. The picture is of a people not just acknowledging Baal alongside Yahweh, but rather who took no part at all in Yahweh worship. Their crying out was not from any vestige of faith or trust but only from desperation.

7–10. Nevertheless, the reader's expectation is that once again God will respond and send another deliverer – but the pattern changes and that expectation is thwarted. The writers present us with both a recurring pattern and a development in Israel's response to the situation and God's response to them. There is no sense of an inevitable and unavoidable recurring cycle. God does in fact respond again and sends a messenger, but this time not a leader to deliver Israel; he sends instead a prophet to rebuke them and perhaps, if we have here an echoic preview of John the Baptist, to prepare them for what is to come. The implication is that God's patience, although extensive, will not last for ever. The Lord will not allow himself to be seen only as a last resort. He has already spoken and acted, and they have taken no notice. It must be clear that they have learned some of the lessons of history before he can be expected to act again. It is sometimes asserted that verses 7–10 were added into the text at a later stage, but the prophet's message fits well with the overall themes of Judges and forms an integral part of the text that has been handed down to us.[24] The prophecy can be seen as a summary of the law: it sets out what God has done for Israel and what he has asked of Israel. The conclusion that they have taken no notice of either who God was or what he has asked is reinforced by the unfolding story.

11–16. At this point we are introduced to Gideon. There is tremendous rhetorical skill in the storytelling here. In this instance no promise of a deliverer is given,[25] but we do have, without any direct reference to what has gone before, the immediate introduction of the angel's approach to Gideon. The writers emphasize both the point that God cannot be taken for granted and that he is a delivering God who takes action on his own initiative, not simply responding to their cries but showing mercy beyond anything they might deserve.[26] The narrative is ironic and probably intended to be humorous. Gideon may be defying the Midianites by doing his own threshing, but he is doing it hidden away in a winepress. Threshing – separating the seed, the edible part of a crop, from the chaff, the inedible straw and husks – was usually done, as can still be seen in some developing countries today, using animals in an open field, not by hand in a confined space. Gideon's actions indicate not only that the harvest must have been quite small but also that the one doing the threshing is afraid, and certainly not a rebel seeking to change society! In complete contrast the angel approached and *sat down*. There is no sign here of the nervous fear of powerful oppressors

---

24. One ancient text does omit these verses, and the assumption of those who take this view is that that text must be an earlier, and therefore more accurate, version of the original document (cf. Martin 2007: 113–140).

25. It may or may not be significant that although Gideon was clearly sent by God, the terms used elsewhere for leading and delivering are not used in relation to him.

26. 2 Kgs 17:7–23 describes the repeated pattern throughout Israel's history of God sending deliverers and prophets to a rebellious and evil people and constantly being rebuffed. But it also shows that God's patience with the northern kingdom of Israel really was eventually exhausted, and we have the repeated and final conclusion: 'The LORD removed them from his presence' (vv. 18, 23).

seen in Gideon and his fellow townsfolk; this is someone who is
relaxed and in control. His comment to Gideon may be ironic, but
it is also stressing that God's view of the situation is not that of the
Israelites. He sees the Midianite oppression not as something to be
afraid of but as something that can be dealt with. He sees Gideon
not as a frightened farmer but as the *mighty warrior* who, because
Yahweh is with him, he has the potential to become. Whether or
not Gideon recognized the man as *the angel of the LORD* is unclear,
but his defensive response ignoring the *mighty warrior* ascription
perhaps indicates that he was more aware of the irony than of the
prophetic possibilities for his future. He depersonalizes the angel's
statement, *The LORD is with you* (sing.), to *if the LORD is with us . . .* and
questions its accuracy, saying, in effect, 'If God really were with us
and really did do all the things we have been told about, then surely
he would have done something about our situation.'

It is worth noting that Gideon reflects knowledge of the prophet's
words (6:8–10) about what God has done for his people in the past,
but includes no acknowledgment that the reason for their current
state was in fact Israel's own sin, confirming the prophecy's conclusion
that they had not listened to God. Gideon takes the line that so many
of the Israelite people had taken over the years: 'If things are going
wrong, it must be God's fault, not ours.' It is interesting that there is
no criticism, explicit or implied, of Gideon's questioning, even though
it could well be seen as impertinent. However, the only answer given
is that implicitly provided in Yahweh's challenge to Gideon to *go in
the strength you have*. Gideon's initial premise is wrong. God has done
something about it: he has provided a solution to the situation; he has
equipped Gideon! The identification between Yahweh and the angel
of Yahweh is evidenced by the alternating use of the two terms.[27]
Whether or not the person Gideon saw was an angelic visitor or God
himself is to some extent irrelevant. There is no doubt at all in the
writer's mind, or in Gideon's, that the words spoken are the words of
Yahweh. Gideon's second response shows that he remains sceptical
and that he has still misunderstood the situation. His question is not

---

27. Cf. vv. 11, 14, 16, 17, 20, etc. Note that *the angel of God* and *the angel of the
LORD* (vv. 20, 22) are also synonymous.

'how will Yahweh save Israel' but *how can I save Israel?* His concentration on himself and the expectation that his own ability will be the determining factor perhaps explains why God spent so much effort later on in making sure that neither Gideon as leader, nor the army he led, could be given credit for the victory over Midian. Both the pattern and the content of Gideon's questioning reflect Moses' response to God in Exodus 3, and it seems probable that the writers are deliberately structuring the account both to emphasize the parallels and to bring out the differences. The fact that in Exodus 3 the Midianites helped Moses, whereas here they are the enemy, is an added irony. God's reply to Gideon reflects the reply that he gave to Moses. Gideon's weakness is of no account because God says, *I will be with you.* In fact, Gideon's claim to be the weakest link in a weak chain is somewhat exaggerated. We know that Gideon's father owned land, including the oak tree that may have been the centre of the troubled community (v. 11), and animals (v. 25), that his household was not small (v. 27) and that he appeared to have influence within the town.[28]

17–24. The parallels with Moses' call continue as Gideon asks for a sign (cf. Exod. 4:1), although for Gideon the point of the sign is not to confirm the task but rather to validate God's identity. It seems at first sight a fairly innocuous request and not obviously convincing. If the one talking to him is still there after an offering is brought, then Gideon will accept this as proof that it really is the angel of Yahweh. Presumably, his thought is that anyone who is willing to stay around for the length of time it would take to kill, prepare and cook a goat and who has not been chased away by the Midianites during that time must be both confident and powerful. The offering is eventually brought and miraculously consumed by fire. Gideon is petrified, but does accept the validity of the sign.[29]

---

28. We cannot be certain about the location of Ophrah. Its link not just to Gideon's father Joash but also to the Abiezrites in general (6:24) means that it is likely to be within the territory allotted to Manasseh, Abiezer being one of Manasseh's sons.

29. Note the parallel with Manoah's reaction to similar circumstances in Judg. 13, although here, where there is no sensible wife to provide reassurance, the angel himself speaks again!

Whether the conversation in verses 22–23 happened before the angel
had disappeared (v. 21) or whether this time God spoke in a different
way is not clear. Gideon's eventual belief and trust in Yahweh is
confirmed by his calling the altar he built *The LORD is peace*. At that
time there was nothing like peace in the area, but Gideon is at least
beginning to have confidence that with Yahweh's help peace just
might be something more than an impossible dream. The editorial
comment that the altar still stands indicates not only that the final
account was produced some significant time after the events in question, but also that Gideon's confidence was repaid – the Midianites
never did have the chance to destroy it. God did bring peace.

25–33. The existence of Gideon's newly discovered confidence
in Yahweh, and also its frailty, is evidenced in the next stage of the
narrative. Perhaps the fact that God spoke to him again on *that same
night* indicates God's awareness that his confidence might not last too
long. The nature of God's ongoing communication with Gideon is
not described, but whether it was through more angelic visits, dreams,
an audible voice or a mental conviction, the text is clear that although
Gideon had many doubts, he apparently never again doubted that it
was Yahweh who spoke to him. It appears he was no longer afraid
of the Canaanite gods and was confident that the God of Israel was
stronger than they were; he had no hesitation in destroying the Baal
altar and the Asherah pole. But he was afraid of the reactions of his
own people, so he did it at night when they were all asleep.

There are a number of textual difficulties in verses 25–26. Some
variants seem to refer to two bulls in verse 25, but as only one bull is
mentioned in the rest of the passage, the approach of most translations that the reference is to a specific bull, perhaps one of a pair,
is probably correct. The variations in the translation of verse 26 show
the difficulty of knowing whether it was the method of building, the
type or the site of the altar that was significant, but the new altar was
clearly distinguishable as dedicated to Yahweh, not Baal. It was built
on top of the height, or the rock or the stronghold, which means
that it would have been immediately visible to all. This is already a
declaration of war against Baal, if not yet against Midian. The use of
the sacred Asherah pole as fuel for the burnt offering dedicated to
Yahweh shows how far Gideon had come in recognizing the weakness
of the gods his people had been worshipping, but also explains the

horrified reaction of the Israelites who had not yet understood the power of Yahweh. The description of the torn-down altar as *your father's*, alongside the angry reaction of the townsfolk, points to Gideon's father, Joash, being the manager of the town's Baal shrine. It appears that Joash was a ˙pragmatist who served Baal because it was convenient and possibly profitable to do so. His loyalty to his own family seems to have been stronger than any loyalty he might have had to either Baal or Yahweh. The response he gives to the people's hostility reveals that Gideon was not the only talented member of his family. Joash's immediate grasp of the meaning of the situation and his ability to calm and convince the crowd were almost as significant in bringing the people to the point where they began to question Baal's power and be willing to face up to the Midianites as Gideon's own actions. Elijah in 1 Kings 18 makes use of Joash's technique, 'If Baal really is a god, he can defend himself', to convince the Baal-worshipping Israelites of his own day.

Readers are left to fill in the gaps. We are not told why the Midianites thought it necessary to assemble the whole of their allied forces for a major attack on Israel. Presumably, the story of Gideon's destruction of the pagan altars without any apparent negative consequences spread quickly throughout the region. Perhaps the new name for Gideon as Jerub-Baal, 'Baal-contender', helped this to happen.[30] This was not just a single act of courageous rebellion; it enabled the people to think the unthinkable. Perhaps Baal and the Midianite forces claiming the support of Baal could be defeated after all. Perhaps Yahweh really was still around and really could do something to help Israel. That kind of thinking would certainly prompt a response from Midian. They sent a large combined army, and when this aggressive approach from Midian and their allies

---

30. It has been suggested that Jerub-Baal was Gideon's original name and the narrator changed it to avoid a servant of God having a name that could perhaps be translated as 'possessed by Baal'. There is evidence of such name changing, as Merib-Baal (1 Chr. 8:34) became Mephibosheth (2 Sam. 4:4). However, in this instance it seems more likely that the name was seen as having a positive connotation. The explanation in 6:32 makes perfect sense.

came, Gideon was ready to fight and the people were ready to follow him. Not only those from his own Abiezrite clan but also forces from the rest of Manasseh and the three northern tribes responded to the call-up. Israel was once more a force needing to be dealt with, if not yet seen as a force to be reckoned with. Why Gideon sent the call for troops to only four of the tribes isn't clear. Was it because he trusted God and thought that would be enough to defeat the Midianite army, or because he did not trust the other tribes to come so it was better not to ask, although when the men of Ephraim were eventually called the response was quick and effective (7:24–26)? Or was it because the southern tribes were too far away and would not arrive in time? The text does not provide answers to these questions.

34–40. The fearful Gideon of earlier verses has been transformed into an army commander. The writers make the cause of this transformation unambiguous: *the Spirit of the LORD came on Gideon* (6:34).[31] This was what gave him the courage to blow the trumpet and issue the call to arms. However, Gideon's confidence in God did not yet stretch to the belief that God could give the weakened Israel the ability to defeat powerful human armies. He asks for another sign, this time one that might be seen as miraculous, an indication that God could control the forces of nature. But then his natural scepticism makes him think that perhaps a wet fleece could have happened by some natural means, so he asks for yet another sign – he could not envisage any way that a fleece could remain dry when the ground all around was wet. His hesitancy in asking for this extra sign shows his awareness that such a request does have problematic implications. It evidences an ongoing failure to accept that God can be trusted, and it is probably significant that there is no record of his response to the signs being given. God is portrayed as recognizing and responding to human weakness, but this cannot

---

31. See comment on the Spirit of the LORD coming on Othniel (p. 64).
In fact, although many versions use the same phrase *came on* to describe the way in which the Spirit empowered both Othniel and Gideon, the Hebrew terms used are different and the ESV translation that the Spirit 'clothed' Gideon is more accurate. This difference may or may not be significant.

be seen as an affirmation of Gideon's requests. Gideon's need for God's repeated action shows that signs per se are rarely really convincing.[32]

Meaning
The four chapters setting out the stories relating to Gideon and his sons form the longest narrative subdivision within the central section of Judges by quite a margin. The stories relating to Samson and his parents also take up four chapters, but they are considerably shorter. The writers clearly see this narrative as playing a significant part in getting across their message. The motifs that we have already seen are continued and developed, and the scene is set for the later stories, which confirm the overall theme emphasizing that life in Israel at this time was not how it was supposed to be. This narrative forms a turning point in the central section. The stories of the first three major 'deliverers' – Othniel, Ehud and Deborah – have left the reader with some sense of hope that in spite of Israel's recurrent 'doing evil', God's provision of effective leaders would eventually bring them back to the right path. At the end of chapter 6 this hope still remains, although even here perhaps the flame burns a little less brightly. It is made clear both that Israel has not in any way responded to the previous actions of God in saving and helping them through the leaders sent before this point, and that God is aware of this fact and this is affecting the way he will respond to them in the future. Nevertheless, it is equally clear that Yahweh is still the God of Israel and still taking action that will make it possible for them to live in the land as his covenant people. Just as we have seen that God can gift and use professional soldiers like Othniel, left-handed diplomats like Ehud and effective women judges like Deborah, he can also gift and use fear-filled and doubting farmers like Gideon. Whether this leader will not only defeat the current enemy but lead the people back to genuine service of Yahweh will be revealed in the following chapters!

---

32. Jesus' somewhat sceptical approach to signs was perhaps influenced by reflection on this passage (see Matt. 12:39; 16:4; Mark 8:11–12; Luke 16:31).

b. Gideon's campaign (7:1–25)

Context

The geographical area of Midian is usually assumed to be south of Edom on the north-eastern shore of the Red Sea. But the term seems to be used broadly for a collection of peoples from southern Arabia. In Genesis 37 the Midianites are traders in luxury goods and in slaves. In Exodus 2 Midianites provide sanctuary for Moses. Here they are seen as a cruel and oppressive enemy. We cannot be sure exactly who was included in this group, and it is clear (6:3) that they were allied with other eastern tribes that had troubled Israel before.

Chapter 6 ended with the signs that Gideon thought were necessary to reinforce his confidence in God. Chapter 7 continues the theme of confidence as the armed forces are reduced to such a small number that there could be no doubt at all that it was Yahweh, not a reinvigorated Israelite army, who brings victory and deserves the confidence of the people. If Yahweh's delivering action was not recognized, then no lesson could be learned and, in the context of these narratives of deliverers provided by Yahweh, there was no point in Yahweh taking action or in the story being recorded.

Comment

7:1–2. The geographical references are again difficult. Harod cannot be identified with any certainty, and no Mount Gilead is known west of the Jordan. It would make sense if the reference here were to Mount Gilboa, just a few miles across the Jezreel Valley from the hill of Moreh. It is worth noting that the action seems to be taking place in the territory assigned to Issachar, although Issachar is not named as one of the tribes to which Gideon sent out the call for troops (6:35). The account mirrors the standard ancient pattern of two opposing forces gathering in neighbouring areas, often at different sites in the same valley, before a mass fight takes place and one or other of the forces is destroyed.

3–8a. Numbers are always difficult to validate in early Old Testament writings because of the extensive use and acceptance of numbers in a symbolic way. Israel had no standing army until the time of Saul; fighting forces were raised as and when necessary. As every able-bodied man was expected to respond to the call to fight,

32,000 is not an impossible number. However, if this number of men, coming from only a few of the tribes, responded, it indicates that Midian's control was probably as much maintained through fear and Israel's resultant lack of confidence, as through any genuinely unbeatable power – in spite of the exaggerated description of the Midianite forces in 7:12.

One wonders how the instruction that all who were afraid could go home was delivered to the gathered men. That more than two-thirds of the group were willing to admit to *trembling with fear* could be further evidence of the extent of the oppression and an under-lying assumption that Midian was going to win anyway. But it may not be quite as devastating an indictment as it appears. Most countries, when conscripting an army, allow for what is sometimes called 'reserved occupations', which are deemed necessary for the ongoing running of the community. Only in a situation of absolute desperation would people doing these jobs be called to fight. The primary statement being made here is that Yahweh, not the army, is their redeemer, and because of that the situation is not desperate and the reserve troops are therefore not needed. The irony that seems to be a strong element in these narratives resurfaces here. To human eyes, the huge Midianite force is far too big ever to be defeated; in God's eyes, the small Israelite force is not yet small enough to achieve Midian's defeat in the way he is intending! But the retention of only a relatively small proportion of the potential fighters also makes the statement that the community will continue: it is worth the rest going home and looking after the animals and crops. However, for God's purposes the 10,000 brave men who remain are still far too many.

The method of distinguishing between those who will finally remain and the rest, that is, those who lapped and those who knelt down, remains obscure. Dogs use their tongues to lap from a stream – the illustration provided – which for humans would involve kneeling down or lying flat. It is sometimes assumed that the chosen ones scooped up the water with their hands, thus remaining more aware of their surroundings, and that this was the reason for their selection. But dogs do not scoop up water and the text does not draw that conclusion. It may just be that whatever the precise differ-ence was, it marked out a small minority. Three hundred men against the massed Midianite forces is meant to be seen by any reader as ridiculous. God tells Gideon to send all the others back *home* to their 'own place'. Gideon sent them, 'each to his tent' (ESV), which seems to imply that although they were not to form part of any battle, they remained in the camp 'just in case', perhaps indicating Gideon's ongoing fears.

9–15. God certainly recognizes these fears, and this time he provides a sign for Gideon without being asked. The focus on confidence continues. Gideon might not have been convinced that God was powerful enough to defeat the Midianite forces, but at least one member of those forces believed that that is what would happen. Perhaps the rumours about Gideon's destruction of the Baal altars had reached beyond Israel. If this was seen as a defeat of Midian's gods by Yahweh, as it might well have been, then the interpretation of the dream, which otherwise seems far from obvious, makes sense. Even a loaf of bread can be seen as an effective means of destruction, and the fact that Israel's army is known to be completely ineffective is irrelevant. Gideon, although unable to trust God's word, is finally convinced by the word of a Midianite soldier. His response to the dream and the interpretation given is to bow down and worship God. It may or may not be significant that this is the last time that Gideon is described as worshipping God.

16–22. The description of the 'battle' is dramatic, and the parallels with the account of the fall of Jericho (Josh. 6) can't be missed. The 300 men, equipped only with trumpets and hidden torches, spread out around the enemy camp. The change of guards in the middle of the night[33] meant that two sets of men who did not necessarily know or trust each other were around at the same time, one set very tired and one set only just awake. It is perhaps not surprising that the sudden onset of noise and light sent them into a panic. Those who were not on guard would have been woken by the noise, adding

---

33. If there were three watches in the hours of darkness between 6 pm and 6 am, then it would have been around 10 pm. In that context this would count as the middle of the night, and it is very likely that the new guard had snatched a couple of hours' sleep before they started and those on the third watch were also already asleep.

to the confusion. Whether there is significance in the fact that Gideon told the Israelites to shout (presumably when they had stopped blowing the trumpets!) *For the LORD and for Gideon*, and they actually shouted *a sword for the LORD and for Gideon*, is not clear. There is probably deliberate irony in the fact that they shouted about swords when they were not carrying them and that the enemy turned their own swords (specifically mentioned) on each other. Chaos followed the panic; the amalgamation of Midianite, Amalekite and other armies may have resulted in a massive army, but it was not coordinated. It would not have been easy to distinguish between friend and foe. The Israelites were not involved in the fighting at all; they simply stood around the camp (v. 21) while the Midianites fled in disarray. In this kind of warfare the chasing of the defeated army was almost as significant as the fight itself, as it had a huge effect on what might happen next and how quickly a new army might be formed. The towns mentioned are not all identifiable but are generally seen as being on the eastern side of the area. The soldiers were heading towards the Jordan, most of them originating from the other side.

23–25. We cannot be sure whether a new call went out to summon the Israelites from Naphtali, Asher and Manasseh or whether the 10,000 troops who remained in their tents now came into the picture. But a further call went to Ephraim to guard the Jordan fords and pick off the fleeing Midianite allies as they tried to cross. Younger (2002: 196) suggests that the killing of Oreb and Zeeb at a rock and a winepress is a fitting ending to the battle, as it was in a winepress that Gideon heard the call from God and at a rock where he first worshipped.

Meaning
In terms of the overall interest in how far Israel was living up to their covenant responsibilities and carrying out God's command to occupy and govern the land, then chapter 7 is something of a 'so far so good'. The picture of Gideon as a complex character, a paradoxical mixture of courage and fright, of belief and unbelief, of humility and arrogance and of acknowledging and not acknowledging his dependence on God, continues throughout this chapter and beyond and is maybe intended to further the writers' aim of

showing that God really can use all kinds of people. We see further evidence of the ongoing interest in the relationship between God's sovereignty and human responsibility. The Israelites need to recognize that only God is able to deliver Israel, that he certainly has that ability but that he also calls them to cooperate with him in the actions he is taking.

c. Emerging problems (8:1–35)

Context

The decisive victory over the Midianites, which we are told removed them as a threat and brought a further forty years of peace to Israel (8:28), should have been a high point for Gideon. He had achieved what God had asked of him. However, the underlying problems within the nation remained. The jealousies and rivalries between the different tribes, the rampant idolatry and the neglect of covenant responsibilities had not yet been dealt with, and all of these raise their heads again within the next chapter.

Comment

8:1–3. The Ephraimites, who had not taken part in the earlier fighting, were now called up by Gideon and commissioned to hold the Jordan River. They did this apparently not just at one crossing point but along a whole section.[34] They not only held the river, but also captured and killed two of the key Midianite commanders. However, they expressed anger towards Gideon (8:1) that they had not been given the opportunity to take a greater part in the overall campaign. Their reaction shows the somewhat shaky relationship between the Israelite tribes that is illustrated several times in Judges. This supports the view of those who see Israel at this time as a collection of loosely associated states probably not even united enough to be called a federation, and certainly not a coordinated grouping that could in any way be described as a united nation.

---

34. The location of Beth Barah (7:24), like that of most of the places mentioned in these chapters, cannot be identified with any level of certainty.

Ephraim's attitude does reflect some sense of responsibility to the whole community, but their jealousy and need to be affirmed as a significant tribe show that external oppression was not the only cause of Israel's failure to live together as God's people. Gideon's answer mentions God in the context of what he has enabled Ephraim to do, but makes no attempt to argue that God's involvement means that individual achievements are irrelevant, nor to explain the restriction of the first group to 300 men. Rather, demonstrating either his diplomatic skill or his knowledge of how the Ephraimites thought – and perhaps both – he concentrates on what they have done, stressing that on balance this outweighs the contribution of all the rest, including Gideon himself. There is perhaps a possibility that Ephraim was concerned that they might not get their fair share of any spoils of war, but the text does not put any emphasis on that.

4–21. The relationship between 7:23–24 where the larger army was involved and 8:4–21 where Gideon appears to be accompanied by only the original 300 is not clear. The story of the chase, capture and eventual death of two further Midianite leaders is told in graphic detail, which may reflect a separately circulating story incorporated by the writers into the final account. Gideon's group pursued the fleeing Midianites across the Jordan, presumably encountering the Ephraimites guarding the fords (7:24–25) on the way. The story of Gideon's defeat of Baal had either not reached Sukkoth and Peniel on the other side of the Jordan in the territory assigned to Gad, or had not convinced them. Certainly, the people of neither city were ready to risk the wrath of the apparently not finally defeated Midianites by providing supplies to Gideon's force. They clearly did not see Gideon, although a fellow Israelite, as their own leader but as a dangerous invader from another tribe. However, without their help, the decimated Midianite army –still numbering 15,000 – were caught, ambushed and defeated on the road to the south-east. The implication is that this further triumph was accomplished by Gideon's 300 men, but they are not specifically mentioned after verse 4 and other troops may also have been involved. The two kings were finally captured and taken back to the Gadite towns, where Gideon carried out the humiliating and violent revenge that he had promised on the two towns that had refused to help him. The town leaders at

Sukkoth were humiliated by being beaten with thorn and brier
branches – as he had warned them would happen. In the case of
Peniel he went much further than he had originally said, not only
pulling down their tower, but killing all the men. His own original
fears and need for many signs before he felt able to take action, even
for God, seems not to have given him any sympathy with others
who were afraid to support the coup. His revenge on these towns
seems to have been the first thing on his mind, but eventually he
killed the two kings he had been chasing. The text seems to show
a particular interest in Gideon's extended family. His expressed
willingness to have allowed the two kings to live if they had killed
only Israelites unrelated to him seems to show that his loyalty to
family is stronger than that to Israel as a whole. If the Ephraimites'
primary loyalty was to their tribe, Gideon's appears to have been to
his family. Gideon's son Jether is not mentioned by name elsewhere,
and the reference here is perhaps included to show the way in which
Gideon has progressed from a fearful youth to a confident man.
Alternatively, given the people's request in verse 22, this could be a
sign that Gideon wants to present his son as a warrior fit to rule with
him or after him. Jether's failure to meet this expectation perhaps
gave Gideon a reminder of the lessons he had been taught relating
to dependence on God and may have been influential on his reply
to their request. This story is told without editorial comment, and
there is no mention of God except in Gideon's own speech. He does
suggest to the people of Sukkoth that it will be God who enables
him to defeat Zebah and Zalmunna (v. 7) and later uses Yahweh's
name in an oath (v. 19), but unlike the earlier narratives there is no
real recognition of the victory being God's or of Gideon's ongoing
actions being part of God's call on his life. It may be that we are
being led to consider whether Gideon's diplomatic skills might
actually have been put to better use in this situation.

22–27. Verses 22–27 begin well; Gideon does refuse the people's
request for him to found a royal dynasty. The basis he gives for this
refusal, whether or not it was affected by the demonstrated fear of
his own young son, was that *The LORD will rule over you*. It seems that
even if the people had not, Gideon had grasped the lesson that was
supposed to have been learned from the use of only 300 soldiers to
defeat the Midianites. It was Yahweh, not the army, not Gideon and

not Gideon's son, who was their real Saviour. However, even here there is irony, and Webb's comments (1987: 152) on these events are worth noting:

> The danger is that the Israelites will fail to give Yahweh the credit for the deliverance . . . if the rationale of the offer is that he who saves is entitled to rule, that entitlement belongs to Yahweh, not Gideon. The irony . . . is that the impiety from which Gideon recoils is of his own making. From the moment he crossed the Jordan he has acted more and more like a king, especially in his dispensing of summary punishments on those who resisted his authority.

As the story unfolds, we see another parallel with the exodus story, this time not with the call of Moses but with the sin of Aaron (Exod. 32), in making an image out of golden earrings, this time from the plunder gained from the Midianites (v. 24).

Gideon's already demonstrated need for visible evidence of God's presence possibly made him believe that the people would be more likely to accept that Yahweh was with them, and specifically with Gideon, if they had something to look at: hence the gold ephod. The same word is used in a very different sense to describe the simple garment worn by the young Samuel and by David (1 Sam. 2:18; 2 Sam. 6:14) and also the jewel-encrusted part of the high priest's ceremonial clothing (Exod. 28:6–14). We do not know what shape this particular ephod took; the term is used in a parallel way to describe the idol made by Micah in Judges 17:5. But even if Gideon intended the ephod to represent Yahweh, the worship of all images is seen as idolatry. Thus, the Israelites who did worship the idol are seen as prostituting themselves, turning away from Yahweh who could never be represented by such an image, however beautifully made. The description of the image as a *snare* to Gideon and his family may simply be implying that they too worshipped the idol. However, it could also be suggesting that they thought that as they possessed the idol, which people came to their home town to worship, they therefore in some sense possessed Yahweh. Whether or not they also believed that this was what gave them a right to rule remains an open question, although it is clear that they did assume such a right. Gideon began by destroying the pagan shrine overseen by his own family, and he ended by creating an alternative and equally pagan shrine, also overseen by his own family (see Butler 2009: 222).

28–35. These verses provide the standard ending for the narrative, telling us that the threat from Midian had been decisively dealt with and the land, presumably under Gideon's ongoing leadership, was at peace. But the presentation of the two sides of Gideon's character continues. Verse 28 is sandwiched between two other short sections that appear to come from unrelated sources, neither showing Gideon in a particularly good light, but the second is less obviously critical than the first. The three previous occasions where the phrase *the land had peace for . . . years* occurs (3:11, 30; 5:31) are all closely followed by the information that *the Israelites did evil*, that God therefore handed them over to a given enemy, that they eventually cried out and new leaders (Ehud, Deborah and Barak, Gideon) were provided. In this instance the pattern is different. Although it is clear that the evil was present, the formal phrasing is missing, and there is no mention in the following verses either of the crying out of the people or of the sending of help from God. In fact, the phrase *the Israelites did evil* does not appear again until the beginning of the Jephthah narrative in 10:6 – perhaps providing further evidence to support the view that the story of Abimelek is meant to be seen as a continuation of the Gideon story.

Verses 29–35 tell us more of Gideon's family life, which involved many wives and many sons. It is ironic that although Gideon had apparently turned down the offer to 'rule over Israel' and in effect to be king, the son born to him by his concubine at Shechem is called Abimelek, meaning 'my father is king'.[35] We are explicitly told that it was Gideon himself who gave the boy this name, which makes something of a nonsense of his earlier claim to have turned down kingship. The ironic twist here is that Shechem is the place where

---

35. If one were to assume that the meaning is 'my [divine] Father is king', then obviously this would put Gideon's choice in a more positive light. However, although it is common for God to be presented as the Father of the nation, evidence for him being seen as the Father of individuals is less convincing – hence the problem that the religious leaders of Jesus' time had with his claim that God was his Father.

in Joshua's time the people made a solemn covenant committing themselves to Yaweh (Josh. 24). This section of the narrative makes no mention of the ephod and does not hint that Israel's turning back to the Baals as soon as Gideon had died might have had something to do with his own behaviour. But if they had been led to identify Yahweh with an image, it is perhaps not surprising that they turned so easily to other such images. Once Jerub-Baal, the Baal conqueror, had gone, then the Baals might once more be seen as powerful. In fact, Gideon had been instrumental in bringing a final end to any military threat from Midian, but his contending against Baal had proved far less successful. The editorial comment in verse 35 does seem to imply that the failure of the people to show loyalty to Gideon's family should be seen as blameworthy, but how that loyalty should have been demonstrated and whether the writers are suggesting that it should have involved acknowledging Gideon's sons as rulers is not made clear. It certainly reflects the line that the only remaining brother, Jotham, takes in his speech to Shechem in 9:7–20.

Meaning
The story of Gideon and his sons leaves us questioning whether there is any real basis for the hope that leaders provided by God would eventually lead Israel back to the covenant commitment seen in the time of Joshua. Yes, there are high points where Gideon shows that he is capable of demonstrating both trust and obedience, and which mean that the hope for genuine change is not yet destroyed. But after these stories, we are not surprised at the way in which the next set of narratives develops. So by the time we get to the end of the Samson stories, the hope that this particular structure of the community and this (or these) particular forms of leadership will ever enable Israel to live in the way God intended as his covenant people lies in ashes.

The ongoing interest in the narrative that God can use all kinds of people continues in the Gideon narratives, but here it is more clearly indicated that because a leader has been chosen, appointed and gifted by God does not mean that that leader should automatically be seen as a man of God. Unless that leader actually lives out a commitment to the covenant and guides the nation into also taking up that commitment, there will be inevitable consequences following on from his or her bad behaviour.

ii. Abimelek (9:1–56)

12a[36]

Context

Only one of the identified characteristics of the leader/deliverer narratives (see Introduction, pp. 59–60) occurs within this chapter, that is, the description of Abimelek's death. This does raise questions about the inclusion of this story at this point. The link with Gideon's family clearly makes it appropriately placed here, but as a narrative it seems to have more in common with the stories of individual corruption in chapters 17 – 21 than with those in this central section of Judges. However, the repeated mention of Gideon's alternative name, Jerub-Baal, which occurs nine times in this chapter, including in the first and last verses, does indicate that this section is intended to be read alongside the previous chapters as part of the Gideon narratives.[37] It is possible that the writers inserted this material to illustrate the ongoing consequences, including the death of Abimelek, of the trap that had ensnared Gideon and his family (8:27). This is not made explicit within the text, but there is no doubt that attention to actions and their consequences is a theme that can be traced throughout the chapter. Abimelek is described as the son of Gideon's *concubine, who lived in Shechem* (8:31). It is not easy to determine the exact status of a concubine, but in a polygamous society concubines were probably regarded as legitimate secondary wives. The fact that this one did not live with the others in Ophrah and that Jotham refers to her disparagingly as Gideon's female slave could indicate that Abimelek was not acknowledged by the rest of

---

36. The list of numbers at the start of each of the twelve accounts shows which of the elements listed above on pp. 59–60 is found within that particular account.

37. Whether or not this was originally a separate narrative is somewhat irrelevant to the purposes of the writers in the text as we have it.

the family. It is possible that his actions were a consequence of their rejection of him.

As Butler points out, the narrative is 'anchored by dialogue' (Butler 2009: 234), with the speech of various characters and groups of characters constantly recorded. This indicates that the chapter needs to be seen very much as a single story. To make it easier for readers, we have split this into four sections, but as with all the narrative sections in Judges, these need to be seen together, and although reference to individual verses is included, to try to find detailed meaning in those individual verses within the overall narrative will not always be helpful.

Comment

9:1–6. The implication of the dialogue in verses 1–6 is that the seventy sons of Gideon were claiming, or were threatening to claim, some kind of joint sovereignty over Shechem. This makes sense of the decision of the local council to accept Abimelek, rather than his half-brothers, as king, and of Jotham's claim that making Abimelek king was an act of rebellion against Gideon's family. The whole impact is again to lessen somewhat the force of Gideon's affirmation that neither he nor his sons would rule over Israel. The account begins not with any approach from God in response to their expressed need, nor even with the approach of the people to a desired leader, but with Abimelek putting himself forward. In the context of the overall interest in the appointment of leaders seen within the book of Judges, that must be significant. For the citizens[38] of Shechem, Abimelek not only had the advantage of being the son of the famed Gideon, he was also a local boy related to at least some of them through his mother. Given that they had been used to oppressive control from outside and had little experience of good governance, the local connection obviously had a real impact on

---

38. The Hebrew text in vv. 2 and 6 speaks of the *baals* of Shechem, using the word in its original sense of 'lords' rather than referring to the gods. The LXX has 'all the men', perhaps deliberately avoiding any association with the Baal gods, and the NIV's *citizens* is a good reflection of the meaning here.

their thinking. Shechem was in the heart of Israelite territory, close to the southern border of Manasseh. It had played a significant part in their early history, since Abraham had built an altar, Jacob had camped nearby and Joshua had led the covenant renewal ceremony there (Gen. 12:6–7; 33:18; Josh. 24:1–25). There is no direct reference here to that history, but the writers of Judges and later readers would almost certainly have been very much aware of it. Gaal's reference in verse 28 to *Hamor, Shechem's father* (cf. Gen. 34:2ff.) suggests that there were still Canaanites living in the city who could be persuaded to turn against Abimelek, but Jotham's claim that Gideon had *risked his life to rescue* Shechem *from the hand of Midian* does indicate that they saw themselves as an Israelite town. Gaal's argument certainly suggests that Abimelek was seen as an Israelite rather than a Canaanite leader. Whether the town leaders were primarily Israelite or primarily Canaanite is not clear. Their acceptance of Abimelek as a 'brother'[39] does not really tell us which community his uncles belonged to. The fact that they provided resources for him from the temple of Baal-Berith shows the extent to which Baalism had infiltrated the town, but then that was true across the whole of Israel, not least in Gideon's own home town of Ophrah. Abimelek is clearly happy to accept resources from that source and shows no sign of knowledge of, let alone allegiance to, Yahweh.

There is no indication that Abimelek's authority ever stretched, or indeed was ever intended to stretch, beyond the regions of Shechem.[40] He became king of a city-state rather than of a nation or even a region. It was not until Shechem turned against him and was destroyed that he even tried to take over the nearby town of Thebez (v. 50). Unless his half-brothers were claiming that Shechem was part of the territory that they controlled, there seems to be no reason at all for Abimelek to kill them other than for personal revenge. The writers, by describing Abimelek's troops as *reckless scoundrels* (v. 4), certainly express disapproval of his actions. However,

---

39. Translated in NIV as *He is related to us.*

40. Beth Millo (9:6, 20) may be a nearby settlement but is just as likely to be a distinct section of Shechem itself – possibly the same area described in v. 49 as the tower of Shechem (cf. Gray 1967: 243).

it does seem as if the town supported his plans, and it was not until he had killed all Gideon's other sons except one that they crowned him as king. Whether the other sons' deaths were a consequence of their (or their father's) underlying desire to rule the nation, or their attitude to Abimelek, or simply an indication of Abimelek's violent nature, the fact remains that they did, with the exception of Jotham[41] the youngest, all die. That they were all killed *on one stone* could imply that they were captured and executed, rather than killed in any battle, but we are not given enough details to be sure. It is possible that the *stone* mentioned is the 'height' on which Gideon built an altar to Yahweh (6:26), and if so, there could be sacrificial implications, but that can only be speculation. That Abimelek did not simply slide into leadership but was 'properly' appointed by the people is indicated by the description of his coronation in verse 6.

7–21. Jotham's impassioned speech is not, as one might have expected, addressed to Abimelek, but to the city of Shechem. His introductory statement, *Listen to me . . . so that God may listen to you*, is unusual and somewhat opaque. It is worth noting that Jotham's position was on the heights of Mount Gerizim, almost certainly not literally on the summit, but on some vantage point where his voice would project and be audible to those well below, yet far enough away for him to be able to escape easily. Mount Gerizim was where the tribes stood who were called upon to pronounce God's blessing on those who honoured their covenant relationship with God (Deut. 27:12). It seems possible that Jotham is saying, 'Listen to me so that God may bless you.' If this is so, then implicit in Jotham's statement is that, otherwise, the call from those tribes who stood on Mount Ebal and pronounced a curse on all who broke the covenant requirements would come into effect. However, Jotham actually shows no interest in whether or not they have turned away from God; his only concern is over what he sees as the betrayal of his father. In fact, this is the only mention of God in the speech, and the whole credit

---

41. Cf. 2 Kgs 11 where Joash (the namesake of Jotham's grandfather), the
youngest son of King Ahaziah, was rescued when all the other potential
heirs were killed by Queen Athaliah.

for the defeat of Midian (v. 17) is given to Gideon rather than to God – perhaps reflecting the way that the story was told by Gideon to his sons.

The story Jotham tells is clearly intended to be a fable or a parable.[42] The specific mention of anointing a king shows that leadership is the point at issue and specifically the introduction of a monarchy.[43] Three trees whose value as fruit-bearers is obvious; the olive, the fig and the vine are offered the role of king but all refuse – on the grounds that production of good things for the community is better than authority over the community. Are these trees meant to represent Gideon's family and his willingness to serve Israel while refusing to be king? Probably, but if so, Jotham's conclusion that Shechem's crowning of Abimelek is a revolt against Gideon's family does not seem an obvious tie-in. The story goes on to describe the reaction of the thorn-bush who, when offered the crown, appears to accept, but this also is not absolutely clear. The assumption is that the thorn-bush represents Abimelek, and the parable therefore suggests that to make him king is foolhardy. However, the statement by the thorn-bush that if you do want me as king, *come and take refuge in my shade* is ambiguous. As the thorn-bush has little space for shade, the likelihood of this happening is negligible. Is Abimelek himself supposedly recognizing this? Does *but if not* in verse 15 refer to the anointing as king (i.e. 'if you don't want to anoint me then . . .'), or does it refer to the not wanting to shelter? Is the reference to fire coming *out of the thorn-bush* (v. 15) related to the fact that in general the only use for that kind of wood is to be burnt in order to bring warmth or for cooking? The bramble bush was generally seen in ancient times as, in contrast to the fruit-trees, almost useless.[44]

---

42. Cf. Nathan's story in 2 Sam. 12 and Jehoash's illustration in 2 Kgs 14:9.

43. This is sometimes seen as adding weight to the opinion of those who see Judges as having been compiled to support the role of the monarchy; whether it actually does do that remains debatable.

44. Soggin (1981: 172, 175) points out that such bushes in fact have a very significant use in preventing erosion on the lower slopes of mountains, but that was not recognized in ancient times and the story clearly indicates a distinction between useful and useless.

Of course, parables of this kind are intended to be impression-istic, and detailed analysis is not necessarily helpful, but the relevance to the situation of Jotham and Abimelek does not seem quite as clear as is sometimes assumed. Perhaps this is a well-known story being quoted here simply to back up the point that if, as Jotham is clearly implying, Shechem has not kept faith with Gideon by appoint-ing Abimelek, then may the consequence of that appointment be their destruction. It is easy to see how the killing of Gideon's sons is a breach of faith with Gideon, but without that, to understand why the appointment of one of his sons as king, rather than the others, should be regarded as betraying Gideon is more difficult. Jotham and his brothers may not have been happy to acknowledge Abimelek as Gideon's son, but by giving him a name (8:31), Gideon himself clearly accepted his role as parent. After delivering his speech, Jotham disappears from the scene and is mentioned again only in passing (9:57). There is no more indication that God had called or enabled Jotham than there is that he had called or enabled Abimelek. The text presents the whole story simply as internecine strife – in effect, a family row.

22–49. Abimelek clearly governed 'in Israel' and over 'some Israelites' but was never in control of the whole of Israel, as verse 22 could be seen as suggesting. Several of the 'judges' are also described as leading Israel when their sovereignty was similarly limited.[45] This is simply an example of the Hebrew idiomatic over-statement. Perhaps unsurprisingly given its violent beginnings, the relationship between Abimelek and the citizens of Shechem deteriorates after only three years. The text is clear that this conflict was *stirred up* by God himself (v. 23). The Hebrew tells us that God sent an 'evil spirit'. In other narratives – of Othniel, Gideon, Jepthah and Samson – God sends the *Spirit of the LORD* to strengthen them for battle (3:10; 6:34; 11:29; 14:6, 19). Here, the evil spirit affects both sides and brings only dissension. The writers apparently want to make sure that readers understand that God is involved in all that

---

45. In fact, Israel per se plays little part in this narrative, which focuses on the local leadership struggle and shows no interest in the 'state of the nation'.

happens to Israel, whether good or bad. It is interesting that the reason given for this 'stirring up' is not that Shechem appointed Abimelek as their leader, or even that they made him king, but that they and he conspired together to murder Gideon's other sons. Both parties were to blame, and that perhaps explains why the evil spirit was sent between them rather than just on Abimelek. However, the surface reason for the disagreement is that Abimelek had apparently instituted a positive policy towards visitors and opposed violent attacks. The Shechemites ignored this policy and surrounded the city with brigands so that no passing groups were safe. The implication could be that Abimelek was actually ruling well but that his previous desire for revenge over his brothers had encouraged the violence that he now wished to control. The books of Samuel pick up this theme when the consequences of David's own actions are seen in the behaviour of his sons, which David himself then found completely unacceptable (2 Sam. 13 – 19).

Gaal,[46] a new resident of Shechem (v. 26) and aware of the growing dissatisfaction with Abimelek, identifies himself with the pre-Israelite residents of the area (cf. Gen. 34) and organizes a rebellion against Abimelek and the current governor of the city who supported Abimelek's rule. The citizens of Shechem *put their confidence in him*. The easy moving of their trust from Abimelek to Gaal brought disastrous consequences, and perhaps the mention of it is intended to show that trust placed anywhere other than in God himself is misplaced. A further implication could be that loyalty easily given (i.e. to Abimelek rather than to Gideon's other sons) can easily be taken away. The description of the resulting conflict has parallels with several other Old Testament stories (e.g. the fight between Abraham and the forces that attacked Sodom and captured Lot, Gen. 14; the destruction of Ai, Josh. 8; the attack on the Benjaminites, Judg. 20:29–36). In this case, Gaal and his supporters are soundly defeated, although unlike the other cases cited there is no mention of God's involvement or of any credit

---

46. Gaal is described as *son of Ebed*. However, whether Ebed is a proper name, as the NIV implies, or a derogatory term, 'son of a slave', is not really clear. Cf. Butler 2009: 245.

being given to him. Who Abimelek's troops (v. 34) were is not explained, although verse 55 implies that they were Israelites and presumably shows that Abimelek did have some influence outside the city of Shechem. Abimelek's tendency to take violent and extreme revenge against those who act against him is illustrated once more. Zebul, the governor, clearly remained loyal to Abimelek, and there must have been others who supported him.[47] But Abimelek apparently took no note of that, and so, because some of the citizens had backed Gaal and in spite of the fact that all Gaal's relatives had now been thrown out (v. 41), he wiped out the whole city.

Exactly what happened is not entirely clear. Verses 40–41 speak of the defeat and expulsion of all Gaal's supporters, but in verse 42 the people of the city went out into the fields as if nothing had happened. Why this should arouse Abimelek's wrath is not obvious, but it clearly did. Perhaps he was looking for some kind of reaffirmation of his lordship, which was not forthcoming. So he destroyed them as well. Spreading salt would mean that there would be no possibility of crops being planted in the area for a considerable period. This destruction was complete and intentional. Presumably, even the property of Abimelek's own family would have been made uninhabitable. Abimelek and his forces may have won the battle but, in doing so, he had also destroyed his own role! There was now no city over which he could be king. In terms of Jotham's parable, the fire coming out of the

---

47. Gaal speaks of Zebul as Abimelek's *deputy*, which could imply that he
    had been appointed by Abimelek and was not actually from the city, but
    could simply mean that as he was a supporter of Abimelek he should be
    seen as in Abimelek's pocket and therefore discounted. It is somewhat
    ironic that Gaal, who moved in from outside, identifies himself with
    the city and tries to get them to see Abimelek, whose mother and uncle
    came from there, as outsiders. Scholars vary as to whether they see
    Gaal as a genuine outsider or a returning resident of Shechem – the
    text does not provide clear evidence either way – but there is no doubt
    that he had not been an integral part of the community any more than
    Abimelek had.

ruling thorn-bush to destroy the city had also destroyed the thorn-bush.[48]

The *tower of Shechem* is clearly a fairly large area, possibly distinct from the city but adjacent to it, that in itself contained a *stronghold*[49] dedicated to *El-Berith*, meaning 'god of the covenant', who is presumably to be identified with Baal-Berith, 'lord of the covenant' (8:33; 9:4). This is clearly seen as a pagan god, and the covenant in question could be that between people and land (Baal often being associated with fertility). However, the use of the term so closely associated with Israel's relationship with Yahweh could have led to confusion in the minds of uninformed Israelite peasants and encouraged the worship of this particular Baal.[50] But those who sought refuge in this stronghold did not escape; the tower was burnt and the people inside were incinerated.

50–57. The reason for Abimelek's siege of Thebez, a few miles north of Shechem, is not stated. Was it simply to find a new base now that Shechem was no longer there? If so, then his attempt again to destroy the city seems counterproductive. Had Thebez joined Shechem in their revolt? This is usually taken as read, but the only actual evidence for this is the attack itself. Whatever the reason for the attack, the citizens of Thebez also took refuge in the town's large stronghold. This time a woman from the town, a forerunner of many other wise women described in Scripture (e.g. 2 Sam. 14:2; 20:16), foresaw that Abimelek would again try to burn down the tower and was ready for him. The upper millstone which,

---

48. Soggin's conclusion (1981: 194) that the intention is to contrast Gideon's pious refusal to take kingship and Abimelek's attempt 'to hold on to it at any price' becomes less convincing when one realizes that Abimelek's own actions ensured that even had he not died, he would no longer have had any subjects to rule over.

49. Many cities built such strongholds in order to ensure survival in case of attack by a stronger enemy. The large community nuclear fallout shelters built in some towns, particularly in Switzerland, would be a modern equivalent.

50. The incident certainly provides a clear rationale for the law's requirement that children be adequately taught about their faith (Deut. 4:9; 11:9).

when rotated on the top of another larger stone, was used to grind grain, would have been just light enough for the woman to drop from the wall, but certainly heavy enough to cause serious damage to anyone below (see Herr and Boyd 2002: 34–37). There is irony in the fact that the text records Abimelek's unwillingness to be known as having been killed by a woman, at the same time ensuring that is exactly what would be known! David appears to have used this woman's actions when training his men to keep away from the city walls when fighting in a siege situation, but when Joab quotes this, it is obvious that the story is told mentioning only the woman and not the armour bearer who actually struck the final blow! The identity of the *Israelites* who *went home* (v. 55) is somewhat obscure but appears to refer to the troops who had been supporting Abimelek. The comment confirms that these events were not about the safety of Israel herself, but about the power of a particular leader.

Jotham's call for Abimelek and the citizens of Shechem to destroy each other (v. 20), described in verse 57 as a curse, is seen as having been answered. However, it is clear that it is the independent action of God himself that lay behind the events. God's action is presented as the consequence of their murderous activity, not a consequence of Jotham's curse. So at the end of Gideon's short-lived dynasty Midian was no longer a threat to the Israelite tribes, but whether Israel herself was in a better place is very much left as an open question.

Meaning

Chapter 9 is a prime example of the overall theme of Judges that how they were living was not how it was meant to be. The writers' interest in the people's relationship with God and the extent to which they adhere to the covenant is shown largely by the lack of that relationship. It should have been there, but was not! However, the writers also demonstrate concerns about human relationships, about family and community loyalty and how these affect the ongoing well-being of Israel as a whole. We are provided with evidence of the way in which leadership can be used both to benefit and to destroy communities. We were clearly shown that Gideon did have the potential to be the kind of leader that God wanted, and there is a possible implication that this was true for Abimelek as well. Things could have ended differently, but they did not! The Abimelek story in particular shows the futility of life lived without reference to God, that the acquisition of power per se does not bring fulfilment, and that leadership is about a lot more than the ability to exercise military power and the expression of gratuitous violence.

G. Two 'minor' leaders (10:1–5)

Context

The timing of all the accounts of the work of different leaders in Israel is not easy to determine. The reference to Abimelek in 10:1, when subsequent accounts of minor judges (here and in 12:8, 15) just say that *he was followed by* or *after him*, may indicate that this was originally the start of a separate document. Whether or not this is so, the chronological marker at the beginning of each of the five accounts makes it clear that the writers are intending the overall work to be seen as arranged chronologically. It has to be said that there is not really enough external evidence to confirm whether or not this is correct. The amount of information given in reference to Tola and all the other minor judges is so limited that most conclusions about their lives can only be tentative. Nevertheless, there are a number of comments that can be made, not just the fact that the existence of these so-called 'minor' leaders reminds us that life in Israel was not just about a series of well-known 'heroes'.

Comment
i. Tola (10:1–2)

9a, 10, 11, 12a, 12b[51]

The reason for the extended genealogy provided for Tola is not clear, but he is the only one of the twelve deliverer/leaders where

---

51. The list of numbers at the start of each of the twelve accounts shows which of the elements listed above on pp. 59–60 is found within that particular account.

both the father's and the grandfather's names are listed.⁵² Both Tola
and Puah were names given to Issachar's sons and therefore referred
to clans within the tribe. The ascription *a man of Issachar* may be
included to make it clear that in this case a specific individual is
involved. Although explicitly described as belonging to the tribe
of Issachar, Tola, like Deborah, was based within the territory of
Ephraim.⁵³ We are told that he *rose to save Israel* (v. 1). It is sometimes
assumed that this was from another armed assault from outsiders,
which may be correct, although this time we are given no details of
the oppressors, the nature of the oppression or Israel's reaction to
it. It is also possible that Tola and the other minor judges were more
concerned with ongoing local government – perhaps 'holding court'
in the way that Deborah did (4:5) – saving Israel in the sense of
'preserving existence' (Boling 1975: 187), maybe putting right
problems left behind by Abimelek (cf. Butler 2009: 257). Tola
remained in office for twenty-three years. Whereas the forty- and
eighty-year time periods for previous judges could be seen as
symbolic, this non-rounded number is presumably intended to be
accurate – a further pointer towards the writers' interest in giving a
sense of historical progression. The information that Tola died and
was buried at his home in Shamir indicates, although the fact is not
explicitly mentioned, that during his time the land was at peace. It
also supports a view that his area of control was probably restricted
to the region around his home. If a wider area of influence was
involved, it seems more likely that his body would have been returned

---

52. Of course, we do know the names of Abimelek's father and grandfather,
but they are not listed together. The name Dodo is related to the word
for paternal uncle, and the LXX translates the phrase as 'son of his uncle'
rather than listing it as a name. What that would imply in this particular
context is not clear.

53. This provides confirmation that the tribal boundaries were not
sacrosanct; people did live and work outside the territories assigned to
their own tribes. How far they were accepted and whether or not they
were regarded as 'foreigners' remains a matter of debate, but it does
mean that speculation about the tribal origins of Deborah, for example
(see p. 61), is legitimate.

to the land of his fathers in Issachar's territory. The precise location of Shamir is unknown; its similarity to the name Samaria, also in Ephraim, is often assumed to be significant.

Michael Wilcock (1992: 103–104) suggests that this little pericope is linked to the narratives concerning Deborah by the three terms: *rose* (v. 1; cf. 5.7 where Deborah *arose, a mother in Israel*), *lived* (v. 1; the word used here can also mean 'sat' or even 'presided' in the way that Deborah did under the palm tree in 4:5), and *led* or 'judged', a term which has so far been used only in reference to Othniel, the first judge, and Deborah. This seems a little tenuous, but if Wilcock is right, then there could be an implication that Tola's period in office was positive, bringing the kind of peace that was achieved during Deborah's time.

ii. Jair (10:3–5)

9a, 10, 11, 12a, 12b[54]

Jair is described as coming from Gilead,[55] that is, in the area east of the Jordan occupied by the tribes of Gad, Reuben and half of the tribe of Manasseh. However, we are not given details of either his father's name or his tribe. It is possible that the eastern tribes had much more of a joint identity than the rest, and therefore the specific tribal identity was seen as of lesser significance than the fact that he came from the trans-Jordan group. The information that his thirty sons rode thirty donkeys and controlled thirty towns is almost certainly included to convey the extent of Jair's wealth and influence. The same kind of statement might be made today in relation to the number of cars owned within one family. It is possible that this

---

54. The list of numbers at the start of each of the twelve accounts shows which of the elements listed above on pp. 59–60 is found within that particular account.

55. Gilead was one of Manasseh's sons, and the name is assigned to one of the clans of Manasseh as well as to the wider region. Thus, although it seems most likely, we can't be absolutely certain that the usage here is in the broader sense.

should be seen positively as an indication that the land as a whole was at peace and relatively prosperous. Donkeys would not normally be able to be ridden freely across the countryside under the kind of oppressive regime that Gideon, for example, faced. It could, on the other hand, be seen negatively as leaders building up wealth in a way that was frowned upon by the Deuteronomist (Deut. 17:14–17).

Numbers 32:41 states that Manasseh's descendant Jair captured an unknown number of settlements in Gilead that were also known as 'Havvoth Jair'. We cannot be completely sure whether these two accounts are referring to the same person or whether two separate people have been confused. The twenty-two years is again almost certainly not intended to be symbolic, and once more, the description that he had died and was buried in Kamon, presumably his home, gives a further indication that it was a time of peace. Kamon is usually identified as a town in Gilead on the border of Manasseh and Gad territory.

Meaning

The accounts of the six major leaders all begin with a reference to the fact that *the Israelites did evil*, whereas there is no mention of this in the six minor accounts. This may of course simply be because of brevity. However, it seems possible that the writers are suggesting that there were periods of peace and stability during these times, and if only Israel had acted or responded as they should have with regard to the covenant, then things could have been very different. Israel's failure to keep the covenant and the subsequent periods of disasters and oppression were not to be seen as inevitable. Whether the evil Israel did that caused God to take further action was absent or lessened while Tola and Jair were in office is unknown, but that could be the impression that the writers want to leave. Shamgar (3:31) is the only one of the minor judges who is portrayed as having any kind of military role. Webb (1987: 161) suggests that the description of the wealth of Jair's sons is an indication that they were pampered and unfit for military service, hence the stress on the need for a warrior in the following account. However, we do not have enough information to judge whether or not the sons did a good job in governing the towns assigned to them or whether they deliberately avoided necessary military tasks. The writers' presentation of the events as in chronological order suggests that the services of a military commander were necessary because of further action taken by God, rather than because of any deficiency on the part of Jair and his family.

H. Jephthah (10:6 – 12:7)

1, 2, 3, 4, 5, 6, 7, 8, 9a, 10, 11, 12a, 12b[56]

The overall thrust of the Jephthah narrative will determine whether the identification of the Gideon stories as a turning point in the central section of the book is correct. If it is, then we will expect to see the situation getting worse, evil increasing and the possibility of any real ongoing commitment to the covenant with Yahweh decreasing. If it is not, then we will expect to see significant changes in a positive direction. What we do find is not quite so clear-cut! Although the overall presentation gives us no reason to doubt that Israel was definitely on a downward spiral, it is still clearly a spiral rather than a straight slope. We will see here, as previously, high points alongside the low points, providing some indication, or at least a hope, that the Deuteronomic vision of Israel living out the covenant might be diminishing, but it has not yet been extinguished.

Webb (1987: 41–78) provides an extended discussion of the structure of Judges 10:6 – 12:7, where he divides the narrative into five 'episodes': 10:6–16; 10:18 – 11:11; 11:12–28; 11:29–40; 12:1–7. I have included verses 17 and 18 in the first section and separated Webb's fourth episode into two halves, but this does not negate the validity of most of his arguments. It is worth noting the extent to which dialogue dominates the text. Thus we have dialogue between Jephthah and his brothers (11:1–3), the elders (11:4–11), the king of Ammon (11:12–28), God (11:29–31), his daughter (11:34–38), and the men of Ephraim (12:1–4) – followed by a final dialogue between the men of Gilead and the men of Ephraim (12:5–6; see Butler 2009: 27).

---

56. The list of numbers at the start of each of the twelve accounts shows which of the elements listed above on p. 59 is found within that particular account.

i. Preface (10:6–18)

Context

The picture of Israel in the context of the wider region is clearer here than elsewhere in Judges. There are references not only to Canaan itself but to Aram in the north-west, Sidon in the north-east, Moab in the south-east, Ammon in the east and the Philistines in the south-west. Egypt was not an insignificant influence at this time but is only mentioned in Judges in relation to the exodus (2:1, 12) and God's earlier rescuing of Israel (6:9; 10:11). There was no over-riding regional superpower such as Assyria, Babylon and Persia became in later centuries. The balance of power between the various small nations of the region seems to have changed constantly, not only when the Israelite tribes were involved. Israel's particular foes at this point are the Philistines and the Ammonites. The story of Jephthah concentrates on problems from Ammon, whereas the Samson story, which comes later in the accounts, deals with the Philistines. The main action in this section appears to take place in Gilead, on the eastern side of the Jordan River. It is worth noting that all the other accounts seem to be implying that the judge in question had a role across the whole of Israel, whereas there is never any suggestion of that for Jephthah. Perhaps this is influenced by the awareness of Samson's role elsewhere.

Comment

6. As with all the other extended accounts, the story of Jephthah, or at least the preface to the story, begins by emphasizing the evil behaviour of the Israelites. Jephthah himself is not mentioned until 11:1, but the information in chapter 10 is necessary for readers to understand his story, and the formulaic *the Israelites did evil* shows that the writers intend the narrative to be seen as beginning here. The minor leaders may have presided over a time of relative peace, but it did not outlast them any more than it did for the major leaders. In this instance we are given more detail about the nature of their evil. Israel betrayed Yahweh by worshipping gods from all the different groups and nations surrounding Israel. The only notable omission is the lack of reference to any Midianite gods. This is presumably intended to emphasize Gideon's success in removing that particular threat, even if he then went on to support the worship of other gods. Here verse 6 is stressing that they were willing to worship any possible god they could find rather than Yahweh. In no sense could they be described as adhering to the covenant.

7–8. It is not surprising that God was upset, *became angry* (v. 7). As Butler puts it, 'Anger is a faithful response to Israel's rejection. All efforts to erase divine anger from Scripture fail, because God's anger continues to reappear in Torah, History, Poetry, Prophets, Apocalyptic, Gospels, Letters, and the Apocalypse' (Butler 2009: 262). He again *sold them into the hands of* those who would oppose and oppress them. His action is portrayed as following on from his anger, but the ongoing narrative points to the intention being as much educational as punitive. Both the Philistines and the Ammonites are mentioned in verse 8, but Jephthah only faced the Ammonites. It seems likely, although not certain, that *that year* of verse 8 does relate to attacks from Philistia as well as Ammon. This means that the events described in the Samson narratives may be envisaged as occurring contemporaneously with those of the Jephthah narratives,[57] but we are given no indication of any overlap between the particular problems in the different parts of Israelite territory.

9–10. The Ammonites sought to exercise complete control over Israelite territory on both the east and west sides of the Jordan, but it was in the east where the pressure was greatest. The specific mention of western tribes, beginning with Judah, may have been included to indicate to later readers from these tribes that although this particular narrative centres on Gilead, it was not irrelevant to them. The Israelites might have thought or hoped that worshipping the gods of the surrounding nations would protect them from attack by those nations, but this hope had already proved groundless on several occasions. Their tactic was no more effective in this instance. The editor of the Judges stories wants to stress that the only reason

---

57. The Samson narratives are set on the coastal plain region assigned to the tribe of Dan, but the Danites left that region and moved to the north (Judg. 18). It seems likely that that happened at a fairly early stage, and assuming that Samson was around before that happened, it is possible that he was one of the earliest of the recorded leaders and actually preceded Jephthah chronologically.

for the Israelites crying out to Yahweh was pragmatism, based on their eventual and limited recognition that serving other gods had not in fact helped them at all. Without the oppression, there would apparently have been no turning back. To allow them to be oppressed seems to be the only tool God could use that would have any effect on them. In this instance they suffered for eighteen years before they decided that perhaps it was worth seeking Yahweh for help.[58] Again, there is no indication that this is intended to be seen as anything other than a genuine time period. The cry of the Israelites in verse 10 shows they understood clearly that serving the Baals as they had done did involve forsaking Yahweh.

11–14. In the Othniel and Ehud accounts Yahweh's response to their cry was to send a deliverer; in the Gideon account it was to send a prophet to remind them that this response could not be taken for granted, but he sent a deliverer anyway. We have already seen that the Gideon/Abimelek narrative is a turning point in this section of Judges, and it is therefore not surprising to read that this time God's response is even more negative. The description of their previous oppressors and the reminder of the number of times Yahweh had already saved them is more extended than in the Gideon account. The foreign gods have not proved worthy of their trust, but history should have shown them that Yahweh was trustworthy and was able to rescue them as he had done so many times before. The conclusion of the speech to the Israelites prior to the equipping of Gideon (6:10) was simply: *But you have not listened to me.* This time the reminder of God's previous actions reinforces that point, but the speech goes further and explicitly states that God *will no longer save* (v. 13). In effect, he is saying, 'As you are no longer my people, I will no longer be your God', perhaps responding to their confession to forsaking *our God* in verse 10. The instruction to go for help to the gods they have chosen to serve (v. 14) perhaps indicates a scepticism about their sincerity, suggesting that their reaction was based entirely on self-interest, with no real desire to serve God involved, only the hope of gaining support from him.

---

58. The relationship of *that year* and the *eighteen years* in v. 8 is not clear. Presumably, it was in *that year* that the eighteen years began.

The alien gods have already proved to be ineffective, and God's instruction is reminiscent of Elijah's call to the Israelite Baal worshippers of his own time (1 Kgs 18:24ff.).

15–18. At this point the Israelites again acknowledge their sin, recognize that they do deserve to be punished, but affirm that they would rather take their punishment from Yahweh than remain in their current distress. They also provide evidence of their sincerity by getting rid of all the foreign gods, the only time in Judges when this is recorded as having happened. Is this a genuine sign of hope for the future? Has Israel really changed this time? These questions can only be answered as the narrative progresses. There seems to be at least a residual awareness not only of the Mosaic teaching that God is merciful (Deut. 4:31) but also that his own people's relationship with him must be exclusive (Deut. 5:7) and that his mercy does require response and action on their part (Deut. 13:17). There are fewer links with Deuteronomy in the Judges accounts than we find in Samuel and Kings, but they are still there and it is not difficult to understand why Judges is placed within the material described by scholars as the 'Deuteronomic History'.[59] A further link with Deuteronomy (26:7) is seen when God finally relents, not because they deserve it, but because *he could bear Israel's misery no longer.* The relational element within the covenant is very clear. What Israel does and what happens to them matters to God, and it can make him angry (10:7) or, as here, profoundly affected. The Hebrew verb used here, *qṣr*, includes the sense of exasperation but does not make clear what effect that exasperation will bring. The same word is used in Judges 16:16 where Samson's exasperation causes him to give in to Delilah. In Numbers 21:4–5 it led the people to turn and speak out against God, and in Zechariah 11:8–9 it caused the God-appointed shepherd to resign his post (see Webb 2012: 307). In fact, verse 16 simply records God's exasperation, and we need to read the rest of the account in order to find out how he reacted.

Whether the Ammonite call to arms was in response to a particular situation, or just a regular occurrence at a particular time of year, is not made plain. What is clear is that they are making a further

---

59. See Introduction, pp. 11–12.

attack on the already beleaguered area of Gilead on the eastern side of the Jordan, west of, and overlapping with, what the Ammonites regarded as their territory. In spite of the description of Israel as *shattered and crushed* (v. 8) and *oppressed* for eighteen years, they seem not to be as dispirited as is described in the Gideon narrative. The army exists and gathers at Mizpah, apparently ready to move, even if there is no-one available to take charge of it. A further parallel with the later Deuteronomic History is seen in the situation when Saul's army was gathered, but until David appeared there was no-one ready to fight Goliath (1 Sam. 17). In this instance the clan leaders are all seeking a champion, but clearly no-one wants to volunteer. The picture is not an address to the gathered assembly, but the clan leaders debating with 'each other' (Boling 1975: 194). The statement in verse 18 is usually assumed to be the announcement of a reward for anyone who does volunteer, but it could be simply a recognition that, as has happened several times before, the consequence of anyone stepping forward and successfully concluding a military campaign will be that they will then take over the government.

Meaning
Webb's conclusion in relation to this chapter is that we see an 'interplay of three different conflicts; the conflict between Israel and Ammon brings to a head the conflict between Israel and Yahweh and the conflict within Yahweh himself' (Webb 1987: 48). Given this latter conflict and the content of earlier narratives, one might have expected a statement that because of their repentance, or at least because of their misery, God sent them a deliverer. But such a statement is not included. Indeed, what happens next is only implicitly related to God's reaction to their condition. The events are described with reference only to the actions of Ammon and Israel. The writers seem to have introduced a deliberate ambiguity – is this situation another part of God's selling them into the hands of the Ammonites, or the beginning of yet another act of salvation? Is the action of the tribal leaders in setting up a search for a new leader a response to the fact that God has said he will no longer save them, or the way in which God worked his purposes out because of their need? Readers are left to determine this for themselves.

ii. Jephthah is appointed (11:1–11)

Context

This section gives some insight into the different ways leaders were appointed in Israel. In general, Judges concentrates on those who are, or can be inferred to be, appointed directly by God, but it is always clear that leaders did exist outside of this. Clan leaders took up their position by birth, although this was not always undisputed. Military leaders appear to have been appointed on merit either from within the armed forces or, as here, by groups of elders. Some of the elders seen in this chapter will probably have been clan leaders, but we cannot really be sure how others were appointed and whether those roles were a matter of seizing power or of recognition from within the community.

Comment

11:1–3. Unlike Gideon, Jephthah is already known as a *mighty warrior* before the recorded events unfold. The parallels with the story of Abimelek are obvious. Like Abimelek, Jephthah was the son of *another woman*, in this case specifically designated as a prostitute, and estranged from his brothers.[60] Unlike Abimelek, he appears to have reconciled himself to this situation, and when forced to leave his own area, he had apparently gathered a collection of malcontents with him and organized them into a force that was recognized by the *elders of Gilead* as effective, probably having already had some successes against the Ammonites. Although 11:34 indicates that Jephthah had retained his base in Mizpah, he had for the moment moved with his troops away from Israelite territory. Tob was just north of the region controlled by Ammon, in the territory of Aram,

---

60. The suggestion has been made that his father is described not as 'a man named Gilead', but simply as 'a Gileadite', unknown because of Jephthah's mother's role. However, this would make no sense of the following verses referring to his paternal relations. The brothers do not dispute the identity of Jephthah's father, which means that Gilead must have in some way acknowledged Jephthah as his son. If so, then his exclusion from all inheritance rights can clearly be seen as an injustice, even if it had been backed by the authorities.

but probably near enough for an organized band of insurgents to cause problems for the Ammonite army. Again, parallels can also be seen with David and the band he gathered when thrown out by Saul (1 Sam. 22 – 23).

4–11. Whether or not the Jephthah narratives were originally a collection of separate stories, it seems clear that the editor is intending 11:4–6 to be seen as following on from 10:18. The result of the leadership consultation described in that verse was a delegation sent to recruit Jephthah. Verse 2 indicated that the reason for Jephthah's expulsion from the community was concern about inheritance, but verse 7 could imply that prejudice against the children of prostitutes was also involved. Such children would not normally be accepted into society, especially in a leadership position. The ongoing motif of God using all kinds of people to work out his saving purposes is reinforced here. The writers may have had a subsidiary motive of showing that any reservations about Abimelek's leadership were not related to the circumstances of his birth. Jephthah's initial response to the leaders' offer is not negative but certainly guarded. Whether one or more of his brothers was included among the elders, or whether the local authorities had been complicit in his banishment, even if only by turning a blind eye, cannot be determined, but it is clear that Jephthah did view them in this way. His response, in effect, saying, 'You didn't want me before, so why should I help you when you are in trouble?', can be seen as reflecting the statement made by God in 10:11–14, and the writers are almost certainly intentional in pointing to that link. Jephthah is convinced that they want him to lead the army at this point, that is, be their commander. However, he is clearly not convinced that they will accept him as their *head* once the military campaign has been successfully completed. The change of leadership terminology here may be significant, indicating that they preferred not to use traditional leadership terms, or may simply signify that the terminology was not fixed, and the variety of terms used in Judges might substantiate that view.[61]

---

61. Willis (1996) provides an interesting discussion on the nature of the authority being offered to, and taken by, Jephthah.

Jephthah evidently kept in close touch with what was going on in his home territory and was well aware that their original job description (10:18) included a reference to ongoing governance, even though their first approach to him does not mention this. Although it appears that Jephthah was specifically 'headhunted' rather than applying for the job, he, having suffered from injustice once, wanted to make sure that he was treated fairly in the way that any other Israelite would have been treated. It may be that his knowledge of, and desire for, the prosperity Jair achieved during his period in office influenced Jephthah's negotiations, but the text only brings out the question of just and unjust treatment. The elders make no admission of guilt concerning his banishment, but they do recognize Jephthah's qualms and confirm that their offer of an ongoing leadership role does apply to him, reinforcing the offer by calling on Yahweh as their witness, in effect making a vow before God that they will fulfil their obligations to make him their *head*. It is possible that this is reflecting their renewed commitment to Yahweh, or it might be an indication that Jephthah was known as an Israelite who had remained faithful to Yahweh rather than following the Baals. If this is so, it could be a further reason why Jephthah was viewed as an appropriate leader at this particular point in time. This could be interpreted positively as 'we really do want to turn back to Yahweh, and appointing a leader who serves Yahweh will help us do that', or more negatively, as 'we are more likely to be able to twist God's arm if we appoint a leader who pays him allegiance already'. Jephthah's reiteration of the agreement that took place *before the LORD in Mizpah* reflects his desire to make sure that it really was 'signed and sealed'. Mizpah was the place where Jacob reinforced his agreement with the possibly untrustworthy Laban (Gen. 31:49).[62] There is no mention of Jephthah's call

---

62. The reference in 11:29 to Mizpah in Gilead possibly distinguishes it from the Mizpah mentioned here, although all four references in the Jephthah narrative (10:17; 11:11, 29, 34) might refer to the same place. There are several towns named Mizpah mentioned in the OT, including one in Judah (Josh. 15:38) and one in Moab where David sent his parents for safety when he was alienated from Saul (1 Sam. 22:3). This may not be the same Mizpah, but it could be argued that the symbolic parallel remains valid.

coming directly from Yahweh, but there is no doubt that Jephthah himself saw any role in battle (v. 9) and government (v. 11) as being dependent on, and in the presence of, Yahweh. The writers are perhaps at least pointing to the possibility that Jephthah was sent by God to save Israel.

Meaning
Given the Israelites' apparent repentance and turning back to God (10:15–16) and the explicit involvement of God in Jephthah's leadership (11:29, 32), it seems likely that this chapter is, at least to some extent, reflecting on the relationship between God's sovereignty and human responsibility in the appointment of leaders. Alongside this, of course, is the ongoing interest in the variety of skills and background of the people whom God does choose to use.

iii. An attempt to find a solution through diplomacy (11:12–28)
Context
International relations within Judges is almost entirely a matter of oppressive control one way or the other, or of military conflict. Jephthah's approach to the Ammonite king, although ultimately unsuccessful, indicates that diplomatic encounters or solutions were understood and available. But it seems in general that the concept of cooperation rather than control was as hard to achieve in the international community as it seems to have been within Israel itself. The nearest we get to genuine international cooperation not based on joining forces on a temporary basis to suit joint military targets was the relationship between Hiram of Lebanon and David (2 Sam. 5:11; 1 Kgs 5:1).

Comment
12–13. Jephthah's first act as leader was not to organize the army for the fight ahead but to seek for a possible way of avoiding the fight in the first place. Jephthah is best known, and often only known, for his disastrous vow recorded in the next section, but the narrative as a whole makes it clear that he was a gifted man, perhaps the most gifted of all the leader/deliverers described in Judges. Not only was he a good fighter, an able military commander and a strategic thinker, he was also a diplomat. His initial question sent to

the Ammonite king is carefully phrased. It does call for an answer, and contains the possibility of a positive diplomatic solution to conflict. However, his use of the words *me* and *my country* (v. 12) implies that Ammon already knows of him and his abilities, and contains the veiled threat that he is a man to be reckoned with who will act in defence of his country if so required. Ammon has perhaps known him as an Israelite exile, a problem on their northern border but not part of the 'Israel situation'. His words also assert Israelite sovereignty over disputed territory: 'This is my country that you have attacked.' The phrasing of the question *What do you have against me?* (lit. 'what to me and to you') is a common idiomatic way of saying, 'What precisely is the issue here?'[63] Not surprisingly, the first response from the king of Ammon is uncompromising. He asserts Ammon's claim to this area and suggests that it has a historical base. They are fighting for what they see as their rights. The land is theirs; Israel has occupied it illegally and should therefore give it back. The territory he names is that to the south and south-west of the area currently fully controlled by Ammon.

14–27. Different interpretations of history from opposing sides in a land dispute have been common throughout the world for as long as tribes and nations have existed, and often the facts become lost in the emotions and the myths. But Jephthah, showing a further sign of his varied gifts, this time as a scholar historian, has done his homework. He begins the long defence of Israel's position by asserting his own authority: *This is what Jephthah says* (v. 14). Whether he studied Israel's history solely for this particular exercise, or whether his desire to understand the way that Yahweh had brought Israel into the land provides further evidence of his personal allegiance to Yahweh, cannot be determined from the text. What is clear is that detailed information about Israel's history, whether from oral or documentary sources, was available to him. The way he retells that history also shows great skill. He starts with the way in which, in spite of provocation, Israel did not encroach onto the territory of either Edom or Moab. They travelled round the eastern side of

---

63. 2 Sam. 16:10; 19:22; 1 Kgs 17:18; 2 Kgs 3:13; 2 Chr. 35:21; cf. Boling 1975: 202.

those countries and then camped north of Moab across the River Arnon, which was and remained the recognized northern border of Moab. That territory was occupied at the time by Amorites, who, because they not only refused Israel safe passage through their land but attacked and were defeated by Israel, forfeited their rights. As Jephthah puts it, Yahweh, *the God of Israel*, defeated the Amorites and therefore gave the land to Israel. He repeats the Ammonite king's phrase, *from the Arnon to the Jabbok*. The implication of the ongoing argument is that this land has never belonged to Ammon because they had no grounds for arguing historical occupancy and their god never defeated an army in order for them to obtain it. Jephthah is in effect saying that Yahweh gave them the land and Yahweh will again decide between the claims of Ammon and Israel – presumably by ensuring that Israel will be successful in any battle for the territory between the two peoples. His argument that Ammon would be better off making peace is strengthened by mentioning that Balak, Moab's famed and successful leader, did not think it wise to attack Israel (Num. 22 – 24), and that Israel had actually already been in the territory, unhindered by Ammon, for centuries. Jephthah's final statement referring to *the LORD, the Judge* is one of the most profound theological pronouncements of the whole book. He is asserting that Yahweh is the one who has the right to determine the future not only of the Israelites but also of the Ammonites. We have here another of the recurrent 'high points' in these narratives which have so many 'low points'. It certainly raises questions as to whether Jephthah is, in speaking of Chemosh in verse 24, assuming both the reality and the power of the Ammonite god. In the final analysis only Yahweh has authority.

28. No further diplomatic response comes from Ammon. Jephthah's view of the historical situation is neither agreed nor accepted. But the implication of Jephthah's message, that the outcome will be determined by the relative strengths of Chemosh and Yahweh, is left in the air, and it seems to be taken for granted by both sides that a battle will now take place. The close relationship between the Ammonites and the Moabites is evidenced here. Chemosh is consistently described elsewhere as the god of the Moabites, with Molek being the god of the Ammonites (cf. 1 Kgs 11:5, 33; 2 Kgs 23:13). The worship of both Chemosh and Molek involved human sacrifice

(2 Kgs 3:27; Jer. 32:35). It is possible that worship of the different gods spread throughout the area; this was certainly true within Israelite territory, although the evidence for its occurrence elsewhere is not overwhelming. It is also possible that Jephthah's knowledge of Ammonite history and religion was not as thorough as his knowledge about Israel, and he simply got confused. If this is so, Ammon's lack of response to his overtures is even more understandable.

Meaning
The writers' main emphasis within this section seems to be the fact that God is in control of history – not just of Israel but also of the surrounding nations. He is the one who will decide who will take control. The way in which throughout the book we see God both handing Israel over to be ruled by oppressive forces and also rescuing them from such rule has already made that point, but it is explicitly reinforced within Jephthah's speech. One could also say that the importance of understanding the history of God's past acts and its implications is also being indicated.

iv. Victory and vow (11:29–40)
Context
In the previous passage we saw the diplomatic encounter between Jephthah and the Ammonite king, with both parties attempting to persuade the other that they had the greatest historical claim to the land under dispute. Whether either party thought there was any chance that the other side would actually be persuaded is not clear. But by including this material, the writers do seem to be suggesting that diplomatic means are always worth trying first. However, the recognition that such means do not always achieve positive results is also found here. Once the king of Ammon *paid no attention to the message Jephthah sent him* (11:28), then a military conflict was assumed to be inevitable.

Comment
29. Judges describes the *Spirit of the LORD* coming on Othniel (3:10), Gideon (6:34) and four times on Samson (13:25; 14:6, 19; 15:14), as well as, in this instance, on Jephthah. This describes a

God-given inspiration and enablement to take action, almost always military action, against enemies – although elsewhere it also involves the right to rule as king or the ability to understand God's intentions or proclaim his words (1 Sam. 10:6; 16:13, 14; 2 Sam. 23:2; 2 Chr. 20:14; Isa. 11:2; Ezek. 11:5). In this instance Yahweh's Spirit coming on Jephthah confirms that whether or not his call to leadership was divinely inspired, his ongoing work was certainly divinely supported. In 10:17 the Israelite army had camped at Mizpah. Jephthah, empowered by Yahweh, apparently travels across the western areas of Israel, presumably gathering more followers on the way, picks up with the original force at Mizpah and sets out to fight the Ammonites.

30–31. At this point, that is, after receiving the information that Jephthah had received *the Spirit of the LORD*, which presumably Jephthah himself was aware of, readers are told about Jephthah's vow. This parallels the vow made by the elders in 11:10, which probably means that such vows were common ways of reinforcing commitments (Robinson 2004: 331–348). Whether this vow was made before his journey started, at some stage on the way or at its completion is not made plain. Clearly, Jephthah's knowledge of the requirements of the law is by no means as great as his knowledge of Israel's history. Offerers did have a certain amount of choice as to what might be brought as a burnt offering, but that choice was limited to certain 'clean' animals, and there is no indication that to make a vow where the potential sacrifice might turn out to be outside those limits would ever have been seen as acceptable. However, there is no doubt about his confidence in Yahweh – he clearly did expect to return in triumph – or his dedication to Yahweh, even though there may be a suggestion of doubt here about his theological or legal understanding. This relates partly to the issue of human sacrifice. It is made implicitly (Gen. 22) and explicitly (e.g. Jer. 7:31) clear that this was not what God wanted, in spite of its use within surrounding nations. It did occur within Israel at a late stage (e.g. 2 Kgs 16:3) but was always seen as an abomination. However, this is not the only problem here. Throughout the whole of the Old Testament as well as the New, there is an emphasis on God's grace. His covenant people are called to respond to that grace, to keep the law because that is the right thing to do, to bring sacrifices to atone for sins and to give thanks to God. Although in the rituals of the nations and tribes surrounding Israel it is often assumed that gifts given to gods would ensure the granting of any request, there is never any indication in the Torah that God could be coerced by promises or vows of any kind. If Jephthah intended his vow as a kind of bribe to make victory more likely, then he had misunderstood the nature of God and of his relationship with Israel. If, on the other hand, he intended it as a thanksgiving offering, he has misunderstood what God sees as an acceptable gift. Jephthah's knowledge of Yahweh does not, in fact, seem to be much clearer than his knowledge of the gods of Ammon and Moab.[64] The vow was made *to the* LORD, but although Yahweh's involvement in the campaign against the Ammonites is clear, there is no mention of his reaction to the vow or any sign of his involvement anywhere in the vow narratives. Even though there is no explicit condemnation of the vow within the text, the implication once more is that this is not how life in Israel was meant to be.

32–33. The description of the battle or battles is limited to two verses, which again stress the involvement of Yahweh in Jephthah's victories. The location of the named towns cannot be determined with any certainty, although Aroer is mentioned in 11:26 as one of the settlements along the Arnon in the south of the disputed zone, and Abel Keramim is likely to be a town further north. Whether the subjugation of Ammon was limited to the area claimed by Israel or also involved undisputed Ammonite territory is a matter for debate. Ammon certainly remained a threat to Israel until after the time of David. The writers seem to be more interested in what happens next in the 'vow story' than in Jephthah's military triumph. It is worth noting that there is no indication that the victory was in any way related to the vow.

Webb (1987: 63–65) concludes that Jephthah's use of 'my' in his vow is deliberate and significant. The address to the Ammonite king speaks of God's actions on behalf of Israel, but here Jephthah is concerned primarily with his own triumphant return and, by implication, with the confirmation of his own position of leadership (vv. 30–31). This conclusion may or may not be justified by the text,

---

64. See comment on 11:28 above.

but it is interesting that verse 32 speaks of Yahweh giving the Ammonites into Jephthah's hands – repeating the words used in his vow – but verse 33 concludes by stating, *Thus Israel subdued Ammon*, making it clear that any victory did not belong to Jephthah alone.

34–35. There has been significant debate as to whether Jephthah expected the first to cross the threshold at his arrival to be an animal. However, the grammar does imply that it would be a human being.[65] It also seems likely that if he had intended the sacrifice to be an animal, then his daughter's approach could have been seen as irrelevant to the vow. However, if he intended a human sacrifice, then the fact that it was his daughter rather than another member of his household seems to be a sad twist of fate for him, but no more of a tragedy than the death of the other person would have been for his or her family. It should be noted that, aside from all other questions, even if Jephthah had intended to sacrifice an animal, the fact that the animal in question could have been legally 'unclean' makes his vow inappropriate. Although the text makes no comment on any of these things, it does make it clear that the results of Jephthah's vow are to be seen as tragic. It is worth noting that Saul made a similarly foolish vow placing a curse on anyone who ate that day (a curse that was interpreted as implying that any offender should be killed) which his son Jonathan inadvertently transgressed. When the army refused to allow the requirements of the oath, there were no consequences to that refusal and no hint of condemnation within the text (1 Sam. 14:24–25). The implication is that God does not treat as valid vows that in themselves transgress his purposes. The importance of keeping vows is stressed in Numbers 30:2ff. (cf. Deut. 23:18–23), but this must be seen in the light of Leviticus 22:18ff. Certain sacrifices are not acceptable, even in fulfilment of a vow (Lev. 22:23); God makes it clear that to bring them is to 'profane' his 'holy name' (Lev. 22:32). But these considerations did not occur to Jephthah. He had made a vow, Yahweh had given victory and therefore the vow had to be kept. There is no doubt that he was horrified when the consequences of his vow – that is, that it would

---

65. For example, the word used in v. 31 for 'to meet' is not normally used in reference to animals.

involve the sacrifice of his only daughter, indeed, his only child – became clear. The narrative detail is beautifully told. The charming picture of the loving daughter coming out dancing and rejoicing at her father's victory, quickly followed by the pathos of his devastation and her resignation, leaves the reader, as was surely intended, with a number of disturbing questions. That Jephthah's distress recorded in verse 35 is concentrated on his own loss rather than on hers, and indeed seeks to put the blame for this distress on her, may confirm Webb's view of his behaviour generally as self-centred (2012: 330–332).

36–39. Again, there has been much scholarly debate regarding the nature of the daughter's fate.[66] Does the stress on her virginity and the mourning because she would never be married imply that the sacrifice did not involve death but rather a dedication to Yahweh, which would mean the equivalent of permanent incarceration in a nunnery? It is true that the law calls for the dedication of all first-born males, human and animal, and that the first-born sons are redeemed by animal sacrifice (Exod. 13:12–15). But although that point is sometimes brought into the argument, it is not clear that it has relevance in this case. When first-born sons were redeemed, they were then free; there seems to have been no suggestion of further permanent dedication of any kind. It could have been possible to apply the same logic here, but that would have left Jephthah's daughter free, redeemed by an appropriate animal sacrifice rather than living in permanent seclusion.

However, there is no discussion of such ideas in the text, and although the references to Jephthah doing what he had vowed in verses 36 and 39 could be seen as vague, the reference to the burnt offering in verse 31 is not. In any case, although a number of ancient cults did have young girls who were dedicated to permanent virginity, there is no evidence for this within the Old Testament or any hint that virginity in itself was something that might be seen as especially pleasing to God. Nor is there any reasonable explanation as to what benefit two months spent weeping with friends in the hills would be before such a dedication; there would surely be plenty of time

---

66. Cf. Beavis 2010; Houtman 2005; Robinson 2004.

for such weeping afterwards. Barrenness was seen as a terrible tragedy, and the lack of any opportunity to have children would be understood as something to be mourned. Indeed, it is not clear that early readers would have seen the denial of that opportunity as any less tragic than the death normally involved in the burnt offering called for in Jephthah's vow. The suggestion may make the passage slightly more acceptable to some modern readers, but there is no real reason to suppose that the daughter's fate involved anything other than death. Indeed, it is likely that the lack of clarity regarding the meaning of, or motivation for, the daughter's time in the hills is deliberate and again relates to the authors' desire to portray the whole process as meaningless. This is not how covenant life was supposed to be. It is interesting that unlike Jonathan (1 Sam. 14:29–30, 43), when he might have been expected to face death following his father's foolish vow, the daughter in no way criticizes her father but accepts her fate without question. Whether or not her apparently willing acceptance of the fact that fulfilling his vow will have fatal consequences for her means that she should be viewed as a participant in events rather than as a victim remains a debatable point.

Attention is sometimes drawn to parallels with the account of the sacrifice of Isaac (Gen. 22), which was prevented from taking place. Trible (1984: 105) highlights the fact that whereas the son was saved, the daughter was not, and Robinson, although he questions the relevance of the parallel with Genesis 22 (2004: 348), nevertheless accepts the validity of Trible's reasoning by concluding that 'the text does indeed perhaps assume that women are more expendable than men' (2004: 343). However, as the stress in this instance is on the belovedness of the daughter and the grief caused by her loss, conclusions about relative expendability can, at best, only be seen as tenuous. There is no suggestion that if Jephthah's only child had been a son, the result would in this case have been any different.

40. In general, it was through their descendants that people were remembered.[67] Jephthah had no descendants, and the writers may

---

67. Cf. 2 Sam. 18:18, where Absalom erected a monument to himself
    because he had 'no son to carry on the memory of' his name.

be deliberately making a point when they record that the commemoration was not of Jephthah but of his daughter. The four days' holiday given to young girls in memory of her is not mentioned elsewhere, and it is impossible to know whether it was something that happened on a regular basis in early times.

Meaning

It is interesting that within this section the discussion of the vow and its consequences takes priority over the description of the victory over Ammon. God's will for Israel was clearly not just about whether they achieved military successes, but also about how their life was lived in the context of those successes. The stress on the fact that, in terms of their required adherence to Yahweh's covenant with them, they were still way off the mark is part of the ongoing interest in the life of Israel not being what it was meant to be or could have been, in spite of military victories.

v. Problems with Ephraim (12:1–7)
Context

Disputes between the tribes have already been recorded. The similarities with the Ephraimites' dispute with Gideon must have been in the mind of the writers as they included this story. However, the two accounts are very different and there are no obvious signs of one being dependent on the other. Ephraim's territory was in the main west-bank section of Israel's territory but near enough to the trans-Jordan tribes to make their call-up realistic. They were separated only by the southern section of Manasseh's western half, and their close relation to the tribe of Manasseh, both being descended from Joseph, may be significant. Manasseh was the only tribe to have territory on both sides of the Jordan.

Comment

12:1–3. Sadly, victory over the Ammonites did not bring an end to the troubles of Israel or of Jephthah. Verse 1a could imply that the call was sent out to Ephraim to fight against Israel's enemies, but the unfolding account makes it clear that the call was sent within Ephraim for them to come and fight against their fellow Israelites, specifically Jephthah and the Gileadites whom he led. Judges contains several instances of tension emerging between the tribes of Israel. Ephraim seems to have been particularly sensitive, especially prone to jealousy concerning who could take the credit for victories, or perhaps just exceptionally awkward. Once again, as they had with Gideon (8:1–3), the Ephraimites express serious discontent with the part assigned to them by the current leader of the Israelite forces. Whether the Ephraimites thought that because the geographical position they had been assigned within Israel was central they should take a central role in everything is not clear. However, the accusation is the same: 'We have not been as involved as we should have been.' But this time the response of the leader in question is very different. Whereas Gideon had been conciliatory, Jephthah reacts angrily with a counter-accusation. We are not told what the 'vigorous challenge' of 8:1 involved, but here their threats are explicit. There is no doubt that they have come prepared to fight. In fact, the threat from the Ephraimites is exactly the same as that from the Ammonites. It is perhaps for that reason that Jephthah is less willing to mollify them – if they behave like foreigners, then they deserve to be treated as foreigners. In fact, he refutes their claim that they had not been called and suggests that they had ignored the appeal that had been sent out. Yahweh had been with Jephthah's army, but Ephraim had not. So when the Ephraimites refused to back down, Jephthah responded to their aggression by recalling the forces of the Gilead tribes of the trans-Jordan area.

4–6. Verse 4 makes it clear that there were racist overtones in this clash between the tribes. The Ephraimites clearly saw themselves as superior to their fellow Israelites whose territory lay on the other side of the Jordan, and as having claims to that territory. The Gileadites were motivated to destroy them because of their insults more than because of the issue they had raised about who had been called to fight against Ammon. Ephraim was defeated, but that was not enough for Jephthah and his troops. A quirk of their dialect meant that the Ephraimites were easily identified, and none of those who had presumed to come into Gilead with violent intentions was allowed to return across the Jordan alive. The decimation of the Ephraimite forces must have had effects that lasted for many years, not only for the development and prosperity of that tribe, but on the ongoing relationships between all the tribes. It appears that the editors of Judges want their readers to understand just how divided the tribes were. It is probably also significant that, as in the vow narrative, there is no indication in the text of any involvement by Yahweh in the conflict between the tribes.

7. It seems clear that Jephthah's six-year leadership was confined to the region of Gilead. The account finishes as it began by referring to Jephthah as *the Gileadite*, and we are told that that is where he was buried. There is no indication of activity in the west-bank tribal areas, and after his defeat of Ephraim any such activity is unlikely to have been welcomed. The fact that he is referred to in this way may be deliberately emphasizing his final acceptance as the son of his father. Whatever else he did or did not achieve during his time in office, the rejection of his brothers had been reversed. The concluding statement is very brief and there is no mention here, or indeed in the whole account, of the land being at peace under Jephthah's control. Robinson (2004: 332) concludes that this, and the fact that Jephthah died without leaving any children, indicates that the writers – and by implication God – disapproved of Jephthah: 'Our impression is confirmed that the narrator views Jephthah with some distaste.'

Meaning
This final section of the Jephthah account concentrates on the tribal rivalries and further emphasizes the consistent picture of Israel as disunited, bound up in self-interest, whether tribal or regional, and a long way from looking to serve Yahweh.

When we look at the Jephthah narratives as a whole, it is difficult to speak confidently about the 'meaning' of a section which, as Butler points out (2009: 299), 'thrives on ambiguity'. What we are not told, for example, about God's involvement in the vow narrative or the intertribal clashes may be as significant as what we are told. We cannot be completely certain as to how far the western tribes were involved, whether Jephthah really intended a human sacrifice or whether his daughter actually died. The writers describe events and rarely give any indication as to how God, or they themselves, viewed what was happening. On the one hand, Jephthah is presented as a gifted diplomat, soldier and leader, with a greater awareness of, and commitment to, Yahweh than is evidenced in any of his Israelite contemporaries. On the other hand, he can be seen as self-centred, determined to forward his own ends and with no real awareness of what it is that God wants from Israel. In the ongoing decline seen in the book as a whole it could be said that if Gideon's family was destroyed by rivalry and idolatry, Jephthah's was destroyed by wrong-thinking religious understanding that led to human sacrifice. However, we also see that even if Jephthah's vow is regarded as wrong, this did not stop Yahweh from using or blessing Jephthah in the context in which he was called: the Ammonites were defeated – if only temporarily (cf. 1 Sam. 11; 2 Sam. 8:12). God can use people with suspect theology as well as he can use left-handed men, women or unconfident weaklings. In Hebrews Jephthah is certainly seen as a positive example of a faithful man, but in a general context where it is not clear for which aspects of his life and career he is being praised. The inclusion of the clash with Ephraim possibly indicates that one purpose of the account is to show just how necessary an accepted monarchy was if the disparate tribal groups were ever going to function as a united nation, but there is no specific discussion of, or reference to, this in the text. What we can say, once more, is that the situation presented in the Jephthah narratives shows that God was continuing to be involved in the life of Israel even as Israel moved further and further from the ideal picture of covenant life portrayed in Deuteronomy. As Butler puts it (2009: 289), 'God retains his freedom to act as he chooses, no matter how faithful or unfaithful the earthly leaders, as will be seen in even starker clarity in the Samson narratives.'

I. Three more 'minor' leaders (12:8–15)

Context
There is no real evidence provided of the timing of the leadership of the three mentioned in this section and little information about the geographical location of their work, although the burial sites of all three are specifically mentioned. The spread of the minor accounts between the longer narratives may be a deliberate ploy on the part of the final editors of the book of Judges, although whether the reason is simply to bring variety or something of more significance is not completely clear.

Comment

i. Ibzan (12:8–10)

9a, 11, 12a, 12b [68]

Ibzan held office for a year longer than Jephthah did, but we know nothing at all of how he functioned. We are not explicitly told his tribal origins,[69] although we know he lived and died in Bethlehem, which could refer to either the well-known town in Judah or, perhaps more likely, as the Judean Bethlehem is usually referred to as 'in Judah', to that in Zebulun (Josh. 19:16). The mention of Ibzan's sixty children could be presented as a deliberate contrast to Jephthah's death without issue, but may be no more relevant than implying that he must have had several wives and therefore been a prosperous and significant figure. As with the case of Jair's sons and their donkeys, this could be seen as a positive indication of the peace, stability and prosperity of the time, or a negative sign of the tendency for leaders to concentrate on building their own empire. In either case, the picture of twenty-five years of peaceful government under Ibzan, Elon and Abdon does provide evidence that Jephthah had done an excellent job during the six years that followed his defeat of Ammon and suppression of the threat to Gilead from Ephraim. Furthermore, following on from the clash between the tribes under Jephthah, the specific mention of Ibzan's policy that all his children should be married to those from other clans is possibly an indication of a deliberate strategy to build relationships between clans and perhaps also between tribes. The reason for this may have been simply to reinforce his own control of a wider area or could indicate a real desire for unity and cooperation. The writers' concentration on what otherwise might be seen as an obscure fact certainly emphasizes the interest in the relationship between tribes and the need to find ways of strengthening a sense of national identity. If this is

---

68. The list of numbers at the start of each of the twelve accounts shows which of the elements listed above on pp. 59–60 is found within that particular account.

69. See the note on the tribal origins of the leader/deliverers (pp. 60–61).

correct, it would indicate that these accounts are meant to be seen as following on chronologically from Jephthah. Jephthah is the only other of the twelve judges where a daughter is mentioned. This is unlikely to mean that Jair (10:4) or Abdon (12:14) had only male descendants, but that only in this case are daughters seen as relevant to the overall discussion. Given the interest in daughters in Judges as a whole (see pp. 43–44), it is possible that the writers are pointing out that although their society, as many others, normally sees only male descendants as significant, nevertheless female descendants do play an important part in ensuring the cohesion of a society.

ii. Elon (12:11–12)

9a, 11, 12a, 12b[70]

Elon is the only one of the twelve named leader/deliverers of whom we are told nothing at all other than his tribe, the length of his leadership and the fact of his death and burial. It may be that he is included simply to make up the twelve and to add to the range of tribes from which the leaders came. It is worth noting that Aijalon in the Hebrew consonantal text takes the same form as Elon. The further reference to Zebulun is to differentiate between this Aijalon and the one situated in Dan (Josh. 19:42).

iii. Abdon (12:13–15)

9a, 11, 12a, 12b[71]

Abdon's home town of Pirathon is stated, both here and in reference to Benaiah, one of the significant officers within David's

---

70. The list of numbers at the start of each of the twelve accounts shows which of the elements listed above on pp. 59–60 is found within that particular account.

71. The list of numbers at the start of each of the twelve accounts shows which of the elements listed above on pp. 59–60 is found within that particular account.

army who also came from there (2 Sam. 23:20), to be in Ephraim. It is impossible to identify the site with any certainty, although possible links have been made with Pharathon (mentioned in 1 Maccabees 9:50) and with a number of similar-sounding places (Fer'ata, Fir', Fer'on) in the region. Where the identified town is in southern Manasseh, the suggestion is made that the borders were fluid and Ephraimites may at times have taken over that area. This is of course possible. However, any such identification involves unnecessary speculation. The reference to *the hill country of the Amalekites* is also obscure. It is possible that the name has endured from previous residents or that there was an enclave of Amalekites living in the area. As with Jair (10:4; cf. also Ibzan 12:9), the extent of Abdon's personal wealth is emphasized by the number of his sons, suggesting a number of wives, and the number of donkeys owned within the family. Not only his sons but also his grandsons (the KJV 'nephews' is not correct here) had their own mount. It would be interesting to know why forty sons produced only thirty grandsons, but the text makes no attempt to answer that question! As in the case of Jair and Ibzan, 'the question has to be raised whether mention of such possessions refers to a positive position in the community or a selfish accumulation of goods at the expense of those he "judged"' (Butler 2009: 298). Certainly, the stress on wealth here, as previously, is on the wealth of the leaders rather than on that of the community as a whole, although it is possible that the former implies the latter. Nothing further is revealed about Abdon's eight-year period in office, and the lack of mention of any military activity is likely to indicate that it is meant to be seen as a time of peace.

Meaning
The detail in these accounts is too scanty to be sure of the intended 'meaning'. However, it is possible that the writers intended to emphasize that life in Israel was not all about major 'heroes', that leadership was spread between different tribes, and that – although this is an argument from silence – the minor judges were no more successful at leading Israel to unity or to long-term covenant adherence than some of their more famous colleagues.

J. Samson (13:1 – 16:31)

1, 4, 5, 9a, 10, 12a, 12b[72]

As with Gideon, four chapters are dedicated to the story of Samson and his family. There is general scholarly agreement that the writers' skill in telling this, or these, stories is exemplary. Each incident stands in its own right and yet is blended together with the others to make a coherent whole. The reader's attention is held throughout and drawn by both what is included and what is omitted to the various implications and motifs that the writers want to highlight. The whole narrative is again set in the context of a nation viewed by God as 'evil'. The foreign power in this instance is the Philistines, and it seems likely that the events described overlap the disputes between Jephthah and the Ammonites in the east. The area around which Samson travelled seems to be mainly in the territory that Joshua 19:40–46 assigned to the tribe of Dan, but verse 47, confirmed by Judges 18, makes it clear that the Danites were never able to consolidate their settlement there (see Soggin 1981: 225–227). The precise borders of the various tribal territories are unclear, and it is impossible to determine whether there was a defined border between land claimed by Philistines and Israelites and, if so, where that border was. In any case, there are no battles described between Israelite and Philistine armies. Although we have here a collection of self-consistent stories, it is a very worthwhile exercise to read the whole account in one go in order to observe the way in which the stories interact and build up the wider picture.

i. Annunciation and birth of Samson (13:1–24)
Context
With Gideon, the final chapter describes events relating to his sons that occurred after his death. With Samson, the first chapter describes events relating to his parents that occurred before his birth. Samson's

---

72. The list of numbers at the start of each of the twelve accounts shows which of the elements listed above on pp. 59–60 is found within that particular account.

childhood is briefly mentioned only in verse 24. The picture is of a farming community in general able to conduct their lives in relative peace. There is no real sign of any reason why the tribe of Dan should have had any more difficulty than the other tribes in taking over the land assigned to them.

Comment

13:1. The information given at the start of each of the six major leader/deliverer narratives, that *the Israelites did evil in the eyes of the LORD*, is found at the start of the account of Samson's parents' encounter with the angel of the LORD. It tells us that this story is intended to be part of the ongoing narrative, and that although he is not yet present, our understanding of Samson and our assessment of his calling and role must begin here. In this instance the Philistines are clearly intended to be seen as the oppressive enemy, and their dominance over the Israelites had lasted forty years. In fact, the timing of the Philistine overlordship is by no means clear. No explanation is given as to how the forty years of this verse relate to the twenty years of Samson's leading (16:31), or to the 'subduing' of the Philistines by Samuel (1 Sam. 7:13) or indeed to the Philistine threat during Eli's time that continued through Saul's reign and well into the reign of David. However, it is made clear as the story unfolds that at this point any Philistine control was by no means absolute. There is no sign within this chapter of the Philistines causing any particular problems for Samson's parents. Perhaps this is why, although the Philistines were clearly in the ascendancy and Israel was not functioning as an independent nation, they seem to have felt no need or inclination to repent of their *evil* or to turn to Yahweh. On this occasion there is no mention of Israel 'crying out' to God.

2. There is no specific reference to Samson having been sent by God, but the adjacency of this story to the introductory statements and, as in the case of Gideon, the appearance of the angel of the LORD to Samson's mother, do indicate that she, and by implication, the child she was to bear, were chosen by God. One might have assumed that the one to whom the message came was in fact the chosen deliverer, but here the message makes it clear that it was her son who would be entrusted with the potential of saving Israel. This chapter is unique in the central section of Judges in that its focus is on characters other than those who are directly described as leading Israel or those fighting with them or against them. As we have seen in the earlier accounts, the writers are interested not only in the big picture of the 'state of the nation' in terms of its independent functioning as the covenant people of Yahweh, but also in the details of everyday life for the people at this time. There is more to this chapter than simply the information that Samson was born. We are introduced to an Israelite couple apparently functioning reasonably adequately as small-scale farmers. Their clear allegiance to Yahweh indicates that although the Israelites in general were doing *evil in the eyes of the LORD*, not every Israelite was necessarily involved in this.

The start of verse 2, *a certain man of Zorah*, implies to the reader that this is the key character, perhaps the one who will be the next deliverer of Israel, but it is in fact his unnamed childless wife who takes centre stage in this chapter. As Butler (2009: 323) puts it, 'The inclusion of a name would seem to afford more importance to Manoah that to his nameless wife but this is an element of the narrator's art in leading you to expect one thing only to discover another.' The motif of the barren woman who through God's help eventually gives birth has already been seen in Genesis and will be seen in the early chapters of Samuel. Here it seems the writers are stressing that God acts to deliver individuals from their troubles, not just the nation as a whole. It seems likely, given the attention already paid to Jephthah's daughter and her feelings, that there is a deliberate emphasis on the importance of unnamed characters. It is also possible that the writers are drawing attention to the fact that these significant unnamed characters are more likely to be women. But what is clear is that God is not concerned only for those 'named' characters that are seen as significant by society.

3–5. The angel – introduced to readers as *the angel of the LORD* – appears, and informs the woman that she is to have a child. In fact, he begins by reminding her of her barrenness, which at first sight could be seen as a cruel way to start his message. In Israel, as in many societies, childlessness was seen as a huge tragedy. Her barrenness would have been a constant wound for her, a thought never far from her mind. However, it is possible that the angel begins in this way in order to make clear God's awareness of just how significant

this was to her. The good news quickly follows that her despair[73] will
be a thing of the past. She will have a son,[74] who will 'begin to deliver
Israel from . . . the Philistines' (ESV). The hesitancy of the 'begin'
maybe indicates the limitations that we will see in Samson's 'leadership', and it is interesting that the woman does not repeat to her
husband the information regarding the boy's future role as deliverer.
The rest of the angel's message informs the woman that she and the
boy are to take up the Nazirite vow. Numbers 6 gives details of
this, the most significant of the vows available to those who were
particularly dedicated to God's service. Its openness to both men
and women is specifically referred to (Num. 6:2), as is the requirement to abstain from both alcohol and shaving. The use of the razor
is mentioned only in reference to Samson and not his mother, presumably because it would have been extremely unlikely that a woman
would be using a razor anyway. The third element of a Nazirite vow
– to have no contact with a dead body, even that of a close family
member – is not referred to at all in this context, but there is no
reason to suppose it would not also have applied, and this may have
relevance to the later account of Samson's encounter with a dead
lion. None of the other leaders from this time was expected to be
a Nazirite, and the text does not give any reason for the requirement
for Samson to take up the vow. It could be seen as providing a
constant reminder to Samson of the meaning of the covenant and
an encouragement and an opportunity for this remarkable young
man to expend his energy in serving God. However, given Samson's
lack of concern for keeping the law in general, it seems that if this
was the reason for his being brought up as a Nazirite, the intention
did not come to fruition. It is usually assumed that the vow for the
woman would be temporary, in effect, only for the period of her
pregnancy, although there is nothing in the text that necessitates that
assumption. However, it is made explicit that for Samson at least

---

73. In fact, the despair has to be inferred as the text gives no indication of
   the woman's previous feelings, and unlike several other 'barren women'
   accounts, she makes no request for a child.
74. The grammar at this point could indicate that although she hadn't yet
   realized it, she was actually already pregnant.

the dedication would be lifelong, although in Numbers the assumption seems to be that the vow would generally last for a specific period of time (Num. 6:5).

6–14. The woman's first action on hearing this message is to go and tell her husband about the visit. Her intelligence and spiritual discernment, which become clearer as the chapter progresses, are evidenced by her recognition that this was an awesome encounter, that her visitor was a *man of God* and probably *an angel*, and also her awareness of the inappropriateness of questioning him.[75] Apart from her omission of Samson's potential ministry, she conveys to her husband the full message given by the angel. He accepts the validity of the message and her conclusion that it was a *man of God* who had spoken to her, but her word is clearly not enough. Manoah therefore prays that the angel will return to teach *us*. The strong implication is that only if he hears the message himself can he be sure about what was said. As many commentaries over the years have pointed out, verse 8 reflects the common understanding that a woman's testimony was not considered valid. However, it is only in very recent times that the much more significant fact that the angel clearly did not accept the validity of this concept has also been noted! The narrative is obviously very aware of the culture of the time, but it is also clear that God does not always share, or approve of, the presuppositions of the cultures described in Scripture.[76] The

---

75. Cundall (1968: 157–158) assumes that the woman's failure to ascertain the messenger's identity was an accidental omission resulting from her lack of composure. His later statement that on the second occasion 'she was sufficiently composed to take immediate steps to secure the presence of her husband', implying that she should really have done that the first time, does not seem to me to do justice to the way the story is told.

76. Another illustration of this critiquing of culture in the text is provided in the story of Hagar. She, as a foreign female slave, is clearly of no account. She is never addressed by her name by either Abram or Sarai, but only as 'my/your servant', 'that woman' or 'her'. In contrast, on both occasions when, fleeing or sent away from the camp, she meets with God, her own name is used. She may have been of no account in that culture, but God took a different view!

angel does heed Manoah's prayer. He returns once more, and the writers must have been aware of the irony that in what we are told is a direct response to the prayer of the man for a return visit, so that he, as a man, might more fully understand his message, the angel chooses once more to appear to the woman when she is on her own! She was *in the field*, presumably at work. We are not told where her husband was, but her immediate reaction to hurry and fetch him does seem to indicate a good relationship between them. When Manoah eventually arrives and seeks further clarification about the boy's upbringing, he is simply told that the angel has already informed his wife of everything that they need to know. The irony continues as the angel emphasizes the significance of the woman by repeating for the man the instructions relating to his wife's Nazirite status, but says nothing more about the way their son is to be brought up. The wife's testimony should and must be enough. Manoah must listen to her if he really wants to know what they are to do.

15–23. Manoah then offers hospitality to the angel, not necessarily recognizing his links with Yahweh but fulfilling the expected rules of hospitality of the time. There is no indication at this stage that the *young goat* was intended as anything other than part of a shared meal. The angel refuses the meal but does suggest that instead the animal be used as a sacrificial offering to Yahweh. The editorial comment informing readers that Manoah did not realize the angel's provenance suggests that the angel's intention is to guide Manoah towards that realization. The woman's spiritual insight in not asking for the angel's name is confirmed when Manoah with less discernment does ask and is given short shrift. However, the sacrifice is offered and Yahweh does *an amazing thing* (v. 19),[77] which caused both husband and wife — at this point acting in harmony in response to the same information – to *fall with their faces to the ground*, presumably in worship, although it is the failure of the man to reappear that

---

77. Webb (2012: 349) translates v. 19 as: 'So Manoah took the kid goat and the grain offering, and offered them on the rock to Yahweh who works wonders, while Manoah and his wife were watching.' In either case, it was the ascension of the messenger in the flame that Mr and Mrs Manoah saw as a 'wonder' and reacted to in awed worship.

actually convinces Manoah (v. 21). When it eventually dawns on him that they really have been visited by God, he fears for his life, and it is his wife who, again with more spiritual discernment, sensibly recognizes that if God was going to kill them, he wouldn't have brought them the message in the first place and certainly would not have accepted their offering. The story of Manoah's wife stands as a clear refutation of any impression that the contemporary or indeed future societies might have that women were intrinsically incapable, or indeed less capable than men, of hearing from God, understanding God's ways, or of speaking for God. Any temptation to make judgments about whom God will choose to speak to or through is challenged by this narrative. What is made clear is that both of Samson's parents genuinely wanted to serve Yahweh. There is no doubt that Samson was provided with a good start in life, which would have given him a clear knowledge of who Yahweh was and what he required of Samson. The responsibility for any failure to live up to that start lay with Samson himself.

24–25. The brief record of Samson's birth and childhood has some parallels with the later accounts of the early years of John the Baptist and of Jesus (Luke 1:80; 2:40) and also with the story of Samuel's birth (1 Sam. 1 – 3). But here there is no indication of later ministry, and certainly the future life of Samson had virtually nothing in common with the lives of either John or Jesus. Samson was *blessed* by Yahweh (v. 24), but there is no sign of the growing 'in favour with God and with people' that we see in the young Samuel or the young Jesus (1 Sam. 2:26; Luke 2:52).The 'blessing' may simply be the signs of physical health and strength that became very clear in the young Samson.

The Mahaneh Dan mentioned in 18:12 is described as west of Kiriath Jearim which is a few miles north-east of Zorah and Eshtaol and is almost certainly not the same place as that mentioned here. It is likely that this is not the name of a town as such but a general term – meaning 'Dan's camp' – for places where the Danites stopped on their migration north. Zorah and Eshtaol are on the southern border of the tribal area of Dan, and Kiriath Jearim is in Benjamin's territory, a few miles to the east of the border with southern Dan. The verb used to describe the activity of the Spirit of Yahweh within Samson is not used in relation to the Spirit's activity in other judges and is usually used for stirring up dissension or disturbance. It is almost certainly deliberately chosen and perhaps indicates that as Samson grew, so also did his remarkable strength and maybe his capacity for aggravating and upsetting others. Another view would be that it is used (here in the qal) to indicate that God was pushing Samson towards doing something that he did not want to do. It is worth noting that the stirring of the Spirit of Yahweh is seen as something separate from Samson's Nazirite status, which began at, or before, his birth.

Meaning
It is interesting that although this chapter deals very much with a local situation rather than the state of the nation or even tribal issues, nevertheless the concerns presented in earlier narratives are also reflected here. We see God's response both to the evil within Israel and to their needs, even though the needs here are unacknowledged by the people. His response to the 'need' of this couple for a child is in the context of the people's need for deliverance. We see the concern for, and God's use of, what might be seen as 'ordinary' people, although the clear implication that this particular couple were continuing to follow and worship Yahweh might be seen as less than 'ordinary' at this particular time. We see an ongoing interest in the lives and abilities of women (see Introduction, p. 7). The point that is made abundantly clear in the ongoing Samson narratives – that what was happening in Israel was not how it was meant to be – is not actually noticeable in this particular chapter.

ii. Samson's marriage (14:1–20)
Context
Previous accounts might have led readers to expect an account of military conflict to be introduced at this point, but the reality is far from that. The rest of the Samson narratives consists of a series of stories relating primarily to Samson's sex life and his revenge on those whom he sees as acting against his interests in this area. At no stage do we see him expressing any concern for, or interest in, what might be Yahweh's purposes for him, nor even the well-being of Israel as a whole. He is never pictured as consciously acting in the interests of his people. The text seems to go out of its way to

portray Samson as entirely concerned for himself, the exact opposite
of the commitment to Yahweh that a Nazirite vow was supposed
to express.

Comment

14:1–3. We are not told how old Samson was when he decided
he wanted to marry the unnamed Philistine woman, or whether it
was before or within the twenty-year period during which he is seen
as having 'led' Israel. Timnah seems to have been a larger settlement
than Zorah and, although technically in the territory assigned to
Dan, was at this stage not only within the area controlled by the
Philistines, but apparently totally populated by Philistines. It was
only a few miles from Zorah, on the border of the area where the
Israelite population was now dominant. On five occasions we are
told that Samson *went down* to or in Philistine cities (14:1, 5, 7, 19;
15:8). Webb suggests that the use of the phrase emphasizes Samson's
downward path; he sees 'a series of downward movements as
[Samson] moved further and further away from the lifestyle expected
of him as a Nazirite . . . The unfolding pattern of his career . . . was
to be a downward one both literally and metaphorically' (Webb 2012:
365). The suggestion is worth consideration, but the phrase is also
used three times in reference to others (14:10; 15:11; 16:31), so
probably the primary reference is geographical, as Zorah is higher
into the hills than Timnah or Ashkelon. Samson's visit to Timnah
could have been an assertion of his own courage and confidence in
entering enemy territory, or it could simply be an indication that
there was a certain level of interaction and freedom of movement
within the two communities. Weitzman's suggestion (2002: 158–174)
that the Samson stories were intended to create antagonism, or at
least to emphasize the difference between Israelites and Philistines
in order to counteract any move towards comfortable integration,
makes sense in that context. The involvement of Samson's parents
in the marriage arrangements seems to point towards their cooperation in negotiating with their Philistine counterparts. Their initial
reluctance may reflect the almost universal tendency for parents to
prefer their children to marry within their own ethnic group. But it
may also be further evidence of their own allegiance to Yahweh and
his covenant. The reference to the *uncircumcised Philistines* could relate

to the fact that they are not part of the covenant community, although it could also be simply a term of mild abuse. It does reflect the fact that, unlike several of the surrounding tribes, the Philistines did not use circumcision. It is not clear whether the awareness of the parents that Samson was a chosen child led them to protest against his wishes which would deny his heritage both as an Israelite and a Nazirite, or whether it pushed them to give in to their son's pressurizing on the grounds that 'he is special so maybe he can't be wrong'. However, their eventual agreement may just be that they were conscious of the danger of his going into an uncontrollable rage! Samson's refusal to follow his parents' wishes would in itself have been seen as reprehensible by early readers and the parents allowing it to happen as also blameworthy. It is likely that the writers wanted to emphasize that point. The NIV's translation, *Get her for me. She's the right one for me* (lit. 'she is right in my eyes'), captures Samson's aggressive attitude but misses the link with 13:1. Samson is clearly unconcerned with what might be seen as right *in the eyes of the LORD*.

4. The editorial comment in verse 4 is somewhat problematic. It suggests that the parents' opposition to the marriage stemmed from a desire to serve Yahweh, and it is clear that marriage to non-Israelites was inappropriate for God's covenant people (Exod. 34:16; Deut. 7:3).[78] But the editor's conclusion is that what the parents did not know was that this marriage would enable God's wider purpose of separating Israel from the Philistines to be fulfilled. The verb translated in the NIV as *confront* may be used here simply as a synonym for 'defeat', although it is possible that it was deliberately chosen to suggest that God's way forward for Israel was confrontation rather than the cooperation and coexistence illustrated in these events. The comment must have been added to an existing story at a point when the Philistines could no longer be described as 'ruling over Israel', that is, sometime during or after the reign of David. The comment could be seen as suggesting that as the law is given by God, he has the right to overrule it, or it could be simply stressing that the parents should not be judged too harshly for giving in to Samson as God

---

78. Ezra and Nehemiah both contain strong comments on this issue (Ezra 10; Neh. 13:23ff.), taking it for granted that it was unacceptable.

used the circumstances for the ultimate benefit of Israel. The parents thought that Samson's marriage to a Philistine was wrong because it would lessen the separation between Israel and Philistia, but in God's providence it would actually lead to greater 'confrontation' and greater separation. The book of Judges as a whole has many ambiguities that raise what might be seen as ethical issues for modern readers (see Introduction, pp. 30–36). The question of God using, or even apparently initiating, what can be seen as wrong actions to bring out good purposes, which could be seen as justifying a position that the ends justify the means, is not the least of these ambiguities.

5–7. Whatever the intention of the comment, we are told that Samson's parents did accompany him to Timnah. Verse 5 implies that they travelled together. However, Samson was clearly alone, perhaps having stepped aside to relieve himself, when somewhere on the outskirts of Timnah, the vineyards planted outside the town already in sight, a lion (mountain lions seem to have been fairly common in the area; cf. 1 Sam. 17:34–36; 2 Kgs 17:25) attacked. At this point *the Spirit of the LORD came powerfully upon him* (14:6, 19; 15:14). Three times in chapters 14 and 15 we are told that this happened. On each occasion it indicates a particular demonstration of unusual physical force, which could imply that Samson's strength was not a permanent feature. However, in chapter 16 he is pictured as taking for granted his ability to use his strength to get out of trouble at any time. It is possible that chapters 14 and 15 circulated separately from chapter 16 before being brought together by the final editor(s) of Judges. What is clear is that the kind of strength demonstrated by Samson is seen as only something Yahweh could give. The reason for Samson's failure to tell his parents of this incident when he rejoined them is not clear, although their lack of knowledge does have some relevance in the unfolding narrative. Verse 7 suggests that Samson's original desire for the woman had not come as a result of a personal meeting; whether he had seen her at a distance or heard about her reputation as beautiful, we don't know, but certainly when they did meet, *he liked her.* Whether or not his parents liked her is seen as irrelevant, and whether or not she liked him is not discussed! However, presumably both sets of parents did agree and the wedding was arranged to take place *some time later* (v. 8).

8–9. Unless the fiancée was very young, weddings were likely to take place fairly soon after the engagement. In this case it was long enough for bees to have swarmed into the lion's carcass and formed honey. It seems likely that for this to happen, scavenging animals would have first opened up the carcass – although Samson's own tearing it *apart with his bare hands* (v. 6) may have served the purpose. Certainly once the swarm had moved in, the scavengers probably kept away. It is impossible without knowing the time of year and the likely temperature to estimate how long the lion's carcass would otherwise have taken to decay and dry out.[79] Why Samson decided to look at the carcass is not explained. Maybe he wanted to revel in the thought of his own strength. But he found more than he bargained for and, like Eve in Genesis 3, he saw, he took and he ate. Webb (2012: 369) suggests that the allusion to Genesis is deliberate.

This time also Samson was accompanied by his parents, but as before had wandered off. It is possible that they walked much more slowly than he did and perhaps he took detours simply to use up his excess energy. There is ambiguity in the various references to Samson's parents, but the suggestion given here seems more likely than that they were not actually present and that references to them were added later. Although some do take this view, it is hard to see why such an addition might have been thought necessary. There was enough honey to scoop up and still have some left for his parents after what he himself had consumed as he walked. Anything taken from a dead animal in this way would have been seen as unclean, and touching the animal in order to obtain the honey would in itself have broken Samson's Nazirite vow.[80] His failure to tell his parents

79. It seems unlikely that bees would have swarmed into a carcass unless it had dried out.
80. The instructions for Nazirites in Num. 6 refer only to the prohibition of touching human bodies. However, this is an extra prohibition that they are not to become ceremonially unclean at all – even when this involved leaving others to deal with the bodies of close relatives, which normally non-Nazirite Israelites would be expected to do themselves. It would almost certainly be taken for granted that contact with dead animals – also leading to ceremonial uncleanness – would be prohibited.

at this point what he had done is indeed significant. It is clear that they would have been horrified at his actions and certainly would not have joined him in eating the honey. This is a further indication of their general adherence to the law and of both Samson's awareness of what was right and wrong and his complete disregard for such considerations.

10–11. In most cultures there are a variety of arrangements and celebrations when a marriage takes place. Some of these tend to be linked to the home of the bride and some linked to the home of the bridegroom. We don't have enough clear evidence about early weddings to know what differences, if any, existed between Philistine and Israelite celebrations. Nor, if there was a difference, can we determine whether this particular wedding followed the Philistine or the Israelite pattern. The fact that Samson left the celebrations in a rage also means that we cannot know whether the bride would normally have remained with her family or left to join Samson's household. In this particular situation the role played by Samson's father is especially obscure. When did he leave Timnah and how long was it before he returned? Does verse 10 indicate a particular ritual involving a visit from the bridegroom's father to the bride? Is it simply a friendly visit that has been noted here or has it been added mistakenly, perhaps moved from an original position between verses 4 and 5?

We are told that the week-long, extended celebratory feast was *customary for young men*, with the implication that this involved serious drinking and that Samson was breaking another part of the Nazirite vow. It was apparently organized by Samson himself – although the fact that Samson held the feast does not necessarily imply that he paid for it – but we are told that those who attended were chosen by people other than himself. It is not made explicit, but the assumption is that the thirty *companions* were Philistines. The fact that there were so many might indicate an awareness that Samson would possibly need to be kept under control. Whether or not they were the only guests is again not entirely clear. It appears at first as if this was some kind of extended 'stag night', but it seems as if his bride was present for at least part of the time. Whether this means that the marriage was consummated before the end of the seven-day period, which would be unusual, or even whether the bride's presence was normal for this kind of celebration or specifically arranged in this instance by the guests, cannot be determined. The timing of the different elements of the celebrations is also debatable.

12–17. At some point Samson issues a challenge, which has to be met within the *seven days of the feast*. For three days they make vain attempts to solve his riddle. They approach Samson's bride who, after weeping for *the whole seven days of the feast*, receives the answer from him, which she tells to his companions. In verse 15 the Hebrew has the guests going to the bride on the seventh day (cf. KJV, NKJV, RV, ASV), but some Greek and Syriac manuscripts have the *fourth day* at this point (cf. NASB, RSV, NIV, TNIV, ESV). The former translation doesn't make sense of the extended time that she spent seeking to persuade Samson. The latter translation follows on from verse 14 but does not explain why she cried for the whole seven days. However, the fact that she eventually persuaded Samson to tell her the answer and therefore enabled the fellow-countrymen to 'win' the challenge is clear.

The issuing of some kind of a challenge, either physical or mental, during the celebrations associated with a wedding has been common throughout history. In most instances such challenges take place in a spirit of good-hearted fun, but sometimes, particularly as here when other rivalries exist, they can be taken to an extreme. Often the bridegroom's companions are appointed to protect him from, or help him with, such challenges, but here the challenge is issued by Samson to the companions. There is evidence that the telling of riddles was a regular pursuit around this time in the Ancient Near East. Yadin (2002: 426) sees Samson's participation in this competition as evidence of his knowledge of, and absorption into, Philistine culture.[81] Usually in such competitions there would be some clue

---

81. Yadin argues that the word *ḥîdâ* in fact refers to a 'saying' that has to be capped, rather than a 'riddle' that has to be solved, and therefore concludes that the references to the lion are added later to add substance to the misunderstanding that it does mean a riddle. However, his argument is unconvincing. It does not explain how the bride could be expected to provide an answer or indeed what an 'answer' might mean in the context of trying to find a new saying to 'cap' the previous one.

that would enable good searchers to find a route to the answer –
similar to the clues found in a modern cryptic crossword. However,
in the case of Samson's riddle, although it seems obvious to readers
who already have a knowledge of his encounter with the lion, it
would be insoluble to those who had no idea that such a situation
had taken place or even could take place. To modern readers the
riddle may seem somewhat meaningless anyway, but Samson's Philistine companions, although they are annoyed at the lack of clues,
clearly see the riddle competition as a suitable challenge.[82] As it is
likely that most men would have had only one linen undergarment
and only one good set of outer clothes, the cost of failing to solve
the riddle would have been high. For Samson, to find thirty such
sets from his own resources would have been unthinkable, and it is
obvious that he is convinced of the impossibility of the riddle being
solved. The attempt to find the answer by blackmailing his bride to
entice Samson to tell her the riddle's solution is undoubtedly
cheating, and one can understand Samson's anger. However, in that
context to present them with a riddle that is insoluble to those
without inside knowledge could also be seen as cheating. The only
innocent party here is the bride, who is in a no-win situation. If she
does not give them the answer, her family will be wiped out. If
she does, she will no doubt have to face Samson's anger, which she
may already know could be devastating. Delilah perhaps faces the
same dilemma in chapter 16.

18–20. The answer to the riddle was brought to Samson not just
by the thirty companions but by *the men of the town*, adding support

---

82. A modern parallel would be the way in which a particular style of
    humour or jokes is taken up by one generation or culture and seen as
    completely meaningless and certainly unfunny by others. For example,
    'knock knock' jokes or 'how many . . . does it take to change a light bulb'
    jokes which are appreciated in certain Western countries are viewed as
    incomprehensible in some other cultures. Emmrich's view (2001: 67–74)
    that the riddle was intended to be prophetic, with the lion representing
    the Philistines and the bees the Israelites, would mean that the riddle
    was also intended to be a hidden insult. However, the text itself gives no
    indication that the riddle was meant to be anything other than just that.

to the theory that the thirty had been selected as representatives of the rest and with an awareness that Samson had been a threat to them all. Samson's response to their success recognizes that they could only have discovered the answer through his wife. His reference to her as a *heifer* was almost certainly meant to be as impolite as it comes across in English and illustrates Samson's facility with words. Perhaps he saw himself as an expert in the riddle competition, and part of his rage stemmed from having been outwitted at his own game. He clearly had never intended to pay up on his wager from his own resources. He went to Ashkelon, one of the five major Philistine cities, perhaps because he was more likely to find thirty men with a full set of clothes there. Ashkelon is not the nearest of the cities to Timnah, and it could be that it was also chosen for that reason, to avoid easy revenge on Samson's family. The level of Samson's rage is shown by the fact that he was still *burning with anger* by the time he returned to his father's house after a journey which must have taken at least two or three days. Whether or not the writers of Judges saw this as the *occasion to confront the Philistines* sought by Yahweh (v. 4) is not clear. The violent robbery of thirty innocent men does not really seem to make much of a point. Given the way it is used elsewhere, one cannot assume that the use of the phrase *the Spirit of the LORD came powerfully upon him* in verse 19 automatically implies that God approved of his actions. It may simply be stating that Samson was filled again with an unusual strength.

The abrupt disappearance of the bridegroom from the wedding celebrations would imply his intention to call everything off, hence the father being *sure you hated her*, using 'hate' in the sense of 'had legally repudiated' (15:2). It would have been a devastating slur on the bride and her family. Her father's action in marrying her off immediately to one of those who had acted as Samson's companion is understandable. Whether this was done before or after Samson returned with the clothing and stormed off to Zorah is not clear.

Meaning
The relationship between individual Israelites and individual Philistines is seen in this chapter as uncomfortable and competitive, but there is no concentration here on oppression in either direction. It

is possible that the writers are intending us to see Yahweh's deliverance of Israel 'into the hands of the Philistines' as much in terms
of deliverance over to their culture and values as in military terms.
The relationship Samson wanted to have with the Philistines was
primarily that of mingling and marriage; the concept of acting to
deliver his people from the Philistines, whether in a military or
cultural way, seems to have been the last thing on his mind. When
he did act to destroy the Philistines, it was to satisfy his own self-
interest rather than in actual obedience to God. We are nevertheless
told that it was the *Spirit of the LORD* that provided the strength for
this. Whether this was simply the writers' way of saying that he had
a special strength, ensuring the conclusion that all that happens is
in the last resort under God's control, or suggesting that in spite of
Samson's own brutishness God was using him to bring positive ends,
is left somewhat ambiguous.

iii. Samson's revenge (15:1–20)

Context
Samson is twice described as having *led Israel for twenty years* (15:20;
16:31), but there is nothing in the account that describes him as
taking up any role that involved political, legal or even military
leadership of any kind. He is portrayed as the archetypal 'angry
young man', who acted only to satisfy his own passions, mostly
relating to sexual desires or personal vengeance, and took no account
as to whether those actions did or did not serve the interests of
Israel. In the other five main leader/deliverer accounts we are made
aware of problems of various kinds, but there is always a hint of
valour and glory. Once Samson comes on the scene, we read only
of brute strength in the midst of immorality.

Comment
15:1–2. As we don't know the time when the original ceremony
took place, we don't know how long it was before Samson's return
to Timnah. It is worth noting again that the things we don't know
provide as much information about the interests of the writers and
editors as the things we do know. From their point of view the
overall timing is clearly irrelevant. The wheat harvest would probably
have taken place in late spring or early summer. It is perhaps

mentioned not because of the precise timing but because this would, certainly for the Israelites, normally have been a time of feasting. By this time Samson's rage had evidently disappeared. As sometimes happens with those exhibiting that kind of violent tantrum, once it was over Samson seems to have had no conception that there might have been unforeseen consequences of his own actions. Perhaps because of his unusual physical stature, he was used to getting his own way. The young goat seems more likely to have been a gift to show Samson's largesse and to make the occasion a celebration rather than any kind of appeasement. As elsewhere, Samson shows no indication that he was aware that he might have been in any way at fault! The mention of the wife's room could be evidence that the Philistines did have a pattern of marriage where the girl stayed in her own home and was visited by the husband who lived elsewhere. Or it could mean that the couple shared a room in the father's house. In either case, unlike that with Samson, the new marriage had been completed and could not now be annulled. Samson was barred from entering. It may be that the offer of the still unmarried younger daughter was made because of a fear of a further occasion of Samson's violent rage. As with offers of monetary settlement made to avoid an expensive court case, it does not necessarily imply that the father was indicating that there had been an initial wrong done to Samson when the girl was married to someone else. It is interesting that Samson seems to accept without question the fact that he cannot now have the girl he had wanted. It is also a sad reflection of the times that both Samson and the father take it for granted that the younger daughter's interests are irrelevant. One wonders if the writers are aware that they are drawing attention to this fact. One also wonders whether Samson's statement that *this time I have a right to get even* (v. 3) is an implicit acknowledgment that he had no right to take the action he did in chapter 14.

3–8. Predictably, Samson does fly into a temper, but his anger is directed not at the girl in question, her father or her new husband, but at the Philistines in general. In all of this there is no thought of any consequences of his actions other than that it will enable him to get his own back for having been thwarted. It must have taken time to catch so many animals, even if they were jackals, which are found in packs, and not just foxes (the same word can be applied to both). But as we have seen, Samson's rages did last a long time. It would have also taken a great deal of effort and is seen by some (e.g. Webb 2012: 377) as impossible, even for one of Samson's strength, without divine intervention. Unusually, there is no mention of the Spirit of Yahweh being involved in this incident, although of course that does not automatically mean that there was no such involvement. Samson seems to have taken a delight in causing mayhem by unusual methods. The writers may have been conscious of the cruelty of the chosen method, but that is not emphasized. What is clear is the extent of the damage caused by his fire-raising. If Samson was aware of the Israelite law that anyone who starts a fire that burns sheaves or standing corn 'must make restitution' (Exod. 22:6), he did not see it as relevant to his own actions. At that time of year the fire would have spread quickly and vast areas of Philistine farming land were destroyed. Not only would that season's production of wheat, grapes and olives be completely lost, but also the possibility of retaining seed for production in the future. No wonder the Philistines – presumably in this instance implying the Philistine authorities – wanted to discover the culprit and take their own revenge. The first victims were the innocent girl and her father who had been the inadvertent origin of the mayhem. The identity of *the Philistines* in verse 6, and whether or not they were the appointed government, is not clear. Their actions do appear more likely to be those of a lynch mob distraught at the results of the fire and can't necessarily be seen as a demonstration of the Philistine justice system. Similarly, Samson's ongoing behaviour is by no means an indication of how the law in Israel was supposed to work.

Whether Samson's further violence was stimulated by a sense of injustice, an ongoing desire always to have the last word or at least the last blow, or by any genuine affection he might have had for the girl, is not made clear. However, the writers use terms that seem to point the reader here towards disapproval. The literal meaning is that 'he hit them hip and thigh', which is undoubtedly an idiomatic expression not entirely transparent to modern readers, but the implication of wholesale violent killing is conveyed well by the NIV's *He attacked them viciously and slaughtered many* (v. 8). His subsequent action of going to stay in a cave (the text does not say he was hiding, but the implication is that that was the case) perhaps suggests that he was aware that he had gone too far this time. It is possible that he understood that his uncontrolled burning and killing bouts would inevitably bring action against his countrymen and he wanted to protect them – although there is no sign anywhere else in the text that he ever indulged in that kind of reflection or even cared what happened to other people, whether of his own race or not! He was not afraid of the Philistines or for his own personal safety, but his unwillingness to go home could imply that he did have some fear of what his own countrymen would think of him.

9–11. It is interesting that the Philistines actually show a lot more restraint than Samson himself had done. They do bring a force out apparently to fight against Israel and make their camp near Lehi. Lehi means 'jawbone' and was so named after the next incident; its precise location is unknown. The mention of Judah in verse 9 may indicate that the cave was at a distance from Samson's usual haunts or that the Danites who had originally been assigned the area had already left (cf. Judg. 18). However, the Philistines respond immediately to diplomatic overtures from the people of Judah and make it clear that their grudge is against the known culprit Samson rather than against Israel as a whole. It adds evidence to the picture that any overlordship they exercised in Israelite territory was by no means absolute and the two communities coexisted with cooperation, if somewhat uneasily. Samson's location is clearly widely known among his own people. It is possible that the Philistines also knew where he was but decided that they would be more likely to achieve the result they wanted if his own people were to deal with him themselves.

The size of the force sent to arrest him and organize his extradition is perhaps an indication of his growing reputation both for strength and for irrationality, although the size may have been determined by a desire to match the Philistine force. Samson's unspoken answer to their question, 'Don't you realize what you have done?' is a resounding 'no'. If there had been any indication in the text that Samson was concerned for God's purposes, one could argue that he is deliberately refusing to accept that there can be any ruler over Israel other than Yahweh, but the writers do not seem to draw out that implication. Samson's actual reply sounds like that of a sulky child: *I merely did to them what they did to me*. In other words, 'Why should this have anything to do with you?' The illogicality of his reasoning is brought out: that is, that in spite of his own response in annihilating those with no interest in, or responsibility for, the supposed injustice against him, he had not really worked out that the Philistines might be thought likely to react in the same way. His words could be seen as a challenge to Israel: 'If the Philistines are rulers over us, why haven't you acted against them?' But the text leaves such an implication as implicit. The Israelites' failure to respond to the Philistine threat by taking them on in battle could be a sign of fear, reflecting an awareness that the overall Philistine army was stronger than theirs, and of unwillingness to set a rollercoaster of tit-for-tat battles in motion. On the other hand, it could be a recognition of the fact that in this instance Samson could actually be seen as blameworthy and deserving of the Philistines' wrath, a legitimate target for extradition. Soggin (1981: 249–250) sees the Judeans' behaviour as 'despicable . . . collaboration' and assumes that they should have taken Samson's side against the enemy, but that implies a view of 'my countryman right or wrong', and it is at least debatable as to whether Scripture as a whole supports that position. Jephthah's diplomatic overtures to Ammon are one example of the view that negotiation is not to be seen as a sign of weakness. However, Boling is probably right in describing the Judeans' attitude as one of 'servility' (1975: 238). In fact, 15:11–13 is virtually the only time when Samson is recorded as interacting with any Israelites other than his family. Whether he is ignoring them or they are ignoring him cannot be determined, but it seems he generally lived as a 'lone wolf' and it is hard to see how he can really be described as leading Israel.

12–17. Although Samson seems to have had no thought of serving or protecting Israel, he clearly had no wish for the people to suffer. Having obtained a promise from the Israelites that they would not take action themselves – if the Philistines had demanded that he be handed over to them alive, there could be a dual reason for their agreement to this demand – he allowed himself to be bound. At the sight of Samson, the Philistine group were understandably wound up and rushed forward. As he had obviously expected, Samson experienced another surge of physical power – again attributed to *the Spirit of the LORD* – and effortlessly breaks his bonds.[83] He picks up what is to hand – a donkey's jawbone. It was fresh, probably meaning that it had only recently been stripped of the flesh by predators or scavengers, and much more effective as a weapon than a dried bone, which would be more likely to break during such extensive and violent usage. Incidentally, it would also be seen as part of a dead body and therefore once more a breaking of Samson's Nazirite vows, but that was irrelevant as far as Samson was concerned. The bone became a club and, brandished with such energy in the middle of a crowd, would have done terrible damage. Samson's reputation probably meant that very few would have wanted to take him on in hand-to-hand combat, and in the midst of the crowd it would have been virtually impossible to use weapons like arrows that could be fired from a distance. Given the mention of 3,000 Israelites, it is unlikely that this thousand, possibly in any case a rounded-up figure, was the whole force. However, once it was apparent what was happening, it seems very likely that the rest would want to get out of the way as soon as possible. It certainly appears that the point came when there was no-one else to be found and Samson casts the bone aside. It is noteworthy that this is the first time that Samson takes action against an official Philistine force. Is he at last beginning to function as the judge he was called to be?

His brief poem before dropping the bone indicates again that, although he doesn't show great signs of intelligence in other areas, Samson did enjoy playing with words. It is always hard to convey Hebrew poetry in an English translation. The KJV's 'With the jawbone of an ass, heaps upon heaps' is a more literal translation, but the Hebrew word for 'ass' and the word for 'heap' are linked, and the NIV's translation, *With a donkey's jawbone I have made donkeys of them*, or Moffat's, 'With the jawbone of an ass, I have piled them in a mass', at least indicate a little of the wordplay element of the poetry. Samson is revelling in his own triumph over the Philistines.

---

83. Webb (2012: 385f.) points out the parallels between this account, where the Philistines rush towards him, the Spirit comes on him and Samson acts to destroy, and the incident with the lion in 14:5–6. Also note the similarities with his response to Delilah (16:10–12).

The writers have pointed out that his power came via *the Spirit of the LORD*, but there is no indication that Samson ascribed his success to Yahweh or indeed to anything other than his own strength. The name *Ramath-Lehi* (the heights of jawbone) is not referred to outside this chapter, but its use in verses 9 and 14 probably indicate that it was more widely used than just on this occasion.[84]

18–19. It was Samson's thirst that eventually caused him to cry out to Yahweh. The accounts of Othniel, Ehud, Deborah, Gideon and Jephthah all speak of Israel crying out to God, but this is the first occurrence of such crying out in the Samson narratives, and it is inspired by Samson's personal thirst rather than by any need of the nation. It is possible that his *Must I now die . . . ?* was something of an exaggeration given Samson's difficulty in coping with any kind of personal deprivation. Having said that, it is made clear that his thirst led Samson to admit his realization that his victory over the Philistines had come from God. His reference to a 'great deliverance' (KJV) links back to the angel's message to his mother that Samson will 'begin to deliver Israel' (the NIV's *great victory* misses that link). He also acknowledges that in spite of his strength, he was incapable of finding water without God's help. Having described God's mercy demonstrated several times to a largely unresponsive nation, the writers point out that that mercy is also available to Samson as a – largely unresponsive? – individual. It is perhaps significant that it follows this first indication that Samson did have some kind of faith; he describes himself in his prayer as *your servant*. A spring emerged from a hollow in the ground,[85] and the place was named *En Hakkore* ('the spring of the one who calls') in recognition of this. Not surprisingly, it has been suggested that the account was formulated to match the name, but aetiological descriptions do

---

84. 2 Sam. 23:11 does speak of Shammah, one of David's 'mighty warriors', defeating the Philistines 'at a place where there was a field full of lentils', using a word that with different vocalization could be seen as 'Lehi'.

85. The *hollow place* may be the site of a previous spring that has now dried up. The end of v. 19 indicates that the newly opened spring did not dry up again.

sometimes stem from original occurrences and are not always invented later.

20. That Samson led Israel for twenty years is also mentioned in 16:31. Such a phrase is normally found at the end of an account. Its occurrence here could indicate that chapter 16 originated from a different source and the two were brought together at a later stage by the editors of the whole book. Apart from the final episode telling of Samson's death, the events described in all the three chapters that speak of Samson's activities seem to have taken place over a period of months rather than years. There is no indication that Samson had any role in Israel other than his various killing sprees inspired by personal revenge. The twenty years may indicate a gap between the events already recorded and those of chapter 16, or may refer to Samson's adult life, including the unknown length of his time in prison. The fact that he led Israel *in the days of the Philistines*, whereas other judges are pictured as defeating enemies and leading Israel in periods when they were not under the overlordship of other nations, may be emphasizing the original prophecy that he was only going to initiate deliverance from the Philistines.

Meaning

Samson treats the Philistines as an enemy only when his own personal aims are thwarted; otherwise, he seems happy to live with them in reasonably comfortable coexistence. The writers evidently want to make it clear that not only was God active during this period and that he had provided possibilities which could have had a trans-formational effect on his people, but also that this transformation had not taken place and that any deliverance which made real sense in covenant terms was not going to come in the form of this pattern of leadership. In spite of how the Samson stories are often presented in children's talks, the way in which the different stories have been put together indicates that they were never intended to be read as 'hero stories'; in fact, there is much more of an 'anti-hero' approach. It is easy to get involved in the individual stories so that the impact of the bigger picture is lost. But the Samson narratives as a whole provide further support for the view that life and leader-ship in the times recorded in Judges was not the way God intended it to be.

iv. Samson's downfall and final feat (16:1–31)

Context

So far the picture of Samson provided within Judges 14 – 15 has not been encouraging. We have been told that he 'led' Israel but seen no evidence of this. We have seen his disregard for his parents' opinion, for the Israelite law, for his Nazarite vow and for other people in general. We have seen his desire for vengeance and his uncontrolled violent episodes. Whatever good he might have done has come as a side effect of other decisions and behaviours, not because of any specific virtuous motives or intentions on his part. Whether the final chapter of this narrative will change this picture remains to be seen.

Comment

16:1–3. These verses seem to add little to the ongoing narrative, but they do re-emphasize elements found in the other stories. We see again Samson's cavalier attitude to life, illustrated in his approach to women: he sees, he wants, he takes. His fame, or infamy, is clear. He could not now enter Philistine territory without people being aware of it. Gaza, in the south of Philistine territory, was more than forty miles away from Samson's home, but he was clearly comfortable travelling all over Philistia. His reputation led the apparently large force that amassed to capture him to wait until dawn before they attacked. Presumably, the point here is that only a few at a time would be able to enter the house, and if Samson happened to be alert, they would not have had a chance in any kind of close combat. Again, presumably, their decision to wait for morning meant that they spent the intervening time sleeping. Certainly, when Samson left in the middle of the night, there is no indication of any attempt, concerted or otherwise, to stop him. Whether Samson's decision to leave early was because he was aware of their presence is not made clear. His previous behaviour had not given any indication that he feared such a force or that he would have doubted his ability to overcome them. Again the text does not discuss the question as to whether his destruction of the city gates was a response to having passed the sleeping group who were obviously waiting to attack him, or whether it was simply a statement to say to the Philistines, 'I can come and go as I please. You can't keep me in and you can't keep me out.' Verse 2 makes it clear that there were guards on duty at the gate, but it seems that they did not have the nerve to tackle Samson on their own. However, any hope that the gate would keep him inside until a larger force could be assembled was immediately dashed, as Samson simply removed the gates and took them with him.

It is around thirty-eight miles from Gaza to Hebron. The gates were almost certainly made of wood but with at least some metal studs or re-enforcement. Aside from the difficulty, even for a man of Samson's stature and strength, of carrying something as heavy and unwieldy as the city gate for that distance, it is hard to find any logical reason why he would want to do so. Of course, logic does not seem to have been Samson's greatest strength, but the suggestion that the hill facing or 'before' (KJV) Hebron is simply a nearby hill in the direction of Hebron is not without merit. However, Samson was no ordinary man, and his achievements elsewhere are no less remarkable than this would be, so it is possible that the writers are intending the account to be taken literally. Perhaps there is symbolic significance in his carrying the gates back into clear Israelite territory. Possibly this was a message from Samson to the Israelite leaders who had handed him over to the Philistines, and a message from the writers that if Israel had been able to harness Samson's gifts instead of marginalizing him as an uncontrollable maverick, then things might have been very different.

4–5. The Valley of Sorek is on the northern boundary of the main Philistine territory and goes through regions that were mainly Israelite, the river passing near to Samson's home area. It is usually assumed that Delilah was a Philistine woman, but that cannot be more than an assumption. It is just as possible that she was an Israelite, or even a mixed-race woman who was tempted by the offer of money. For a man of Samson's reputation there was no such thing as a private life, and his liaison with Delilah soon became known to the Philistine leaders. The possibility of defeating Samson in battle or by any kind of normal stratagem had apparently now been discounted. Samson's attacks seem to have been isolated and unplanned, but they had caused the Philistines huge problems not only in terms of the actual destruction caused but also with regard to their reputation. It is very likely that the Israelites in general, and possibly the subjects of other people groups too, were beginning to have less respect for the Philistines and to believe that they could in fact be resisted and even beaten. Samson's exploits would have laid them open to ridicule. His donkey poem, for example, is likely to have been spoken of widely. The only way the Philistines could envisage getting rid of Samson was to find a means of counteracting his strength. Such *great strength* was not normal and therefore must have had some kind of specific source. Who better to find the nature of that source than a woman whom Samson 'loved' and presumably therefore trusted: hence the approach of the rulers to Delilah. The number of rulers involved is not given, but each one of them was going to give Delilah 1,100 silver shekels. Even if the group consisted of only one leader from each of the five main Philistine cities, that would have meant 5,500 shekels or around 140 pounds (65 kg) of silver, a vast sum on any reckoning. There is no evidence of Samson ever being violent towards women, but to persuade Delilah to expose herself to the risk of such violence and to compensate for the loss of her 'celebrity' lover, the sum would need to be high. Delilah's loyalty to Samson would have had to be extremely strong to resist such a temptation. The Philistines of course were also risking the possibility that Delilah really did love Samson in return and would inform him of their offer. This was possibly the reason why the offer was so generous: 1,100 shekels per person[86] rather even than the round thousand.

6–9. We have no way of knowing just how long Delilah's relationship with Samson had existed before the deception was attempted, but it must have been long enough for the Philistines to have heard of it and recognized his genuine affection for her. Whether or not they lived together or Samson simply visited her at her own house is also not clear, but he was certainly present with her on many occasions. He has often been compared to Solomon as being a man of unbridled passion who was defeated because of his inability to keep away from women. Clearly, Samson did like to get his own way, but the three 'relationships' described here, with the second one apparently being a 'one-night stand', are far fewer than we read of in the lives of many other Israelite kings, including David, and can

---

86. This forms a link with 17:2 where the same sum is mentioned.

hardly be compared with Solomon's hundreds. Similarly, the accusation that Samson had already been deceived by one woman and therefore should have been on his guard against the treachery of another could really only be made by a misogynist! One woman, under the threat of terrible retribution for refusal to comply, had been the cause of Samson losing a game. To suggest that he should have concluded from this that he should never again trust any woman because they are all the same, all deceivers, seems at the very least a little 'over the top'. It certainly does not do justice to the women who have so far played a part in the Judges narratives. Delilah was corruptible and the cause of Samson's downfall. Whether he should have been expecting that is a very different question. It is noteworthy that, unlike the girl in Timnah,[87] neither Samson nor the narrator refers to Delilah as his wife. Perhaps that was a significant factor for Delilah and she saw herself as owing no loyalty to Samson. The text does not provide us with quite enough information to determine whether Delilah should be seen primarily as a scheming harlot, a hard-headed, independent business woman playing Samson at his own game, or a victim used both by Samson and the Philistines for their own purposes. Readers are left to determine this for themselves, and there is no scholarly consensus on the matter.

Delilah exhibits no subtlety in her attempts to discover Samson's secret. She simply asks him straight out. Her expectation seems to be that she would be trusted and that Samson would tell her the truth. There has been no indication in the text so far that Samson's power was somehow tied up with his Nazirite vow; the only basis for his strength that the text ever mentions is the Spirit of Yahweh coming on him in power. However, it becomes clear that Samson himself believed, whether or not that belief had a basis in fact, that his strength stemmed not from the Nazirite commitment as a whole – he apparently had no qualms about touching dead bodies or eating the honey that would have been perceived as unclean, and there is no reference in his adult life as to whether he did or did not drink

---

87. She is referred to as Samson's wife five times (14:15, 16, 20; 15:1, 6) by the narrator and once by Samson himself (15:1), even though the marriage was never formally completed.

alcohol – but from the fact that he had never used a razor on his hair. His Nazirite status would not have been a secret in his own community, but it seems unlikely that if there had been any awareness among the Israelites that Samson's strength was dependent on his lack of a haircut, such a rumour would not have already reached the Philistines. It was indeed a 'secret'. Samson's failure to tell Delilah the truth possibly reflected his knowledge that if this information got out, he would lose his edge over the Philistines. However, his already demonstrated hubris suggests he would have assumed that no-one would have been able to get near enough to him to do anything about it. Perhaps it did indicate a lack of trust in Delilah, which would soon be proved justifiable. However, it is possible that part of the reason was simply Samson's love of games and riddles: he liked to tease.

Whatever the reason, he makes up a story about being tied with seven undried thongs or 'bowstrings' (NKJV). Whether Samson was asleep or whether he was awake and thinking that she would share the joke when he eventually broke free is not clear. One would have expected Samson to question where Delilah had obtained the seven bowstrings, but that does not seem to have happened. The fact that she was able to secrete a group of Philistine soldiers in another room could be evidence that Samson did come to visit her in her own house. Once Samson was safely tied, she suddenly cried out that the Philistines were coming. This reference may, but does not necessarily, imply that she was not herself a Philistine and thus saw them as a separate group. Whether Samson saw this as a real threat or simply as part of the game cannot be determined. However, he immediately snapped the bowstrings, not an easy task with strong undried thongs that would still be pliable. For Samson it was as easy as if they had been charred to the point of almost cracking by themselves.

10–14. We are not told whether the next 'round' took place immediately or whether the soldiers left and returned. This time there is no mention of the Philistines supplying the new ropes. It would be much easier for Delilah herself to obtain them. It also seems likely that the Philistines would have known that Samson had already broken free from new ropes (cf. 15:13–14) but that Delilah herself would not – this would make more sense if the soldiers were still waiting in the adjacent room. When the challenge came, the new

ropes, which would certainly hold a normal man, snapped as easily
as they had done the first time. In her second response Delilah uses
virtually the same words as on the first occasion, but it seems likely
that the tone was different. The first response may have been an
acknowledgment of his ability to deceive her, of the 'OK, you got
me there' type. For the second, any sense of relaxed amusement is
likely to have disappeared and been replaced by a tone of stressful
tension. One can imagine Samson's delight at having 'got' Delilah
for the second time and her frustration as she could see the money
slipping away. Samson's third deception is a little more creative. He
uses the *seven* again, perhaps because he saw it as more likely to
persuade Delilah given its reputation as a powerful number. Maybe
the idea came to him as he looked across the room at the loom that
Delilah used to weave cloth. He suggests that if his long braided
hair was woven in as part of the cloth on the loom, he would then
indeed lose his strength. Perhaps the fact that he refers to his hair
and is moving towards what he perceives as the truth made him
more convincing. Delilah is again persuaded, but this time the
procedure is delayed. Maybe Samson was tiring of the game, or perhaps this was later and the Philistine agents had to be reassembled.
On this occasion she waited until Samson was sleeping before
carrying out the procedure, but the result was the same. He awoke
at her cry and lifted up the whole loom as he jumped to his feet.

15–22. We don't know how long it was after that before Samson
eventually gave in, as *day after day* her wheedling became nagging.
The 'How can you say you love me when you won't do what I want?'
argument is always a demonstration of a desire for control rather
than an expression of love in return. But it has been used successfully throughout the ages when there is an element of genuine love
for the nagger from the one being nagged. Samson has grown tired
of the game and eventually he has no more strength to resist, and
the secret, at least as understood by Samson himself, is told. If he
gave up his lifelong Nazirite vow not to have his head shaved, then
his strength would go. It is not stated what persuaded Delilah that
this time it was different. Samson must have known that she would
want to try it out as she had on the other occasions. The text gives
us no clue, but it is possible that unlike the other times he added a
warning that this was not a joke and she really must not do anything

to test it out. There is no indication that Samson was concerned that she would betray him. Whatever it was that had persuaded her, she was also able to persuade the Philistines, who must have been somewhat suspicious that they would be thwarted yet again, to return. Verse 19 is somewhat ambiguous. It is not clear as to whether it was Delilah or the man she called who actually cut his hair. The feminine verb form implies that Delilah did the actual cutting but that she called for someone to help. Maybe the hair was so long and thick that it was really a two-person job. But however it happened, the result was the same: Samson's hair was cut and *his strength left him*. The NIV's statement that she *began to subdue him* is better rendered as 'to torment him' (ESV) or even 'to humiliate him' (as Butler 2009: 310).[88] This does indicate that Delilah was not simply 'in it for the money' when the incident might end with a 'sorry, dear, but no hard feelings' type of reaction. Rather, it does point to her bearing some kind of grudge against Samson either because of a personal slight or because she was indeed a Philistine and in spite of their relationship had felt the pain of her people.

It is interesting that the conclusion in verse 20 is that *the LORD had left him*. Whether or not Samson's exceptional strength was directly tied to the length of his hair, the text makes it absolutely clear that it was a gift from God and that God had the freedom to take it away. Samson had not treated God or his gift with the respect they deserved. His strength gone, the Philistines were able to control him. One might have expected that he would be killed immediately, but instead they *gouged out his eyes* and led him away. Samson would no longer be able to decide what was right 'in his own eyes'. For the Philistines who had been ridiculed by Samson, to be able to show the blind, pathetic wreck of a man set to grinding corn in the prison would be far more useful as a public relations exercise than for people to know that Samson was dead. The latter may simply have led to the growth of any myths associated with Samson's previous domination. The former was more likely to cause such myths to be

---

88. One LXX version has 'and he began to be humbled' (cf. footnote of NRSV and NIV: 'he began to weaken'), but this does involve an amendment of the Hebrew.

dispelled. Samson had perhaps been more than a match for any of the Philistine men, but he had been outwitted by a woman and was now set to do women's work (see Butler 2009: 352).

Samson's strength was clearly gone, but the Philistines were taking no chances, and *bronze shackles* were used to make sure he could cause no further trouble. It is perhaps surprising that they made no attempt to keep his head shaved. It is possible that those guarding at the prison had not seen Samson in his heyday and may not even have been told about the method of his capture. Verse 22 states merely that Samson's hair began to grow again. Possibly this is also meant to imply that he began to realize what was involved in his neglect of his Nazirite vow and to embrace again his commitment to serve Yahweh – but this is not made in any way explicit.

23–27. As elsewhere in these narratives, the timing is vague. We do not know how long Samson was imprisoned before the Philistine celebrations took place. For his hair to grow again even to a reasonable length after having been shaved would have taken at least a few weeks and could have been months. On the other hand, if the ceremonies were directly linked to his capture, that seems a long period of time to wait. Verse 25 implies that the decision to bring Samson out was spontaneous, whereas verse 24 seems to suggest that he was already present. Perhaps the account is formulated to indicate the different perspectives that would have arisen in the kind of chaos found in such a large gathering – both before and after the final carnage. Even if it was some time since Samson's capture, it was a significant enough event to be the focus of their rejoicing. The irony is that more attention seems to be being paid to Samson than to the god Dagon[89] to whom the festival is dedicated. Even their song, reminiscent of, if less crude than, Samson's own triumph song (15:16), tells us more about Samson that it does about Dagon. His reputation for devastating both land and people had clearly been huge. Nevertheless, the credit is being given to Dagon for Samson's eventual capture. The reputation of a country's god and the reputation of the country itself were very closely tied together. The writers almost certainly have that in mind as they draw the narrative

---

89. See Introduction, pp. 21–22.

to a close by making it clear that it is Yahweh and not Dagon who will have the last word. The Philistines had credited their success in overcoming Samson to Dagon, but attentive readers already know that it was only because *the LORD had left him* (16:20).

Whatever the exact circumstances, Samson was brought out for everyone to see. The *high spirits* mentioned in verse 25 is a good indication that more than a little alcohol was flowing, perhaps adding to the confusion. What was entailed in his 'performance' is unknown, but there is no doubt that even his presence involving his apparent humiliation would have excited the crowd. It is possible that the temple was built at the side of an open arena. The rulers and other important guests would have gathered under the shade of the roofing area where crowds of ordinary people stood, all therefore having a view of the open space. The pillars would then be those that held up the roof, probably balanced by a wall at the other side. This would make it possible for those on the roof to watch Samson *perform*. Again, for whatever reason, Samson was brought back between the pillars. Perhaps there was a break in the proceedings; maybe some particular ceremony was going to take place. It is possible that the VIPs just wanted a closer view, but Samson's freedom to speak to his keeper and ask to be moved a little makes one of the other scenarios more likely. If these details of the construction are correct, then the crowd on the roof would probably have surged forward craning for a view. Perhaps the change in weight distribution made it easier for the pillars to be dislodged. The blinded Samson must have been aware of the way in which the temple was constructed. It has even been suggested that he might have planned for this occasion, but although he might have suspected that they would put him into the arena, he could not have anticipated the precise circumstances.

28–31. We cannot tell whether Samson had sensed a growing strength within himself or whether his time in prison had led him to a deeper awareness of just how dependent he had been all along on Yahweh's help. We are told that his final attempt to bring destruction on the Philistines is prefaced by a prayer for strength, which could imply that he did not have such strength before this. Any repentance that might have happened has clearly not changed his basic character! His prayer is not that he might serve Yahweh or benefit Israel in this way, but that he might get personal revenge for his own blinding. A number of versions suggest that a better reading might be 'for one of my two eyes'. If this were correct, it would mean that Samson is stating that even destruction of this kind would not be enough to avenge what they had done to him. Samson grasps the nearest two pillars, perhaps those in the centre of the longer side of the temple bearing the most weight, and pushes. The NIV translation would cause the reader to assume that he pushed against the pillars from the side, forcing them apart from one another. However, the term used implies that his hands went round the pillars and he pushed them in the same direction, either out into the courtyard or inward towards the people, depending in which direction he was standing and leaning. The result was the same. The pillars fell, the roof collapsed and Samson died along with a large number of the Dagon worshippers. Given that most of the key Philistine leaders would probably have been present at these national celebrations, and that the efforts of anybody left alive would have been concentrating on seeking any survivors, it is perhaps not surprising that Samson's family were able to come in unmolested and take away the body. Samson was buried in the tomb of his father. Given the previous references to Samson's mother, the specific mention here of his father's family may mean that his mother had also already died.

Meaning

We are informed twice that Samson had been around as a 'leader' in Israel for twenty years, although the timing of the various events and their relation to this twenty years is unclear. The Old Testament presents leadership, even when leaders are said to have been anointed or appointed by God, as also being affirmed and accepted by the community. It may be that the writers here are pointing out, if not actually drawing attention to, the fact that Samson's leadership was apparently affirmed by the people because of his physical strength and in spite of his character defects. If so, this is a further indication of the people's distance from God's covenant requirements. However, there is so little interaction between Samson and the rest of his people that it is hard to know in what sense he *led* them. It is interesting that when 'all the elders of Israel' came to Samuel to ask him to organize a monarchy for them (1 Sam. 8:4), the main reason was that Samuel's sons whom he had appointed as leaders were leading the people away from, rather than towards, following Yahweh. Perhaps the elders had been reflecting on the mistakes of the era of the 'judges'.

As has already been noted, there is no evidence that Samson's leadership involved anything other than his causing the death of many Philistines. However, the prophecy given to his mother before his birth that he would 'begin to deliver Israel from the hand of the Philistines' can indeed be seen as being fulfilled by his killing spree. These were violent times. The Philistine overlords were seeking to control and ultimately destroy Israel as a distinct community along with all it meant for them to be Yahweh's covenant people. Samson is not portrayed here as in any sense a nice or a good man. However, his undermining of the Philistines' military supremacy, and hence their influence and authority over Israel, did lay the foundation for Saul's defiance and David's later successes over them. It is possible that his final suicide mission, by destroying a generation of leaders, also helped to undermine their governmental structures. The major concerns of the book of Judges are continued within the Samson narratives. They too provide a clear sense that this was not the way that life was supposed to be lived in the land that God had promised to, and provided for, his people. But at the same time they too make it very apparent that in spite of the failure of the people and their leaders, God is still present and active among them, still has an ongoing purpose for them and can still use unexpected people, even those who make no effort to cooperate with him.

The Samson narratives do not contain any major battle scenes between Israel and her enemies, but they do tell of the decisive victory of Yahweh in a battle with the Philistine god Dagon. In many ways Samson was representative of the whole of Israel. He was more inclined to mingle with the Philistines than to keep separate from them. As Webb (2012: 405) puts it, 'He has wanted to mix with them, intermarry with them, and party with them.' But in God's providence Samson's quick temper and violent reactions had constantly brought him into confrontation with the Philistines (cf. 14:4), which had led to an increasing level of separation that neither Samson nor Israel had sought for themselves. It is worth noting that Hebrews 11:32 refers to Samson, along with Gideon, Barak and Jephthah, as an example of a man of faith. No specific reference is given, and it is not easy to see how most of the illustrations of what such men of faith did (Heb. 11:33–34) apply to Samson apart from perhaps 'whose weakness was turned to strength', unless we take 'shut the mouths of lions' in a literal way.

The next major leader in Israel that we read of is Samuel. The parallels between Samson and Samuel are clear (see Blumenthal 2005: 108–112). Both were born to previously childless mothers in a way that is perceived by those mothers to be the result of God's intervention and blessing. Both grew up with an awareness of God's involvement in their lives. But the way in which they built on that heritage could not be more different. As the final editors of Judges were almost certainly aware of Samuel and his leadership of Israel, it seems likely that the Samson story is deliberately recounted in a way that emphasizes that contrast. Perhaps, as the last of the major 'judges' whose story is told, Samson also stands as a final illustration that this method of leadership or governance was not going to succeed in helping Israel to be the people God wanted them to be.

3. STORIES OF INDIVIDUALS: EXEMPLIFYING THE TIMES (17:1 – 21:25)

A. Introductory comments

The main central section of the book of Judges has focused on twelve particular leaders and their families. The final five chapters contain two story cycles, which cover a series of events set in motion by the activities of two individuals. These two, *a man named Micah* (17:1) and an unnamed Levite (19:1), have no particular significance as far as the leadership of Israel is concerned, and yet their activities do have a remarkable influence on the behaviour of others, not only other individuals but tribes and even the whole nation. It is possible that the inclusion of both the young Levite in the first cycle and the Levite in the second cycle is also significant as showing that that tribe, although not involved in seeking their own tribal territory, nor in the local or national leadership stories, nevertheless plays a part in the overall corruption evident within Israel. Corruption in Israel and their failure to live as God's covenant people is not just a result of tribal armies failing to complete their campaigns or of inadequate leadership (or the inadequate following of good leaders); it is also the responsibility of every individual within the nation, including the two groups highlighted within these texts. Thus this section, although sometimes described as an appendix, can clearly be seen as an integral part of the writers' overall strategy.

The two story cycles are also linked together by the sentence, *In those days Israel had no king*, which appears four times in this third section of Judges, twice in each of the two cycles (17:6; 18:1; 19:1; 21:25). The first and last occurrences, towards the beginning of the first cycle and at the end of the second, add the phrase, *everyone did as they saw fit* (lit. 'what was right in their own eyes'). These editorial comments serve to give structure to the whole section. They indicate that the section is intended to be viewed as a whole and provide clues as to the particular interest of the writers at this point. It has often been assumed that their primary interest was to provide support for the monarchy – showing that without the monarchy it was not possible for life in Israel to be lived as God intended. However, it could equally be suggested that the writers' interest is in the possibility of good government and, rather than simply calling on their contemporary readers to support the monarchy, are asking them to assess whether the monarchy as they know it has or has not changed the situation in any way. Did the monarchy in practice actually lead to more people doing what was right in Yahweh's eyes? Certainly the phrase 'right in their own eyes' is parallel to the repeated *the Israelites did evil in the eyes of the LORD*, which occurred seven times in the earlier part of the book but is not repeated in the final section. A further connection between the two stories in this section is the fact that both Levites have some links to both *Bethlehem in Judah* and *the hill country of Ephraim*, and both (18:31 and 21:19) mention Shiloh (see Webb 2012: 419–420), although whether these links are significant or coincidental is less clear.

None of the tribal leaders is mentioned in these chapters and there is therefore no indication of timing. It is sometimes suggested that the second series of stories comes from a time prior to the first series. However, we cannot be sure of that. If 20:1 is seen as an indication that the Danites had by then settled in their own territory, then those events would have to be later than the situation described in 18:1. It is possible that because the first stories involve the Danites, they were placed immediately after the Samson narratives also relating to Dan. However, as Micah himself came from Ephraim, this seems a somewhat tenuous link. There is also no mention in this section of external enemies having control over the Israelites or indeed any evidence of their presence in the land as other than peaceful citizens facing conquest by the Israelites. It seems likely that the writers were clearly aware that this does not tally with what has been previously described and that the omission was deliberate. Without this section it would have been possible for Israel to claim that all their problems resulted from their being oppressed and influenced by outsiders. But here it is made very apparent that corruption, both spiritual and ethical, existed within Israel itself, independent of outside pressures. Surely the writers are intending to suggest that Israel herself must take responsibility for the corruption within her borders – even at times when those borders might not be particularly secure.

B. Stories related to Micah (17:1 – 18:31)

i. Micah's idols and priests (17:1–13)
Context
This story seems to be composed of interrelated layers. We have the account of Micah's family, maybe presented as typical of rural families of the time, with syncretistic worship and theft from each other alongside loyalty and affection. We have movements of the Danites providing more information about the way in which the tribes were and were not able to fulfil their commission to occupy the land. We have an indication of the way in which Levites were viewed at the time. There is no real agreement as to whether this should be seen primarily as a spy story (like those in Num. 13 and Josh. 2 when men were sent to spy out the land), a war story, an occupation story or indeed an anti-spy story (Bauer 2000). Parallels with the account of Jeroboam, who set up altars served by non-authorized priests at Dan and Bethel, have been noted, and questions raised as to whether the account should be seen as a polemic against the later northern monarchy (Na'aman 2005; Amit 1990). It seems clear that although there is little specific editorial comment in the account, the writers do intend readers to come to negative conclusions about what is happening, so to view it as a polemic seems

fair and one can imagine southern readers being particularly pleased with the presentation of corruption in northern shrines. However, whether parallels with the Jeroboam account should be seen as evidence of a date later than Jeroboam is less convincing. It is perhaps just as likely that the Judges passage had some influence on the way the story in 1 Kings 12 – 14 is told, with the implication that there has been no real progress since the time of the initial conquest of the land.

Comment

17:1–2. Chapter 17 seems to begin in the middle of a story, but everything the reader needs to know about previous events can be presupposed from the information given. A countrywoman, probably a hill farmer, had been robbed of 1,100 shekels.[1] This is a substantial amount, and even if it was her whole savings, we are talking here about a wealthy family. Most towns were built in the valleys, and we are specifically told that her son came *from the hill country of Ephraim*. If theirs was a significant property in the area, it explains why travellers commonly approached the home. There is no mention of a husband, and the silver was clearly her own property. This would have been a substantial loss, and she cursed whoever had taken the money. Her uttering the curse in Micah's presence may or may not imply that she did have a suspicion of his guilt. Curses played a major role in the lives of those in the tribes and nations surrounding Israel, and the literature of those nations is saturated with rituals and formulae for dealing with curses, as without such action curses were seen as irrevocable. However, the whole approach stands in contrast with the Hebrew Scriptures where nowhere is there any indication that it was appropriate for God's people to issue such curses and not one curse-revoking formula is to be found. The only curses relevant for God's people were those that stemmed from God himself. David's reaction to Shimei's curse (2 Sam. 16:5–13) indicates his view that if God was behind a

---

1. There is a possible link here with the amount given to Delilah by each of the Philistine rulers (16:5), but it is hard to determine what that link, if it exists, might be.

curse, then let God's will be done, and if not, then the curse was powerless anyway (Evans 1994). We are not told the content of the mother's curse and what evil she had wished upon the culprit, but the fact that she had uttered a curse in itself points to her being strongly influenced by the religion of the surrounding nations and her idolatry shortly becomes explicit. It is not stated whether her curse was issued in the name of one or other of the local gods, although her subsequent references to Yahweh may mean that she had an awareness of him. In either case she clearly has no real knowledge of Yahweh or his requirements, and no sense that the use of his name in this way would have in itself brought the full force of the law down on her. Whether or not her son Micah's sudden fit of conscience was related to the fear of her curse is not made clear, but he admitted to being the thief and returned the silver. It has been suggested (Jost 1996) that her curse against Micah could be seen as an indirect criticism of anyone who wrongly used cultic objects, but in fact the curse here relates to the theft of the silver, not the making of the idol, which she herself initiated.

The record that her immediate response to the son's returning the silver was to say, *The LORD bless you, my son*, is almost certainly deliberate irony on the part of the writers, although probably not of the mother herself. The syncretistic use of the name of Yahweh alongside practices that the law proclaimed to be totally unacceptable reflects the general situation in Israel at this time. Once she got her property back and realized that the culprit was her son, her attitude changed completely. It is possible that her blessing was a deliberate attempt to try to reverse the previously uttered curse. If so, it makes it less likely that she was already aware that he was the culprit. The use of God's name, Yahweh (in English versions usually replaced by LORD), in the blessings and presumably in the curse as well, shows that the concept of Yahweh was present and was a part of their lives. Maybe the fact that in spite of the mention of his name Yahweh plays no part in this narrative is intended to emphasize the reality that, although his name was known, there is clearly no idea of relationship with him and no intention to seek out and follow his will. In fact, it is possible that the writers are drawing attention here to the flagrant disobedience of the commandment not to misuse the name of Yahweh, just as the next verses point back to the second commandment not to make or worship any kind of image.

3–6. Her dedication of the returned silver to Yahweh and the placing of the image she had made in the house may have been a further attempt to frighten Micah into not repeating his theft. Again, her understanding of what such dedication might mean appears to be extremely limited. Two hundred shekels (about 5 pounds or 2.3 kg) were set aside to make an image. Even if this was intended to be something that would better enable them to worship Yahweh – and that is far from clear – the creation of any such image was strictly forbidden. Human attempts to make a representation of Yahweh can never be anything other than idolatrous. There is almost certainly a deliberate irony in the recording of her cursing of whoever stole her silver alongside her causing an idol to be made – an action which itself comes under an automatic curse (Deut. 27:15). The family's lack of knowledge regarding what it meant to belong to Yahweh's covenant people is further exemplified by the description of Micah's shrine (lit. 'house of God' or 'house of gods'). The ambiguity of the term (the plural *elohim* is either a plural of respect, meaning God, or the normal term, meaning gods) may again be deliberate irony on the part of the writers. Yahweh is mentioned in relation to the shrine, but it actually housed idols (see Webb 2012: 425–426). The shrine, which may have been attached to Micah's house or a separate building, contained a selection of gods, the new idol and an ephod – presumably here an item used to determine the best thing to do in any given situation (cf. 1 Sam. 23:9; 30:7). The alternative uses of ephod as a garment (1 Sam. 2:18; 2 Sam. 6:14) or as part of the priestly regalia (Exod. 28:4–12) do not really make sense in this context. One of his sons became the *priest* at Micah's shrine. What happened to the rest of the silver *solemnly consecrated* to Yahweh is not stated. The implication is that it remained as part of the wealth of the family.

The first of the four occurrences in chapters 17 – 21 of the sentence, *In those days Israel had no king*, comes in verse 6. It is generally assumed that the main interest of the writers in this section is therefore to draw attention to the fact, made very apparent in the previous section, that the current method of leadership has not worked and to prepare for the next stage in Israel's history – that is, the monarchy. There is certainly the implication that if there were a king, at least one who functioned according to the principles of kingship set out in Deuteronomy 17:14–20, then the spiritual and ethical horror stories described in these chapters would or could surely not have happened. However, if the authors were aware, as the writers of Samuel and Kings clearly were, of the later failures of the monarchy, it is possible that the phrase here is being used to indicate that the failures of this period could not be blamed on the monarchy, but lay firmly as the responsibility of those who 'did what was right in their own eyes'. In the immediate context of chapter 17 the phrase is also used to provide an explanation, clearly felt necessary by the writers, as to how such a terrible situation as Micah's idolatry and the family's lack of concern about inappropriate cursing or the need for appropriate priests could have existed in Israel. The clause, *everyone did as they saw fit*, or more literally, 'what was right in their own eyes', is added both here and in the fourth and last occurrence of the original sentence. Although it is possible to argue here that the editorial comment is simply descriptive and not judgmental, the direct link with the 'evil in the eyes of Yahweh' of the previous chapters strongly implies that what was 'right in the eyes of' these Israelites was actually 'evil' in God's eyes, providing further evidence for at least a measure of unity within the whole book. As the writers are clearly using the phrase as a structural indicator, it seems surprising that the first instance is found here and not at the beginning of the story. The idea that it was necessary for readers to hear how bad things were before any reason for this was suggested (Harris, Brown and Moore 2000: 263) has some merit. Readers may have been tempted to think that Micah's family were exceptions in a generally godly society, but in fact they were only examples of the general population who were all doing 'what was right in their own eyes'.

7–13. Again, as the *young Levite* arrives on the scene, the impression is given that there is another story yet to be told. What had he been doing in Judah and why was he now moving on? That is not relevant to this story and therefore no information is given. Whether Micah's simple question: *Where are you from?* reflected suspicion or merely hospitable interest we cannot tell. But he responded immediately to the news that this was a Levite seeking a base. In spite of Micah's twisted theology, he did have an awareness that it would be better to have a Levite to look after his shrine than to depend on his own son. There is no indication that this Levite was descended from Aaron and therefore eligible for a priestly role, but then Micah's shrine did not exactly follow the required pattern either! In fact, we learn in 18:30 that the Levite's name was Jonathan and he came from the Mosaic section of the tribe of Levi, not the Aaronic.

It is hard to know the exact value of money at this time, but the Levite seems to have been well satisfied with his ten shekels a year all found. This indicates just how wealthy the family was, if ten shekels plus board – making hardly a dent in the remaining 900 shekels – is seen as an acceptable year's salary. The Levite's willingness to be part of this corrupted religious system is clear evidence that the lack of covenant awareness throughout the tribes was also present among the tribe of Levi. The text stresses that he was treated as a member of the family. As priest, he became Micah's *father* (v. 10). This seems a strange ascription for someone who is clearly presented in verse 7 as a young man. It makes sense that in every other way he was treated as Micah's 'son' – the reaction of Micah's own son, who had been deposed as priest, to this appointment is not recorded! Micah's conviction that as he now had someone from the right tribe, if not the right clan, as his priest, Yahweh would be forced to bless him, is recorded without comment, although given what has gone before, it is hard not to conclude that the writers are pushing the reader towards a critical conclusion. They would expect readers to understand that Yahweh's blessing was not something that could be ensured or bought by carrying out particular rituals, but was possible only through a life of obedience to, and relationship with, him. The awareness that Micah did have of the special role of the tribe of Levi tends to suggest that knowledge of what Yahweh required of his people would have been available to the family. In other words, if they knew this element of the law, it seems that the law as a whole was there to be known. However, there is no indication that Micah or his family had any kind of interest in finding out what might be 'right in Yahweh's eyes', only in seeking to ensure their own well-being.

Meaning
The picture being painted here is not just of the syncretism and idolatry that were taken for granted by all the characters in this

particular story, but of the breakdown of the whole concept of covenant community. Micah's name means 'who is like God', but it is very clear that no-one described here had any idea what Yahweh was like or what he really required of them. Yahweh, when he is thought of at all, is seen as there not to be served and worshipped, but to be manipulated in order to bring gain to those who mention him. The concept of exclusive worship of Yahweh is an irrelevance to Micah and his family. We have here the picture of a family who, in terms of the covenant that the people of Israel were expected to follow, were doing everything wrong. Nevertheless, it could be said that this negative presentation could point readers towards the possibility of how it might have been if people had behaved not as they themselves *saw fit*, but in accordance with the patterns that God had set out for them.

ii. The Danites take Micah's priest (18:1–31)
Context
Chapter 17, telling of the shrine set up by Micah and his family and presided over by the young Levite, provides the immediate context for the account in chapter 18 of the exploratory journey of five Danite spies, followed by the northern migration of a large Danite community incorporating the removal of Micah's gods and priest. The wider background is the failure of the Danites to take over the land assigned to them (Josh. 19:40–46) and described as their inheritance. Joshua 19:47 and Judges 1:34–36 give details of this failure, which explains their need to search for new territory.

Comment
18:1–2. The second occurrence of *In those days Israel had no king* in 18:1 again raises the question as to whether a monarchy would be better than the current situation. The instructions for the appointment of a king in Deuteronomy 17:14–20 show that a king's primary responsibility would be to know and keep, and to ensure the people knew and kept, the law of Yahweh. The events of these chapters make it very clear that at present the law was hardly known and even less kept. The writers may be implying that the events that are about to be described would surely not have happened if a stable overall government including the monarchy had been in place. There is

irony in this thought that may or may not have been intended. If there had been a king who was functioning properly as guardian of the covenant, then Micah would have been able to take his case to the king and gain recompense against the Danites for stealing his property. However, if such a king had been in place, then Micah's idolatry would not have been tolerated in the first place! The question of whether or which 'judges' would have been available to make similar judgments is not raised.

The impression given here is that the Danites were one of the last tribes to settle into their inheritance. This tallies with Joshua 19:40 where Dan was the last tribe to gain their allotment in the ballot, and with Judges 1 where, although not every tribe is included, Dan is the last to be mentioned and apparently the least successful in taking over their assigned land. Zorah and Eshtaol are in the south of Dan's tribal land, so some territory had clearly been claimed, but by no means the whole area. The reason for the Danites being confined to such a small area is related in 1:34 to resistance from the Amorites and was probably also affected by strong Philistine opposition. Joshua 19:47 also speaks of the Danites' acceptance of their inability to occupy the land assigned to them and gives very brief details of their migration to the northern areas. Whether the mention of Dan seeking new land is deliberately placed next to the statement about having no king, and whether readers are therefore meant to question Dan's action, are matters for speculation. The text does not discuss this particular issue, but for one reason or another the Danites were not satisfied with the land that had been assigned to them. Five key leaders are sent out to reconnoitre the land in much the same way as Moses sent out the twelve 'spies' in Numbers 13. We are not told where in the *hill country of Ephraim* Micah's house was situated, but it was apparently on the route to the north taken by the Danite spies.

3–6. In any event they turned up at Micah's home, stopping off there because they recognized the voice of the young Levite. As he came from Bethlehem and they were from around Zorah, it is not obvious how they might have known him well enough to recognize his voice – but that is not relevant to the writers' concerns and we are given no information about it. It is possible, as Brown suggests, that they heard from his accent that he did not come from Ephraim

(Harris, Brown and Moore 2000: 266), in which case their questions about his situation are general rather than personal. The Levite seems to have been perfectly satisfied with his position. There is no indication that his report to the Danites was anything other than positive. It seems likely that Micah's shrine was used locally as an oracle – perhaps even as a way for Micah and the Levite to make money. His replies make it clear that he is paid for being there and give no indication of any sense of God's leading. In fact, he doesn't mention Yahweh at all at this point. The Danites certainly saw the idol as something they could use to their advantage. They clearly had no problem with the idolatrous nature of the shrine, and their request for the Levite to *enquire of God* (using *'ĕlōhîm*) is ambiguous. However, in this case the Levite, now referred to as *the priest*, does give his message to them using the name of Yahweh. The writers make no comment as to whether the message actually did come from Yahweh. The statement that their journey 'will be in front of Yahweh' is more ambiguous than the NIV's *has the LORD's approval* would indicate – it is possible that the Levite was covering all his bases – although it would almost certainly have been interpreted by the Danites as a blessing and the Levite probably told them what he thought they wanted to hear. The fact that they were heading out to look for land in an area that was not assigned to them by Yahweh is not taken into consideration. When their mission was successful, it is likely that they would have seen the priest as bringing them good fortune.

7–10. The Danites travelled to the north of the region occupied at that time by the Israelites, although the area they reached was technically in the territory originally assigned to Naphtali. The town of Laish (Josh. 19:47 calls it Leshem) seems to have remained exempt from the constant fighting between the different people groups that was seen further south. It lay at the northern end of the valley of the Jordan, a fertile area well able to support a reasonably small population but surrounded by much less hospitable mountainous countryside and therefore not a major target for invaders. It had clearly been colonized by the Sidonians at some point but was not near enough to Sidon for the town to have received much interference or support from there. As far as the Danite agents were concerned, it was ideal, good land and easy to conquer. Their report back to their fellow Danites in the Zorah region is probably deliberately reminiscent of the report delivered to Moses by the first Israelite agents in Canaan, except this time there were no reservations about any difficulties involved in the occupation. As far as they were concerned, God had opened up the door and all they had to do was walk through it. The fact that they were going against his specific commission to them does not seem to have had any part in their thinking. The open door must be God-given, particularly as their enquiry of Yahweh's representative, the young Levite, had brought what they saw as a positive response. Again, the writers record the events as they happened and leave the reader to draw conclusions about whether or not this really was part of God's plan.

11–21. So 600 armed Danites, together with all their families and possessions (v. 21), set off to occupy their new home. What proportion this was of the Danite community centred on Zorah and Eshtaol is unknown. They camped at Kiriath Jearim – said here to be in Judah, although part of the territory was actually assigned to Benjamin. The tribal borders were fairly fluid at this stage, and it is possible that either as they moved or at the time when the record was completed Kiriath Jearim belonged to Judah. This was presumably their first main camp, only a few miles from the original Mahaneh Dan (see comment on 13:25). We are told that their stay was remembered but not why this particular camp was significant enough for its presence to have been remembered in this way. Not surprisingly, their journey followed the same route as that taken by the five agents and therefore, as they travelled through Ephraim, the migrating group passed by Micah's house. The comment of the five men, *Do you know that . . . ?*, appears to be spontaneous. However, the *Now you know what to do* and the fact that the whole company of men were armed for battle implies that the decision to take Micah's idols had been made well before their arrival at that point. It seems unlikely that they would have been fully armed while passing through the territory of fellow Israelites whom they had no intention of attacking. Clearly, the silver idol Micah had made was only one of several religious objects kept at the shrine. This was not just one mistaken creation that they thought could represent Yahweh. The writers draw attention to this by mentioning, with only slight amendments, the list of what they took – the idol, the ephod and the household gods – four times in the space of seven verses. This provides more evidence that when the Danites had asked the young Levite to 'enquire of *'ĕlōhîm*' (v. 5), they were really saying 'gods' not 'God'. The reference to *the house of the young Levite at Micah's place* (v. 15) reinforces the impression that the shrine was housed in a separate building and maybe explains why they were well on their way before Micah realized that his property had been taken.

This may have been a fairly simple robbery – the silver and other materials would have been worth something – but the primary motivation seems to have been the removal of the images because of their perceived value in bringing the Danites good fortune. The five men who had already received hospitality in this house were welcomed again without question by the young Levite. To steal after receiving hospitality should have been unthinkable. The irony of the situation is emphasized by the statement that they greeted him, which is literally 'wished for him peace' or shalom. When they began to dismantle and remove the shrine, he did start to question them, but 600 armed men waiting outside would have discouraged any attempt to prevent the robbery! Unlike the robbery itself, the decision to invite the Levite to accompany them appears to have been unpremeditated. He immediately jumps at the chance, delighted with the offer. Their argument that it was better to serve the many than the few could, in another context, be seen as implying that it was morally superior, or even that one could serve Yahweh better in this way. However, here it is more likely that they were implying that an oracular priest could earn more money if there were more people available to come and consult him. It is true that the Levite was about to lose his job, which was to look after the about-to-be-removed shrine. Nevertheless, the previous information that even though he described himself as *hired* by Micah (18:4) he had been treated as a son (17:11) suggests that he might have been expected to show a little more loyalty to Micah. The mention of the placing of the women and animals at the front of the party indicates that they were expecting some kind of reprisal and were prepared for it by keeping the fighting force between their families and those who might attack. It is made very clear that this was not just a random attack by a small group, such as those who had been in the original spying party. The whole tribe was obviously complicit in this offence.

22–26. When the loss of the shrine was discovered, its idols and its minder both having disappeared, there would have been no doubt at all what had happened. The loss affected not just Micah himself but the whole community, who had presumably used the shrine and the priest to discover what behaviour or events might be seen as propitious. The men from the area got together and chased after the Danites, who could only travel at the speed of their families and animals. The recorded dialogue clearly shows that for Micah this was primarily about money rather than about any perceived principle. Possibly, he had suspected that his property had been stolen by a small number, probably the spies who had visited previously, and he could ask the larger tribal group to deal with it for him. Once it became clear that the whole group had supported the theft, he very quickly gave up any attempt to retrieve his belongings. Verse 24 strongly suggests that the shrine was the way in which Micah had made his living. There is no question here of this being a matter of a mistaken but genuine attempt to serve and worship Yahweh. He sees their crime simply as theft, not as sacrilege. What they have stolen is *the gods I made*, and there is no reference at all to Yahweh within this section. With neither the *gods* nor the Levite, who was obviously gaining a reputation, available to him, Micah was left with no other means of earning money. The Danites response in effect says, 'You will lose a lot more than that if you don't go away without causing us any more trouble.' We cannot tell how many men Micah took with him, but both he and they saw the Danites as the superior force. More would be lost than gained in entering into a fight, so Micah's pragmatic decision was to turn round and go home. The irony of the fact that Micah had stolen from his mother and now had himself been the victim of theft is almost certainly being emphasized by the writers.

27–31. Verses 27–31 describe the capture and resettlement of Laish, henceforth to be called Dan. In today's world any kind of territorial aggression is seen in very negative terms. In the times described in the book of Judges this was not generally an issue. In Joshua and most of Judges, when battles involving the conquering of territory seen as given by God to Israel are described, there is very little discussion or any kind of questioning about the morality of such action. Jephthah's argument from 11:24, *Will you not take what your god Chemosh gives you? Likewise, whatever the LORD our God has*

given us, we will possess, reflects the general attitude. It was accepted
that this was what should be happening and that people would die
in these campaigns. It is possible that they were also taking for
granted the concept that the giving of the land to the Israelites was
related to the taking of the land from the Canaanites who had shown
themselves unworthy of possessing it. Israel spent forty years in the
wilderness because of their unbelief and disobedience, but the occupation of the land was also apparently delayed because the Canaanites
had not yet forfeited all rights to it. Whatever the general attitude in
this case, however, the repeated stress on the vulnerability of the
previous residents of Laish and the language used – *There was no-one
to rescue them* – seems deliberately designed to raise questions in
the reader's mind about the rightness of what is going on here. The
point is not made explicit, but the fact that this was not land that
had been given to the Danites by Yahweh did possibly make a
difference to the writers here. They are describing, but not necessarily approving of, what went on in this particular act of conquest.
Nevertheless, they did conquer, the city was razed and then rebuilt
and the Danites continued to live there. They also, although this is
not reaffirmed outside of this chapter, continued to be served for
many years by the Levite, here revealed as Jonathan son of Gershom,
the son of Moses, and his descendants. This may simply indicate
that he came from the Gershomite clan within the tribe of Levi;
'son' is often used in the Old Testament to refer to 'descendant'.
The MT has been amended by the addition of an 'n' over the consonants used in the name Moses – hence the translation 'Manasseh'
in the KJV. The suggestion is probably correct that the amendment
was made either to distance the name of Moses from the activity of
this particular Levite or to associate the Levite with the later king
who was seen as the epitome of evil. The *time of the captivity of the land*
(v. 30) could refer to 733 BC, when Tiglath Pileser of Assyria oversaw
the capture of much of the northern kingdom, leaving only a small
area around Samaria which was eventually also subjected to defeat
and exile in 622 BC. However, there seems to be a direct link being
made between the use of the priest and the use of Micah's idol,
which is said to have continued *all the time the house of God was in Shiloh,*
that is, until the ark of God was captured by the Philistines and after
its release kept at Kiriath Jearim until David took it up to Jerusalem

(1 Sam. 5; 2 Sam. 6). Perhaps the writers, with their Deuteronomic influence, are identifying the captivity of the ark with that of the land. Certainly, when one of Jeroboam's golden calves was placed at Dan (1 Kgs 12:25–30), there is no mention of Micah's idol – although the previous worship of that idol may have made it easier for Jeroboam's image to be accepted in that situation. Clearly, these verses tell us something about the time of the final compilation of Judges (see Introduction, pp. 4–5).

In many ways the account of Dan's accession of the northern land can be seen as a success story (Wilcock 1992: 159). They had the city and the land, where they lived in apparent safety for many years; they had a priest to guide them and the system to go with it. But although there is very little editorial comment, the reader is left with the strong impression, strengthened by the contrast in the final verse between *the idol Micah had made* and *the house of God* which was in Shiloh, that this was not how it was meant to have been!

Meaning

The picture is of a self-serving community with no concern for the way in which Yahweh might want them to live. In their eyes such things as hospitality, loyalty or even justice counted for nothing in comparison with self-interest. As far as they were concerned, their gods were there not to be served but to make their lives easier. The story of Samson's parents told in chapter 13 has already informed us that not all Danites come into the same category, but for the writers of Judges these Danites, alongside Micah the Ephraimite, sum up everything – or almost everything – that had gone wrong with the nation of Israel during this period. There are no heroes in these chapters, only different kinds of villains and possibly victims. The following chapters inform us that what we have seen so far is not the worst of it.

C. Stories related to the Levite from Ephraim (19:1 – 21:25)

i. The Levite's concubine (19:1–28)
Context
This second series of stories begins and ends with the statement, *In those days Israel had no king*, the final verse again adding, *everyone did as*

they saw fit or 'did what was right in their own eyes' (see comment on pp. 185–186). In these chapters the fact that the phrase acts in this way as an inclusio is evidence that it is the key to unlocking the whole. What we have here is a picture of just what depths this community had sunk to and how far they were from living as God's covenant people. Clearly, the writers are strongly emphasizing the point already made in the first cycle of stories. This ought not to have happened, and the implication is that if there had been a functioning king, this would never have happened – although the rape of David's own daughter (2 Sam. 13) raises obvious questions about the validity of any assumption of that nature. It is possible that at this time a movement supporting the appointment of a king was beginning to build up. The final verse of Hannah's prayer at the beginning of the books of Samuel, 'The LORD . . . will give strength to his king and exalt the horn of his anointed', perhaps reflects an awareness of, or even an adherence to, this movement. However, if, as many scholars assume, the material was finally brought together during, or possibly after, the monarchy, then it seems very likely that readers are being asked to appraise the monarchy. Did any of the monarchs they had known actually function in such a way as to ensure that Israel did live as Yahweh's covenant partner?

One of the first stories in Judges is that of the marriage of Caleb's daughter. This last section begins with the tragic story of another 'marriage'. The reader may be being deliberately drawn to contrast the two. As so often in the historical narratives of the Old Testament, we have both a description of a series of events and also, alongside this, an underlying critique of what is happening and of the attitudes and values that lie behind those events. The writers demonstrate a clear understanding of the cultural assumptions of the time from which these events are being recorded, but the reader also appears to be directed towards serious criticism of the unfolding story. There is very little explicit editorial comment, but the reader is left in no doubt about the attitude of the writers towards the behaviour they are recording. It is as if time after time the writers are pointing out that this is what happened but this is not how things should have worked out in the life of God's covenant people, often by the use of irony in the telling of the story (Butler 2009: 438).

Comment

19:1–2. The fact that the refrain referring to Israel having no king occurs at the very beginning of this final series of stories leads readers to expect that the chaotic situation in Israel portrayed in the rest of the book is not about to change (cf. Webb 2012: 454). The introduction of the Levite is not meant to imply the possibility of another new deliverer! Like Micah, this Levite lived in the *hill country of Ephraim*; the addition of *remote* indicates that this was further from the usual routes between towns. At first sight this fact seems to have no particular relevance to the story. His concubine came from Bethlehem, at least a full day's journey to the south. There is irony, which may or may not be deliberate, in the fact that whereas the Levite in the previous stories came from Bethlehem and travelled to Ephraim, this Levite came from Ephraim and travelled to Bethlehem (Wilcock 1992: 151). The exact status of a concubine at different points during Israel's history is not entirely clear. There is certainly no provision made for such a status within the law. Often a concubine seems to have functioned as a secondary wife, sometimes living in a different place (Judg. 8:31). However, in this instance there is nothing in the story that would cause her to be distinguished from a wife. There is no mention of another primary wife, and the responsibilities of and to a spouse are taken for granted. Why the term *concubine* is included here is not explained. One possibility is that the phrase *took a concubine* is deliberately used, in contrast to 'married a wife', to emphasize that right from the beginning the Levite viewed her in terms of property rather than relationship. It is also possible that a tradition had developed, perhaps stemming from Leviticus 21:14, which states that high priests must only marry within 'their own people', that is, within their own tribe. In any event, the relationship was clearly long-term and the obligations of marriage were taken for granted. Exactly what form the woman's unfaithfulness took is not made explicit. Some versions (RSV, NJB, NET), following some manuscripts of the Septuagint, have 'because she became angry with him', and as the two words in the Hebrew are very similar, it is possible and perhaps likely that this was the original meaning. Other versions take it for granted that it involved adultery (cf. 'played the harlot' NKJV), but this seems unlikely given the Levite's intention to 'speak

kindly to her' (more literally, 'speak to her heart') and bring her back
(v. 3).[2] The NIV's *persuade her to return* does not quite catch this
element of his attitude to her. It is inconceivable that that would
be his approach if she had committed adultery. Indeed, the text
itself makes it clear that she returned to her family home, and there
is no indication whatsoever that she engaged in sex with other men.
The reason for her departure is not made explicit but could possibly
have stemmed from mistreatment by the Levite – his treatment of
her in Gibeah makes this not impossible and would explain his
intention this time to 'speak kindly to her'. An alternative explanation is that she found the remoteness of his situation just too
difficult to deal with and wanted to get back to the town life that
she was used to. This would at least explain why we were told both
that his home was *remote* and that she came from Bethlehem.

3–4. Four months later, and again we can only speculate about
the reason for the delay, the husband, taking a servant and two
donkeys, went to see if she could be persuaded to return. Genesis
2:24 implies that the original intention for marriage was that the
man would leave his family home behind, although whether that
is as well as, or instead of, the woman doing so is not mentioned.
However, there is little evidence that within Israel this pattern was
ever followed, and almost always the woman is portrayed as leaving
her home and going to live with the man. The references to father-
in-law and son-in-law use terms normally reserved for relations
within marriage and again emphasize that the girl is being pictured
as a wife. The amount of detail in this story is fascinating – even
if conclusions about the reason for such detail can be only speculative. Are we told about the donkeys to make it clear that he was
providing a mount for her to ride home? And in that case would
the servant then have to walk? Verse 10 tells us that the donkeys
were saddled, so it does appear that they are for riding and not
pack animals. Does it indicate that he was not a man without
resources and thus explain why the father was so pleased to see
him? Or was it just that the writers of Judges had a particular

---

2. The word 'heart' occurs five times in Judg. 19, although the NIV obscures
all of them. See comment on 19:5–9.

interest in donkeys?[3] One-tenth of all the verses in the Old
Testament referring to donkeys are found in the book of Judges!
Whatever the answer, the Levite was received warmly. The fact
that the woman herself is described as taking him into the house
could imply that she did not leave because of his unreasonable
treatment, although it could just be saying that there was nothing
else to be done once he had arrived. Equally, it could be argued
that the specific mention of the father's welcome suggests a
contrast with the woman's attitude, which may have been more
wary. It is interesting that although the girl had shown some initiative in leaving the man in the first place, she plays no active part
in the rest of the narrative and at no point do we hear her voice:
in general, we are told about things that happened to her, that is,
were done to her rather than by her. We are not informed whether
or not she had any choice about returning with her husband,
although the mention of his coming to persuade her might suggest
that she did. However, although there was clearly some kindly
speech between the two men, it may be significant that in spite of
his expressed intention there is no mention at any point of the
Levite speaking to the woman at all, let alone 'to her heart'.

5–9. Whatever it was that the writers wanted to convey here, the
man stayed for three days of good hospitality. Indeed, after that he
was persuaded to stay for a fourth day and night and even well into
the fifth day. It is hard to see why the father was quite so insistent
for the man to keep staying and why again we are given so much
detail. It could be suggested that the father was aware of problems
and was putting off for as long as he could the moment when his
daughter must leave with this man, but the warm welcome described
in verse 3 makes this unlikely, and it could quite easily be that the
two men simply enjoyed each other's company. The quadruple
mention of the father-in-law calling on the Levite to 'strengthen his
heart' (*refresh yourself* NIV, vv. 5, 7) and 'have a good heart' (*enjoy yourself*
NIV, vv. 6, 9) is perhaps drawing attention to the lack of any speaking,

---

3. A similar pattern can be identified in the Joseph narratives where there
seem to be more references to what people are wearing than might
normally be expected!

by either father or husband, to the heart of the girl (cf. Webb 2012: 461). It is possible that the father was concerned for the well-being of his daughter, but there is no real indication of that in the text. However, the fact that the festivities seem to have been restricted to the two men (v. 8) reflects the cultural practices of the time and may not have any other significance here. Hospitality, important in so many cultures, was a key expectation within the covenant community. Often within the Old Testament the presence or lack of hospitality is a crucial marker indicating whether or not Israel were living as they should have been. It may be that the writers here want to contrast the father's lavish provision with what we see later in Gibeah. Just as with the story of Samson's parents in the earlier narratives, before we see something of the worst of behaviour and attitudes in Israel at that time, we are shown that it was not all bad, that right behaviour was a real possibility.

10–14. It was into the afternoon when they eventually set off, so an overnight stop somewhere on the way was going to be inevitable. It is probably significant that although verse 9 makes it clear that the man, the woman and the servant all left together, verse 10 says only *the man left*. Neither the servant nor the woman really counted. Jebus – which was at this point occupied by Canaanites, probably Amorites, and remained unconquered until David took it over and it was renamed Jerusalem (cf. 2 Sam. 5:6–9) – was only about 6 miles (10 km) north of Bethlehem, and even with one of them walking could be reached in a couple of hours. The servant's desire to stop before there was any chance of being caught by the onset of darkness was understandable. The roads were not good, and accidents or attacks by wild animals were as much of a risk as danger from human enemies. The Levite, however, perhaps doubting the hospitality of non-Israelites, wanted to press on to a place that was known to be occupied by Israelites, even though they would not have been from his own tribe. Gibeah was around 3 miles (5 km) further north again, with Ramah about the same distance north of that, both in Benjaminite territory. Darkness fell just as they reached Gibeah, and there was no question then of going on to Ramah. Gibeah was Saul's home area (1 Sam. 10:26), and Ramah was where Samuel's family came from. The mention of both of these towns here may link in with the writers' interest in kingship and the way it might improve conditions in Israel. If, as some think, there is also an anti-Saul, pro-David element in the texts, then the denunciation of Saul's home town may be part of that.

15–21. Many backpackers or budget travellers even today know the experience in some countries of hanging round a central area looking for those who might offer a bed for the night, although nowadays money would almost always be expected. In those days this was usually the only way that accommodation could be found. It should have been unthinkable in an Israelite city that anyone arriving in the city square just after sunset would not be invited to stay in the home of one of the citizens. But many unthinkable things were happening in Israel at this time, and they were left there long enough to reach the conclusion that no-one would take them in for the night. The one who eventually approaches them is not a mainstream resident of the city but an old man from their own region of Ephraim. The old man's late arrival from the fields could indicate that it was harvest time and that everyone was preoccupied by the amount of work needing to be done. His questioning also perhaps reflects the uncertainty of the times and the fear of strangers and even of local gangs, which may have stopped others from helping them. However, once he knew something of their background, this old Ephraimite, in contrast to the locals, was glad to help. He apparently rejected their offer to supply all their own needs and looked after them from his own resources. It is worth noting that the Levite does not at this point identify himself as such and simply mentions that his home is in Ephraim territory. Whether he is going directly home, as the Septuagint, followed by most English versions, implies or via *the house of the LORD* (MT followed by NIV) is not clear and not really relevant to the story. Presumably, he would have seen 'the house of Yahweh' as the centre at Shiloh which was on his way to the north. It is interesting that he does not identify the woman as either his wife or his concubine; the term used here would be understood simply as a maidservant (see Butler 2009: 423). This could explain, although not excuse, the old Ephraimite's offer, but as he in fact does refer to her as a concubine and couples her with his own daughter, there is probably little significance in that.

22–28. What happened next is described in a very similar way to the record in Genesis 19 of the reception given to the angels who visited Sodom. It is very likely that the writers intended their readers to draw the parallels, to remember the condemnation of Sodom and to note that this Israelite town is following their example. There are obvious similarities: not only has the town itself failed to offer any hospitality; these depraved men were seeking to prevent the exercise of hospitality by the old man. However, there is a clear difference between the two situations. In Lot's case his inexcusable offer to allow the rape of his daughters could at least be explained by the thought that failing to ensure the safety of those who had been offered hospitality was worse than anything else. In this case the offer involved the visiting woman, who should also have received protective hospitality, and clearly demonstrates that the woman's safety was irrelevant in comparison to that of the man. It is possible that the Ephraimite also remembered Lot's story and the fact that, in that instance, Lot and his family were protected by the angels. However, his call to the men of Gibeah to do to the woman 'what is right in your own eyes' draws attention to the broader picture and to the unacceptable nature of what is happening. It may be significant that in fact there is no mention of his daughter actually being given to the gang, and it was not the Ephraimite but the Levite himself who got rid of them by sending out his concubine. Whether the fact that the two men are described as *enjoying themselves* is meant to imply that they had drunk so much that rational or moral thought was impossible is a debatable point.

The treatment of the woman is described in horrific detail. That the man who had retaken her from the security of her father's home should send her outside was bad enough – so much for his intention of 'speaking kindly' to her expressed in verse 3 – but the following events were unthinkable. She was raped and abused throughout the night, and we picture her in the morning with no other option than to crawl back to the place where the one who had sent her out into this terror was staying. Whether she would have lived if she had been found between dawn and full daylight, or whether she was alive when the Levite found her, cannot be determined. The text is deliberately ambiguous, although the phrase *But there was no answer* does imply that by this time at least she was dead. In verse 3 the Levite is described as *her husband*; in verses 26 and 27 he is *her master*. Perhaps the text is suggesting that he has forfeited any right to a role that implies care and relationship (Webb 2012: 469–470). The woman was placed on the donkey, perhaps further indicating that she was being treated as simply part of his property. Clearly, all readers should be horrified.

Meaning
This story can be told as an illustration of how badly women were treated at that time, and it certainly functions in this way. However, in addition it seems that the writers, who in this section are deliberately portraying the depths to which Israel had sunk, are actually depicting the mistreatment of women as one of the worst things that could possibly have happened. The next chapter may indicate that the Levite, and possibly the rest of Israel, regarded this as a dreadful offence against him – but the story is told in such a way as to suggest that the writers are also portraying him as an offender; the victim in this case is the woman. In other words, to use the passage as an illustration of the Bible's justification of the abuse of women is completely to misrepresent the intention of the writers here, who clearly wanted to present the behaviour of both the Levite himself and of the Gibean scoundrels as scandalous.

ii. A search for justice (19:29 – 20:48)
Context
The lack of a national government and the rather confused relationship between the different tribes are demonstrated in this passage. There was clearly some sense of unity, some sense of the need to present a united front in the face of unprecedented circumstances, but it is equally apparent that when push came to shove, at least for Benjamin, tribal loyalty outweighed intertribal responsibilities. The key interest in chapters 20 and 21 is 'what are we going to do about Benjamin?', but the account only makes sense in the light of the immediate context of the story as told in chapter 19. The whole account makes it clear that the writers are seeing the concubine as the primary victim of both her 'husband' and the rapists, but the attitude of the gathering of tribes is much more ambiguous. Perhaps because of the way in which the story was presented to them by the Levite, they saw him as the victim who had been deprived of his rightful property.

Comment

29–30. The final two verses of chapter 19 lead us into the account of tribal warfare described in chapter 20. The events are clear; the implications drawn out in the account may be somewhat more ambiguous.

The Levite travels home, dismembers his dead concubine so that the body is in twelve parts and sends the parts out throughout Israel. We are not told here that there is one part for each tribe, but it seems that this is what the symbolism of the twelve is intended to indicate. The tribal boundaries were themselves uncertain at this time (see Introduction, pp. 26–28), and the central section of Judges has shown that bad feeling often existed between different tribes. Nevertheless, the Levite is clearly expecting some kind of united action. Saul dissected a pair of oxen and called the tribes together by sending the divided parts around the country. Whether that is an indication that this was a known method of summons within the surrounding areas or whether Saul knew this story and copied the effective methodology cannot be determined. But the implication made explicit in 1 Samuel also seems clear here: failure to respond to the 'gift' would mean the recipients facing the danger of a similar bloody fate.

It may be, given the inclusio referring to the lack of a king, that our attention is also being drawn to that concept here. If there had been a king, then he could have been approached, and could have been expected to lead an attempt to bring the perpetrators of any offence to justice. But as there is no king, the Levite adopts this bloodthirsty way of calling the tribes to attention. The response from the people is described in very general terms: *Everyone who saw it was saying* . . . , and the words uttered by *everyone* are themselves ambiguous. Is the *thing* that *has never been seen or done* the sending out of the twelve body parts, or is it the lack of hospitality and unbrotherly behaviour resulting in the rape and death of the woman? It seems probable that they were thinking of the former but it could be the latter, and in either case it seems likely that the writers intend the latter to come to the fore. It is inconceivable that those who carried the gruesome objects would not have known of, or told of, their origin. Many bad things had happened to and in Israel since they had left Egypt, but the abuse of this woman is seen as the very worst.

Those receiving the body parts are, from the beginning, united, at least in their uncertainty. It is not obvious to whom the 'Think about it! What are we going to do? Who's going to speak up?' (NLT) of verse 30 is addressed. There does not appear to be any thought that the request could be addressed to God. It is perhaps a call for a corporate consultation followed by joint action. Certainly it results in a tribal gathering, presumably of tribal leaders and elders, but again we are possibly being led to think of the at present non-existent king who might have been expected to tell them 'what to do' or at least to 'speak his mind' (KJV).

20:1–3. The phrase *from Dan to Beersheba* became an idiomatic way of referring to the whole nation, much as in Britain one might say 'from Land's End to John O'Groats'. It appears that Mizpah had begun to be an accepted place for the tribes to congregate (cf. Jephthah's actions in Judg. 11:11). Representatives from the whole nation – with the apparent exception of Benjamin – gathered to act as a kind of High Court, undertaking the investigation into the dreadful crime. That this investigation preceded any punitive action shows that some elements of the law were known and taken seriously. We are told that they *assembled before the LORD* (v. 1), but there is no reference to Yahweh's opinion being sought until after the decision to fight had already been taken and then they went to Bethel to seek an oracle. The reference here seems to suggest only that this is a gathering of Yahweh's people. The implication of 20:3 is that Benjamin had also received the summons but had declined to attend, thus giving an initial indication that their tribal loyalty to the men of Gibeah was stronger than any sense of national identity or natural justice.

4–13. The events recorded in much greater detail in 19:14–29 are repeated very briefly in verses 4–6, perhaps told in such a way as to present the Levite to the tribes in a much more positive light. For readers of the whole account, the omission of the information that it was the Levite himself who sent the woman out to the men of Gibeah actually draws our attention to it. Also, where 19:22 speaks of the criminals as *wicked men of the city*, the Levite has changed this simply to *men* (lit. 'rulers'), implying that the whole city was responsible. It is unclear whether knowledge of these facts would have affected the attitude of the assembly. The crime to be considered is clearly the rape and death of the concubine, whether or not the primary attention is to the loss that this brought to the Levite rather than the offence against the woman herself. In either case, it was agreed by the whole assembly that this was totally unacceptable and that something had to be done about it. Webb (2012: 476) raises the question as to who was leading this assembly, and the absence of any names may be deliberately drawing attention to the lack of adequate leadership. But verse 8 emphasizes the fact that the people acted together, thus taking united responsibility for what follows; there is no way that they can 'blame the manager' in this instance.

They were so horrified by what the Levite told them that immediate, united and comprehensive action against Gibeah was decreed. No further investigation into the matter was thought necessary, and again the writers might be drawing our attention to the lack of proper legal procedures. The fact that the whole city was seen as responsible for the actions of presumably only a few citizens is recorded without comment. The sense of corporate responsibility at that time is likely to have been strong, and therefore there would not necessarily have been any awareness that this might be thought unjust. Or there could be an implication that the whole town must have been aware of the violent tendencies of some of their fellow citizens and thus had to bear responsibility because they had done nothing about it. The unity of the tribes, which is strongly emphasized –all the men . . . all the Israelites got together and united as one– serves also to highlight the isolation of the tribe of Benjamin which was not part of this unity. Their first action was to inform the missing Benjaminites of the situation and give them the opportunity to acknowledge the crime, to distance themselves from Gibeah and to ensure that justice was done. The mention of the wicked men of Gibeah in verse 13 may refer to the whole city or may indicate that they were aware of issues of personal responsibility and that justice would be satisfied by the execution of those who were culpable. Benjamin, however, refused to cooperate.

14–25. At this point the focus moves from the actual case to the ongoing relationship between Benjamin and the rest of the tribes, beginning with a battle that was disastrous for both sides, and ending with some fairly dubious diplomacy. In the process of recording the fighting, the writers present us with a very clear picture of the escalating nature of violence. The need to punish a city turned into a desire to destroy a tribe. It could be said that Benjamin's refusal to allow the concubine's death to be avenged made them accessories to the crime and therefore equally responsible and deserving of punishment. The Benjaminites had decided, rightly or wrongly, that loyalty to one's own tribal members was more important than any questions related to justice. However, there is no discussion of these issues, and the way in which the account unfolds does imply that events simply got out of hand. Strategic planning – which may have been the prerogative of an effective king –seems to have come into play only in the later stages of the battles. There is a sad irony in the fact that it took terrible events like this for the tribes to seek out some kind of unity.

The method used for enquiring of God is not specified. We read elsewhere of the ephod (1 Sam. 23:9; 30:7), the Urim and Thummim (1 Sam. 14:41; 28:6) and the casting of lots (Josh. 18:6; 1 Chr. 24:31) all being used to determine God's answer to questions presented to him. It is possible that, as in this instance, they required more than a yes/no answer, and some kind of lot-casting was used. The answer, seen as coming from Yahweh, was that Judah would have the somewhat dubious honour of going first. In the kind of hill country around Gibeah, superiority of numbers was not the advantage it could be on the plain. The Benjaminites were on home territory, and guerilla fighters, especially those skilled in the use of the sling who could kill from a distance, could defend themselves against large numbers of approaching troops. Judah contained similar territory, so the choice of Judean forces to take the lead was a sensible one. It is not clear how this choice relates to the lot casting described in verses 9–10, which appears to envisage a representative group from each tribe going to fight. Certainly, the rest of the account speaks of the actions and the deaths of Israelites in general, so it could be that the Judean contingent was placed in the lead of the rest of the troops. Whoever was fighting, the result of the first attack was disastrous. However, we understand the numbers, and a huge section of the initial force died on the first day – not far off the numbers involved in the whole of the Benjaminite force. It is not surprising that the Israelites were devastated.

It is always difficult to determine the accuracy of numbers in accounts like these when mathematical precision is not the major interest of the writers. In the census results detailed in Numbers 26 there were apparently over 45,000 Benjaminites of fighting age, with more than 550,000 from the other tribes. Given the difficulties Israel faced during the period after the initial occupation of the land and assuming that the assembled forces would not include all available troops, the numbers given here – 26,000 and 400,000 – are not too far out of line. Nowhere near 400,000 Israelites were involved in the actual fighting, and it is possible that these were the numbers committed to be made available if necessary (and represented by their leaders in v. 2), rather than the number actually assembled. However, the force involved at the fall of Jericho was 40,000 (Josh. 4:13), and this number is also mentioned in Deborah's song (5:8) which raises other questions. The word translated *thousand* is sometimes used for an assembled army unit (just as Roman centurions were in charge of a unit known as a century, but which was not always 100 strong), and it is possible that that is what is happening here. Left-handed swordsmen in a predominantly right-handed army would have been a risk to their own side, so it is perhaps not surprising that the group of committed left-handers had formed a regiment of highly skilled sling operators. We are not told of any specific part they played in the battle, so their existence may be noted because of a particular interest of the battle recorder; perhaps he himself was left-handed. Whether there is any relation between the groups of 700 mentioned in verses 15 and 16 is unclear. The number of left-handed people in a population varies with time and place, but it seems unlikely that there were 700 fighting left-handers from one town. It is possible that the numbers here became confused when the account was copied. The battle is recorded in three stages, and there is some repetition within the account, which also makes it difficult to work out the exact numbers involved at each stage. But the sense is clear. Benjamin was vastly outnumbered, and although they initially had great success and caused huge losses among the other Israelites, they were eventually defeated and almost wiped out. Webb (2012: 485) suggests that since it is specifically mentioned that all of the Israelite army that were killed were *armed with swords* (v. 25), Benjamin's success in the earlier battles may be precisely because they did have a battalion of skilled marksmen (v. 16).

26–48. It appears that the main Israelite shrine was at Shiloh both before and after this time (Josh. 18:1, 8; 19:51; 1 Sam. 1:3), and although Bethel had significance because of the links with Abraham and Jacob, there is no record of it being a permanent resting place for the ark of God. The name 'Bethel' means 'house of God', but it would be more likely for Beth Elohim rather than Beth El to be used for the generic sense. However, it is possible that as Shiloh was some distance from Gibeah, the ark had been transported temporarily to Bethel to be in easier reach of the assembly. Mizpah was about 4 miles (7 km) north of Gibeah, Bethel a further 3 miles (5 km) north and Shiloh around 12 miles (20 km) north of that. In any case, we are told explicitly that the ark was at Bethel being looked after by Aaron's direct descendants. If this Phinehas was Aaron's grandson, then these events must have occurred fairly early after the entry into the land. But there may have been other descendants of that name; it is not unusual within Hebrew genealogies for generations to be missed out of the list. We know Eli's son was called Phinehas (1 Sam. 1:3), and if he was involved, perhaps travelling with the ark from Shiloh, then this could be not too many years before the birth of Samuel.

The chronology here is a little difficult. Verse 22 speaks of the forces regrouping in their original positions, whereas verse 23 sees the first day concluding with desperate weeping and further enquiries made of Yahweh. They were seeking justice, they had sought Yahweh's guidance and yet this had happened. How could this be? Confusion and despair were inevitable. But when the word came back that they should fight again, courage and determination took over. As in the whole book of Judges, we see good and bad standing side by side in the behaviour and attitudes of the Israelite people. They were seeking justice and they were courageous, but at the same time they had forgotten the lesson of Joshua 5:14 where the angel of Yahweh made it clear that God could not be manipulated in support of their own cause. It seems a very hard way to learn a lesson when on the second day 18,000 more troops died, but it is possible that the writers also want to raise questions about the kind of justice they were seeking. To destroy a whole Israelite town for the sake of a few wrongdoers is not the way envisaged by the law. There are reminiscences here of Abraham's enquiries of God in Genesis 18 where he is told that God would not destroy a whole town even if there were only ten righteous people left in it. On their third visit to Bethel we learn that they not only weep and enquire of God but also present sacrifices. It is possible that this element is emphasized to indicate that this time they really are taking God seriously. As Butler (2009: 450) aptly states,

> Human plans will not be automatically ratified because people gather at an ancient storied sanctuary. God's people must listen obediently to God before they can expect God to listen to their desperate cries . . . Human desire for victory over an enemy does not necessarily mirror God's understanding of justice and righteousness for the helpless segment of society.

The need to ask again is clear, although the variation in their three enquiries of God is interesting. In 20:18 the question was 'Who will go up first?', taking for granted the need to fight. In 20:23 the question was *Shall we go up again to fight . . . our fellow Israelites?*, indicating that maybe they were beginning to think about the implications of their covenant alliance. The third question indicates even more wariness: *Shall we go up to fight . . . or not?* (20:28). However, their determination to fight for justice at whatever cost can be seen as praiseworthy.

This time the message brings not only the instruction to go, but also the encouragement that this time their attack would be successful. It may also be relevant that on this third occasion we actually see evidence of the kind of strategic planning that might have made a difference in the beginning when they had apparently simply trusted in their superior numbers. The parallels with the successful ambush story recorded in Joshua 8 are striking and may be significant. The narrative here is dramatic and lively. One can picture the scene with ambush following preliminary attack and strategic withdrawal. Its repetitive style serves to bring out the perspectives of both the Israelites and the Benjaminites. The impression given is that the issue now was not merely justice for the Levite and his concubine but revenge for the earlier defeats. God's promise that he would *give them into your hands* had been fulfilled as soon as Gibeah had been taken. They had no mandate for this wholesale destruction. There is no question of mercy for the defeated. Once the Israelites had the upper hand, they killed and kept on killing until they could find no more Benjaminites to kill: not just Gibeah but town after town were razed to the ground, and women and children alike were slaughtered without mercy. The only Benjaminites left were 600 who managed to hide themselves in the rocky wilderness. In the midst of the sense of victory and success we are once more left with the impression that this is not how it was meant to be. There is irony in the fact that although Israel had significantly failed to remove Canaanites throughout the land, they had no problems with the wholesale destruction of one of their own tribes.

Meaning
T. J. Schneider (2000: 245–246, as quoted by Butler 2009: 411) provides an eloquent summary of this section:

> This episode [i.e. ch. 19] is what the preceding stories in Judges have led up to and is itself the catalyst for what is to come . . . Literary motifs and references made throughout the book culminate in this episode. This story contains most of the main questions raised thus far in the book: what happens when there is no leadership, what is the role of Judah versus Benjamin, what is the relationship between Israelites and non-Israelites and more frightening, the relationships between the different Israelite tribes.

The section as a whole deliberately raises these difficult and painful questions, but largely leaves readers to determine any answer for themselves. The 'silence' of God as the events unfold may be the writers' way of emphasizing the fact that God cannot be seen as approving of what went on.

It has often been suggested that the negative attitude to Benjamin in the final chapters is an indication that the book was written to support David's kingship over against Saul's. However, neither within these chapters nor in the book as a whole is the tribe of Judah pictured more positively than the other tribes. And one could argue that Ephraimites and Levites receive equally bad press. There are many victims in this final account but no heroes. The irony in the stories of chapters 17 – 18 centring on Micah, the young Levite and the Danites can at times be seen as amusing, but there is no room for humour in these narratives – as Wilcock (1992: 166) notes, it is a story of 'unrelieved dreadfulness'. The Levite lost his concubine, but he behaved abominably. The tribe of Benjamin behaved badly, but so did the other tribes. How it should have been for Israel, how it could be, remains to be seen, but it is abundantly clear that the events described here do not in any sense reflect the right way forward, the right way for Israel to be governed, the right way for the tribes to relate, the right way for people to behave.

iii. The salvaging of the tribe of Benjamin (21:1–25)
Context
The impression that the writers really want to stress the inappropriateness of the events is reinforced in the final chapter of the book which is so filled with irony that it becomes almost farcical (see Webb 2012: 495). The Israelites are faced with the unforeseen consequences of the decisions they had made at the Mizpah assembly. Their intention had been to punish those responsible for the unspeakable crime at Gibeah. The decisions were as follows:

1. To fight the Benjamites who were supporting the Gibeans;
2. Never to allow their daughters to marry a Benjaminite;
3. To execute all those who failed to obey the summons to a national assembly.

Chapter 21 encourages readers to think through the implications of such decisions.

Comment
21:1–7. The oath referred to in verse 1 is not mentioned in the original account of the Mizpah meeting in chapter 20. Similarities to the story of Jephthah's foolish vow (Judg. 11:29–40) where possible consequences were also not considered perhaps indicate that the writers are providing a general critique of the practice of making oaths of this kind. Certainly, when Saul made a similarly foolish oath (1 Sam. 14) which Jonathan inadvertently flouted, there were no adverse consequences when the army refused to let the

terms of the oath be carried out. Perhaps memories of the consequences of these foolish oaths remained. The Israelites' intention
had certainly not been that the tribe of Benjamin would be wiped
out. But this was the apparent consequence of the uncontrolled
fighting and the thoughtless decisions. It is interesting that once they
came to their senses and realized what they had done, there was no
question of killing the remaining 600 Benjaminite warriors. The
implication is unavoidable: if these warriors did not deserve death,
then why were so many of the rest destroyed? But questions like
this are left hanging in the air. The writers are again indicating the
existence of some kind of sense of national identity, shown by
the desperation at the thought of one of the tribes being lost. At the
same time they re-emphasize the problems of living in a situation
where there was no consistent, organized government able to make
and apply laws after having previously investigated any consequences, that is, where *Israel had no king*.

Butler (2009: 455) suggests that there may be significance in the
fact that in verse 2 the people are described as sitting *before God*
(Elohim), not before 'the LORD' (Yahweh). The Canaanites also
used Elohim to refer to their gods, and the writers are perhaps
indicating the possibility of syncretism. However, Elohim is also a
very common term for the God of Israel, and the Israelites' cry in
verse 3 to Yahweh Elohim makes this suggestion less convincing.
The irony that permeates this section is very clear in verse 3 where
they distance themselves from the events that have occurred. Their
heartfelt question, *Why has this happened to Israel?*, clearly calls for the
answer – although the writers leave it implicit – 'because of your
own stupid behaviour and your failure to consult and heed God at
a much earlier stage'! This repeats the pattern of the previous
chapter where the Levite also distanced himself from the consequences of his own decisions. The irony continues in verse 7 where,
although they have shown very little concern for God's will or for
the law in other situations, they now decide that their responsibility
to keep this oath must be kept to the letter – if not to the spirit – of
the law.

8–14. Their attempts to salvage something from the disaster of
the wholesale destruction of Benjamin is again recorded with little
editorial comment, but it is hard to avoid the sense that the writers

intend to create an impression of mounting horror. For some reason the town of Jabesh Gilead had not sent anyone to the assembly. The town was on the far side of the Jordan in the territory assigned to Gad. Perhaps the distance was the issue; it certainly made it easier for this town to be made the scapegoat. It seems likely that the original decision, that non-attenders should die, was aimed at Benjamin and meant to ensure that all tribes were represented at an assembly. But it was decided to use this law to solve the problem of finding wives for the Benjaminites. A force of 12,000 – perhaps symbolizing the involvement of all the tribes in the salvaging of Benjamin – was sent to kill all those in Jabesh Gilead who were not young female virgins. It is hard to find any justification for the appalling destruction of almost a whole town just to solve a problem caused by previous decisions made without regard for their conse-quences. It may be that those who made this decision justified themselves by saying that they were treating the town as *ḥerem* (dedicated to God, usually by means of total destruction). As Butler points out (2009: 459), exactly how they are to determine who were and were not virgins is left to the reader's imagination, and it is quite possible that this is another deliberate irony added by the writers. The 400 remaining women, all Israelites, were taken, with no con-sultation and no choice, and after having had their families slaughtered, were handed over to the Benjaminite men as if they were merely baggage. The terrible mistreatment of one woman by the Benjaminites had turned into the terrible mistreatment of 400 women for the benefit of the Benjaminites. It is hard not to presume that the irony in this narrative is deliberate. In 1 Samuel 11 we read that Saul, another Benjaminite, in one of the few acts of his kingship that is presented without any obvious criticism, rescued Jabesh Gilead from the Ammonites. It is possible that the town had become repopulated, but it may be that the force sent to abduct the virgins had seen the consequences of the previous wholesale slaughter and did not carry out their instructions to the letter. In fact, it is interesting that the text carefully mentions twice (vv. 10–11) that they are to kill all the rest, but never actually states that they did so.

15–24. But the problem was only half solved. There still remained 200 wifeless Benjaminites, alongside a vow, binding on all Israelites, that they were not to give them their daughters as wives. There was apparently no other city that could, even with dubious legitimacy, be destroyed for them, so a further ruse was designed. At the forthcoming *festival of the LORD in Shiloh*, when unsuspecting young Israelite women were dancing in the fields celebrating before God, the Benjaminites were to seize them, take them back to their home territory and the tribe could then start to rebuild itself. It is not possible to identify this *festival* as one of the required celebrations set out in the law or to know whether it reflected orthodox Yahwism, but it is conceivable that it was the festival that Samuel's family attended each year. On this occasion the fathers and brothers of these unfortunate girls were to be reassured that the taking of their daughters would not bring them under the curse for breaking their vow. The lack of reference to any kind of reassurance for the girls themselves only serves to emphasize again the horror of what was going on. The Israelites saw it as self-evident that the main concern of the men of Shiloh would be their own welfare after breaking the vow, rather than the abduction of their daughters. As far as the men were concerned, it was a problem solved. Everyone went back home as if nothing had happened and got on with life. But readers are meant to see the ridiculous and horrific nature of their thinking as well as their behaviour; this is not how life in the covenant community was supposed to be. It is probably not insignificant that in these final chapters of the book of Judges, which has presented us with the varying degrees of evil and ugliness in the life of Israel, the climax, the epitome as it were, of the evil in the land is portrayed as the abuse of women. The concubine, the young virgins from Jabesh Gilead and those from Shiloh were all treated abominably. The culture did not care, but their fate had been noticed and is recorded in our text. It is also possibly significant that in some compilations of the canon these chapters are followed by the book of Ruth and the early chapters of 1 Samuel, both of which also discuss, and provide some critique of, the treatment of women.

25. *In those days Israel had no king; everyone did as they saw fit.* The account finishes by repeating the sentence found at the beginning of this final section in 17:6. Of course, the comment found in the vast majority of commentaries that this indicates a dissatisfaction with the system described in Judges and a move towards the monarchy must be correct. However, whether the writers, particularly those who eventually brought the various stories together, really thought that the monarchy would be an improvement and enable Israel to live in the way that it should, is debatable. Certainly, the rest of the Deuteronomic History found in Samuel and Kings illustrates very clearly that the writers there were aware that there was much evil and many problems – along with some of the high spots also found in Judges – seen even when there was a king in Israel. Dumbrell (1983) suggests that 21:24 provides a positive ending to the book, with a picture of everyone going home to a secure living, but that seems very much an overly optimistic view. The last word here – that everyone did what was right in their own eyes – does seem to be deliberately placed to emphasize that although what has been recorded is what happened, it was not what was right in the eyes of the LORD.

Meaning

There has sometimes been a tendency for preachers to try to find a way to justify certain events in the narratives of the Old Testament that might seem unacceptable to modern readers. Such attempts may occasionally be helpful, but in many instances, as certainly applies here, they are completely misconceived. There is absolutely no justification for the events described, and even to try would misrepresent the intention of the text. The writers do not explicitly state their own opinion, but the way in which the events are recounted gives abundant clues to their position. Hospitality in Israel is important, treating visitors well is important, tribal cooperation is important, valuing people – women as well as men – is important, and violence against women is completely unacceptable. Justice is important, but the way to justice is never thoughtless overreaction. Commitment to God is important, but thoughtless vows are not helpful ways of resolving situations. Hospitality is important, but the excessive hospitality of the girl's father and the defensive hospitality of the old Ephraimite, which ignored other responsibilities, were both inappropriate. Leaving God out of any equation is never going to lead to an adequate answer. And as Webb notes, the writers of Judges make it very clear in this section that '"Everyone doing what is right in their own eyes" produces a society in which both sexes lose their humanity, but it is the women who suffer most' (2012: 473).

RUTH

INTRODUCTION

The book of Ruth follows Judges in the canon of Scripture and is deliberately placed in the context of Judges, but the two books could not be more different. Ruth is shorter, deals with fewer characters in a much more limited scenario, contains very few textual problems, has no interest in national or tribal politics or warfare and makes very little reference to violence. When one reads Ruth after Judges, it is tempting to view it as the calm after the storm. However, although one does hear of Ruth referred to in terms such as 'a beautiful idyll', 'a lovely romantic story' or 'ideal material for a women's conference',[1] none of these does justice to the story we are presented with, which is much more complex than at first

---

1. Sylvia Roache (2004: 15) cites a number of such descriptions, e.g. Herbert Lockyer in *All the Books and Chapters of the Bible* says of Ruth, 'This Hebrew Pastoral idyll is the most perfect, charming and touching narrative in the scripture.' She herself describes it as 'a delightful, captivating and romantic story'.

appears. The writer is clearly concerned to draw attention to a number of serious issues that readers, male and female, need to consider. We are faced with something of a hermeneutical circle, or a 'chicken-and-egg' situation, in that any decision about the structure and purpose of the book is going to influence how the concerns it presents are viewed, but the structure and purpose can only be determined after the contents have been carefully examined and reflected upon. In this Introduction to Ruth the decision has been made to look at the story first, and the literary issues, including purpose and structure, after that. However, it would make equal sense to read section 4 (Literary issues, pp. 228–235) first. Similarly, a decision has to be made about whether to study the whole text first and look at the 'introductory issues' afterwards, or to read the text having already considered such issues. Whether this Introduction is read before or after the commentary may be irrelevant. However, if the text is to be taken seriously as a whole, then it is vital that the issues dealt with here are seen as key to a full understanding of the story and not just as optional extras.

1. Background

Given the early date and the limited number of contemporary descriptions of community life, much of what can be said about the background can only be speculative. However, it is worth rereading the whole book in the light of the issues and questions mentioned here.

a. Geographical

The locations described in the book of Ruth are fairly limited. Chapter 1 begins with a family located in *the country of Moab* and then covers the journey of Naomi and Ruth from Moab to Bethlehem. We are given no indication of where in Moab the family had settled, or even if they had remained in the same place for the whole of their sojourn there. Moab is situated on the south-east side of the Dead Sea, above Edom and below the land on the east of the Jordan allocated to Reuben. Because we have no information about where in Moab the family had settled, we cannot know whether it would have been easier for them to take the route round the south end or the north end of the Dead Sea. Thus we cannot ascertain the distance of their journey, although it is likely to have been somewhere between fifty and a hundred miles. Because we are also not aware of their method of travel – whether they had a donkey, were able to hire a place in some kind of cart or walked the whole distance – we cannot know how long their journey took. The rest of the book all takes place in and around Bethlehem, a town in the hill country assigned to the tribe of Judah, a few miles south of Jerusalem and around twenty miles west of the Dead Sea. The town later gained significance as the birthplace of David, but at this point all the indications are that it was not seen as an important centre and was probably fairly small.

The close proximity of Israel and Moab means that climatic conditions are similar and a widespread drought could affect both countries. However, the Dead Sea does also provide a barrier, and it is clear that localized weather conditions do exist; areas of Israel suffering drought at the same time as conditions in Moab remaining conducive to good harvests and vice versa is quite possible.

b. Historical

The only clue we have to the period in which the story of Naomi, Ruth and Boaz is set is found in Ruth 1:1: *In the days when the judges ruled.* That is, the events are said to have occurred sometime between the settlement of the descendants of Jacob in Israel and the institution of the monarchy. In other words, there was no national government at the time; Israel remained a collection of tribes. It is hard to be exact about dates at this point, but we are probably talking about a time between 1400 and 1100 BC. The story indicates that relations between Israel and Moab are not particularly strained and that the Israelites were well settled in the land, at least around the Bethlehem area. The book of Judges presents the time when Israel was 'subject to Eglon king of Moab for eighteen years' (Judg. 3:14) as coming fairly early in the settlement era, and that seems to have been well past at the time of the events described in Ruth. There is no indication either that Moab was at this time 'subject to Israel', so although it is possible that the time envisaged was during the eighty years of peace after Moab's defeat mentioned in Judges 3:30, it seems likely that it was later than that. We know that the conditions in

Israel, perhaps more particularly in the northern areas, were unstable for many years after that time, but it is possible that this instability did not have dramatic effects in Bethlehem. Any narrowing of the possible timescale can only be speculative, but it is not unreasonable to suggest that these events are set between 1200 and 1100 BC – this timing also ties in with the genealogy in chapter 4 which has two generations between Boaz and David who, we can be fairly sure, lived somewhere between 1050 and 950 BC.

c. Social and religious
The book of Ruth provides one of the best windows we have on the ordinary life of individual Israelites at this time. The closing genealogy shows that the writer was aware of national issues, but there is no other reference to anything other than local and family concerns. We learn nothing of tribal government or any other formal structures, although we do see that, at least in Bethlehem, local issues that may be described as legal matters were considered by a group of recognized leaders apparently brought together for that specific purpose. It seems clear that decisions made in that context were accepted by the community as binding. Naomi's position may have been unique, partly because of Ruth's presence with her, but the fact that she was not automatically absorbed – even reluctantly – into an extended family unit provides some indication that the so-called 'nuclear family' was perhaps more significant than is sometimes recognized. It is possible, although there is no reference to this in Ruth, that individual families lived and worked on smaller subsistence farms. However, there were clearly a number of larger estates that employed varying numbers of both regular and occasional workers, both male and female, covering a range of jobs. References to the whole town being *stirred*, to the corporate reactions of the townswomen and to the *elders and all the people* gathering at the gate, can be seen as indications both that this was a reasonably small community and that there was some sense of corporate identity within the community (1:19; 4:9–17). There is also an indication that that sense of corporate identity in general excluded those who were not Israelite by birth. The lack of reference to any religious functionaries, or indeed to any religious organization at all, does not mean that these did not exist within the community, but could be

an indication that they were not central to the life and thought of the people. It is possible that the lack of reference to such things is the writer's way of pointing out this lack of centrality. However, this somewhat depends on whether the writer intended readers to view Boaz as typical or untypical of the men of his community. Boaz himself clearly did have an understanding of what it meant to follow the covenant and saw following the law as important.

2. Character studies

The writer's descriptive skills are remarkable and the character delineation in particular is extraordinary. Readers are drawn into the situation and given real insight into the feelings and reactions of the characters as well as descriptions of their actions. The extensive use of dialogue of course makes this easier. Even when larger groups and minor characters like the estate foreman and the closer relative are being described, it is very clear to readers what is happening and why these particular people are reacting in these ways. But it is worth looking more closely at some of the things we are told about the three main characters. In an introduction to characters in a narrative text like this, the main point is not to provide a detailed portrait that might be seen as going beyond what the text says, but to raise questions that enable readers to go back to the text and get to know the characters for themselves.

a. Naomi
The facts about Naomi are fairly clear. She had migrated from Judah to Moab with her husband and sons in a time of famine and had stayed there until her husband had died, her sons married and then both sons had died. She apparently remained for a time in Moab living with her two daughters-in-law, but we do not know how long this lasted. The three women clearly got on well together. However, when Naomi heard in Moab that there was now food available back in her home area (no information is given about how that news was received), she made the decision to go back there. It is sometimes suggested that Naomi's decision was based on a 'yearning for home' (e.g. Harris, Brown and Moore 2000: 305). It is of course possible that this affected Naomi's thinking, but the text speaks only of the

need to find food. Apparently, her first plan was that the two daughters-in-law would go with her, but somewhere on the road Naomi decided that it would be better for them to remain in their own homeland. Orpah agreed to do this, but Ruth was determined to stay with Naomi. The two of them eventually arrived in Bethlehem and received what can only be described as a lukewarm reception from the townsfolk. They managed to survive for a while before Ruth eventually married Boaz and had a child. This circumstance brought renewed status to Naomi as well as personal blessing.

The first picture of Naomi is of a fairly strong, determined woman, more than capable of assessing situations and making decisions. However, the return to Bethlehem did not bring an improvement to Naomi's circumstances, and this seems to have knocked her off balance. At this point, perhaps depressed by the failure of her relatives or fellow townsfolk to provide any care for her, she leaves everything, including the decision-making, to Ruth. However, her ability to assess situations and grasp their implications has not been lost, and once it becomes clear that Ruth's actions have borne fruit, both metaphorically and literally, it re-emerges. She sets out a plan of action, which Ruth adapts. Boaz picks up the family responsibilities that he has been reminded of, buys Naomi's land and marries Ruth. Naomi then takes up an active role as the baby's grandmother and responds very positively to the affirmation that she now does receive from the women of the town.

b. Ruth
No background story is given for Ruth. She enters the narrative as Mahlon's widow. We can only speculate as to whether her determination to remain with Naomi was influenced by an unwillingness to return to what may have been an unhappy home situation. The information that we are given is that she loved Naomi and that her decision to commit herself to Naomi was made with a clear understanding of what might be involved, including the fact that this was a lifetime commitment. That she was also going to commit herself to Naomi's God is also made clear, although whether or not this was a primary factor in her decision is not discussed.

Ruth was a strong, intelligent and kind woman. She does not appear to have been fazed by any of the difficult circumstances she faced. She listened to Naomi and accepted her leadership, but had no hesitation in overriding Naomi's decision to send her home. When, back in Bethlehem, Naomi appeared to have lost her confidence, Ruth quietly took over the reins of the household, while still ready to listen to Naomi's advice. She seems to have had an ability to grasp both cultural and personal implications. She adapted Naomi's plan in such a way that offended neither Naomi nor Boaz yet enabled her to maintain her own integrity. In many ways Ruth can be seen as acting as the family guardian that Naomi's own family had initially failed to supply.

c. Boaz

We are told in 2:1 that Boaz was *a man of standing*. He was a notable citizen, a property owner with many employees, someone respected within the community. He seems to have been a good employer and he certainly knew those who worked for him and, if his treatment of Ruth can be seen as typical, cared for the needs of his employees. He was clearly an older man, contrasting himself with the *younger men* that Ruth could have sought to marry. It would be surprising if he had not been married previously, but we are given no information at all about his previous family life, so although later Jewish literature tells many stories about his background, we have no evidence as to whether he was a widower or if he had any previous children. He was a relative of Elimelek and Naomi who, although not the closest relative, was in the chain of those who could be considered responsible for caring for the needs of the bereaved Naomi. He is portrayed as competent not only as a businessman but as a negotiator who grasps ideas quickly and understands how people react and the implications of their actions. He comes across as kind and generous. The extent of his eventual help and assuming responsibility makes it surprising that it was not until Ruth, apparently by chance, entered his particular property that he took any action to help Naomi.

d. Minor characters

Apart from these three, there are no other named characters who enter the stage, except for Orpah who leaves early and the baby Obed who arrives at the end. Two other individuals have a speaking part: the overseer in 2:5–7 and the nearer relative in 4:1–8. All other characters are in groups: the townswomen, the harvesters, the elders and *all the people at the gate*. Each of these, both individuals and groups, appear to have a function in emphasizing the needs of Ruth and Naomi, the part Boaz was playing in meeting those needs, and the fact that the community as a whole took no action to fulfil their covenantal responsibility to care for the weaker and needier members of that society.

3. Theological themes

The narrative nature of Ruth, telling a story and including extensive dialogue with very little editorial comment, means that it is difficult to be sure just what the author's intentions were regarding theological teaching. Nevertheless, a number of issues seem to be emphasized through how the story has been told. It becomes clear as we consider these themes and the recurring motifs examined in section 4d that although Ruth can be described as a book about the marginalized – in particular, destitute widows and foreigners – and although it can be very helpfully used to encourage and validate those in that category, it would be a travesty to treat it as only that. The lessons of Ruth were just as important, and perhaps even more necessary, for the wealthy and powerful men of Israel as they were for poor women.

a. The nature of God

There are eighteen references to Yahweh in the book of Ruth and five other uses of the terms *God* and *Almighty* which also clearly refer to Yahweh. Three of these are used in parallel with Yahweh: *the Almighty . . . the LORD* [Yahweh] *. . . the Almighty* (1:20–21), and *the LORD* [Yahweh], *the God of Israel* (2:12); and the other two are in 1:16 where Ruth states that Naomi's God, that is, Yahweh, will be her God. As twenty of the twenty-two references occur in dialogue and some are very much 'in-passing' mentions of God's name, it may be argued that it is not possible to draw any conclusions as to how the book as a whole portrays the nature of God. However, it is interesting to note that the two remaining editorial references come very near the beginning and very near the end of the narrative. In 1:6 we are told it was hearing that *the LORD had come to the aid of his* *people* that stimulated Naomi to action, and in 4:13 that *the LORD enabled her to conceive.* Thus, it is possible that the author is encouraging the reading of the whole narrative in the light of God's sovereignty both over the forces of nature that brought and alleviated the famine and over the conception of a child in this particularly needy family. If this is so, then it is worth noting the way in which the various actors do talk about God in their dialogue with each other and examining how far what they say does or does not reflect an understanding of the sovereignty of God.

Six of the sixteen uses of Yahweh in dialogue are using God's name to reinforce a blessing, curse or oath: *the LORD be with you*; *the LORD bless him*; *the LORD bless you* (2:4, 20; 3:10); *May the LORD deal with me* if I don't stay with Naomi (1:17); and *as surely as the LORD lives I will do it* (3:13). Thus, the community did know of Yahweh, and there seems to have been an understanding that God was responsible for good and bad things happening in life, that it was possible to request blessing from him and that the community had a duty to God to fulfil any responsibility he had given them. However, all of these could be almost automatic uses without any real thought as to who God was or what they were actually expecting when they asked for his blessing. In that case it seems likely that the author is implying that the people knew of God, but didn't necessarily know God himself. Three instances (1:13, 21 alongside the two similar references to the Almighty in 1:20 and 21) are of Naomi's assuming her difficult circumstances can be blamed on God – *the LORD's hand has turned against me*; *the Almighty has made my life very bitter*; *the LORD has brought me back empty . . . afflicted me . . . brought misfortune upon me* – and one (4:14) praises God, assuming that the new and improved circumstances can also be ascribed to him. The remaining six references to Yahweh are in what could be described as prayers: *May the LORD show you kindness . . . grant that each of you will find rest* (1:8, 9); *May the LORD repay you . . . may you be richly rewarded by the LORD* (2:12); *May the LORD make [Ruth] like Rachel and Leah . . . May you have standing . . . may your family be like that of Perez* (4:11, 12).

Thus, virtually every reference to God, whether in passing or more deliberate, shows an understanding of God's sovereignty, God's responsibility for everything that happens, good or bad, and of the possibility of bringing requests to God with the expectation that he will do something about it. Whether the community grasped the implications of these truths is a different question, but it seems that the author wanted them to be clearly understood by the readers of the narrative.

b. The nature and responsibilities of the community

The community in Ruth consists of the townsfolk of Bethlehem and the surrounding regions. This community functions in the book almost as a character, or perhaps two or three characters – the women of the town, the elders and the whole people. We first meet the larger group in 1:19 when we are told that *the whole town was stirred* by the arrival of Naomi and Ruth, and we hear of them again in 4:11–12 when they act as witnesses to Boaz' commitments and then pray for his and his new family's well-being. In 4:1–12 we see the elders exercising their role as making and upholding legal rulings within the wider community. The townswomen acknowledge Naomi's arrival in 1:19, but play no further part in the narrative until 4:14–17, when – after Boaz has married Ruth and she has borne a child, thus gaining status in the community – they praise God, assuming his responsibility for Naomi's new good fortune, and acknowledge and praise Ruth for taking on the responsibility of family and being *better than seven sons*! It is hard to avoid the implication, given the lack of any mention of the community in chapters 2 and 3, that the author is emphasizing two facts. First, the community did exist, they were aware of what went on, they had responsibilities as a community and there was a functioning system of carrying out those responsibilities. Second, the community failed completely in its responsibility to make sure that widows, foreigners and other low-status people were protected and cared for within the community. Their care for Naomi and acceptance of Ruth came into play only when they could no longer be seen as low-status people! Given the deliberate setting of Ruth in the time also covered by Judges, it is not inconceivable (and is perhaps likely) that the author is drawing attention to the fact that even in what might be seen as a positive story, the people of Israel, if Bethlehem can be seen as a microcosm of the whole, were not fulfilling their covenant responsibilities in anything more than a perfunctory way.

c. The nature and responsibilities of the family

It could be said that the main focus of the book of Ruth is family life. Obviously, the primary interest is in the story of Naomi and Ruth and their relationship, but we are also provided with insights into wider family concerns. The facts are again clear: the small 'nuclear' family unit of Elimelek, Naomi, Mahlon and Kilion moved from the Bethlehem area to Moab. In the beginning the move brought blessing in the provision of food and the marriages of the two boys, but the death of all three of the men in the little family was an unforeseen disaster. There is no way of determining whether or not the author intended us to see their original decision to move to Moab as positive or whether we are meant to view it as a betrayal of their responsibilities to the wider family and wider covenant community in Bethlehem. If the latter is true, it could go some way to explaining the lack of practical help given to Naomi when she eventually returned home. Certainly, the picture presented is that the family's primary concern was the welfare of the smaller family unit. Orpah and Ruth became part of that family on their marriage, but when Naomi made the decision to return to Israel, it became clear that for Orpah at least links with her original family had not been severed. However, Ruth identified herself entirely as part of Naomi's family, taking on all the implications and responsibilities of that position. Thus, it raises the question as to how far family identity was governed by genetics and how far by relational commitment. As the story develops, we see an awareness of family responsibilities beyond the nuclear family as the concept of 'guardian-redeemer' is introduced. But even here the question of whether it was the official family tree or relational commitment that really counted comes into play, as Boaz, who was not the nearest relative, takes on the responsibility.

d. The nature and responsibilities of individuals

Although the narratives of Ruth raise a number of questions relating to family and community responsibilities, the author presents us with the way in which individuals were also seen as responsible for making decisions on their own behalf. Naomi decides to go home; Ruth decides to go with her. Ruth decides to go gleaning. She follows Naomi's instructions about approaching Boaz but does so in her own way. Boaz decides to help; the nearer relative decides not to be involved. Although there is no actual editorial discussion of the point, the story seems to be told in a way that emphasizes the responsibility of the community for living according to covenant principles. But the community is made up of individuals, and the way in which individual lives are lived is clearly seen as influencing the overall pattern of community life.

4. Literary issues

a. *Structure and purpose*
In contrast to Judges, the book of Ruth, with the possible exception of the concluding genealogy in 4:18–22, consists of one continuous narrative. Discussions about the structure of Ruth tend to focus either on questions relating to how the narrative itself is formulated or on whether the story is deliberately formulated as a lead up to the genealogy of David in 4:18–22, which is sometimes seen as the key passage of the whole book.

Good storytelling does involve patterns and links, and it is suggested that the story in Ruth has a chiastic or symmetrical pattern. Luter and Rigsby (1996) provide a full discussion of different ways in which this symmetry has been understood,[2] and they develop their own argument that a chiasm with seven sections can be seen in Ruth. Their chart of this (ibid.: 16) shown on the opposite page is worth noting. Some of the links may seem a little forced, but there is no reason to doubt that some kind of symmetrical structure does exist.

For those who see 4:18–22 as the key that unlocks the purpose of the rest of the book, the writer's main concern is to provide information on David's background. Block (1999) begins with the assumption that the writing of the book centres on what he calls 'The preservation of the royal line'. He assumes that the structure of the book should be understood via the question of how this relates to that 'line'. He divides the book into four acts: 'The Crisis for the Royal Line', 'The Ray of Hope for the Royal Line', 'The

---

2. Notably by S. Bertman, 'The Symmetrical Structure of Ruth', *JBL* 84: 166–168.

An alternative overall chiastic structure for Ruth

A	1:1–5 – Emptied: family/home/provision lost husband and two sons	no future
	B 1:6–22 – Hopeless widows go back to Bethlehem	1 gone (Orpah) 2 persons commitment
	C 2:1–23 (Deut 24:19–22) – Setting: harvest field Issue: immediate provision	Ruth leaves Naomi Ruth's request Boaz' response: concern/ generosity Ruth and Naomi rest
Central Focus	**D** 2:18–23; 3:1–5 – Interaction	Present blessing by God and Boaz Future blessing by God through Boaz
	C' 3:1–18 (Deut 25:5–10) – Setting: harvest field Issue: longer-term provision	Ruth leaves Naomi Ruth's proposal Boaz' response: concern/ generosity Ruth and Naomi interact
	B' 4:1–12 – Hopeful widows taken care of in the gates of Bethlehem	1 gone (kinsman) 2 persons commitment
A'	4:13–17 – Filled: family/home/provision Ruth, better than 7 sons, and Obed	great future

4:18–22 – Epilogue: family tree of the clan of Perez

Complication for the Line' and 'The Rescue of the Royal Line', with 4:18–22 seen as the Epilogue. However, the lack of any mention of kingship in the narrative itself does raise questions about the adequacy of this approach. Another way is not to see the final reference to David as the key to understanding the book, but rather as a link to the first reference to the days of the judges (in Ruth 1:1). The final reference is then similar to the key phrase in the last part of Judges: there was no king in Israel. Both books can be seen as asking the question: 'Will it make a difference when we have a king?' The writers may be assuming a positive response, but the answer is not contained in either Judges or Ruth, and the answers provided in the books of Samuel and Kings certainly don't give an assurance that a positive answer was found.

However, there is no need to assume that 4:18–22 is there to provide a rationale for the story rather than simply being an addendum to it. We need to look at the interests presented in the story itself. To limit the significance of Ruth to approval of David's kingship or line – or even to showing his direct link to the patriarchs – is surely to undervalue the importance of the story which emphasizes the significance of the lives of ordinary people and in particular the concentration on the feelings, needs of and attitudes to women and foreigners.[3] Section d. (below) looks at some of the recurring motifs in Ruth, and an examination of these is surely necessary before drawing any conclusions about the purpose of the writer in composing Ruth. However, it is worth noting here that the symmetrical structure as identified by Luter and Rigsby would imply that the author was concerned for readers to think about the nature of God's blessing in bad times and in good times. This is almost certainly true, but does not cover the author's parallel concern for the responsibility of the people to live in the light of God's covenant requirements. Richard Bauckham's suggestion (1996) that the writer of Ruth is deliberately telling the story from the perspective of women, allowing their voices to be heard in a way that is not always found in some of the more male-focused narratives, is also worth consideration.

Phyllis Trible's article in the *ABD* 5 (1992: 846) gives an excellent summary of the variety of purposes found in Ruth and is worth quoting at some length:

> Attempts to specify a single purpose falter in the light of the book's richness and complexity. Many levels of meaning intertwine – social, political, religious, and aesthetic. A representative list includes: to maintain Israelite customs, to inculcate legal duties, integrate law and daily life, legitimate David and his monarchy, tell a good story, encourage proselytes, promote universalism over against nationalism, elevate the virtues of friendship and loyalty, glorify family ties, preserve women's traditions, and witness to God at work.

---

3. Hubbard (1988: 21–23) provides a more detailed defence of the view that the function of Ruth 4:18–22 is not so much 'to introduce what followed but in some way to conclude what preceded'.

b. Authorship and dating

There seems no reason then to presuppose multiple authorship. The book itself supplies no details of its own origins, and there is no external evidence for an identifiable author, so any statements here can only be very general. However, we can determine a number of characteristics of whoever the writer was. The evidence in the book itself tells us that the writer was:

1. A gifted storyteller with a clear understanding of human nature;
2. Someone with a good knowledge of Israelite history in and prior to the time of the Judges, who assumes that readers will also be able to identify the characters from that history who are mentioned;
3. Someone who understands the requirements that the covenant relationship with God engenders for Israel and the people of Israel;
4. Someone with a genuine interest in, and concern for, the needs of the underprivileged in society.

We also know that the writer, assuming that the same person was responsible for the final verses, lived in a time when David was well known to all concerned, although it is not possible to tell whether this was during the latter part of David's kingship or much later than that. The Talmud suggests that Ruth was written by Samuel, but as Samuel died before David actually came to the throne and the concluding genealogy certainly suggests that it was written when David was well known, this seems very unlikely (Driesbach 2012: 497).

Any discussion of the precise dating of the story within the *days when the judges ruled* can only be speculative (see section 1b above), and this also applies to discussion of the dating of the document itself. G. R. Goswell (2014) argues the view that Ruth was a late composition contributing to the debates in the time of Ezra and Nehemiah regarding marriage to foreigners and providing a different perspective. However, this does not explain the links in the book with David. It is clear that Ruth does contribute to the debate about exogamous marriages, but it is a big leap to move from that to suggest that this is evidence for its composition in the context of

Ezra and Nehemiah's teaching. The fact that there is no agreement among scholars and the dates ascribed to Ruth vary between the tenth century and the sixth century (see Block 1999: 592) indicate the danger of trying to be too precise.

c. The nature of narrative text

Issues relating to the interpretation and function of narrative texts have been discussed in the introduction to Judges (see pp. 5–7), and it seems unnecessary to repeat that discussion here. However, it is worth restressing the importance of recognizing that narrative is most often simply a record of events rather than a direct assessment of those events, and the lack of editorial comment in Ruth makes that particularly important in this context. Readers are presented with the task of analysing the account and asking questions regarding why particular incidents, and in this case particular conversations, are included and recorded in this particular way. However, the lack of editorial comment does not mean that the author is not presenting a point of view. Like Judges, what we have here is 'preached history', and readers are in fact being led towards some conclusions through the selection of material and the method of presentation. In this instance we are pointed to the context of the wider history – and the references to characters from that earlier history encourage readers to look further into that history. Similarly, as particular themes and motifs are drawn out within the narrative, readers are deliberately encouraged to work out what they can and should learn from these particular stories. This is obviously an especially important task for those of us who understand the whole of the Bible to be the inspired and authoritative Word of God, that is, as 'Scripture'. In this case it is at least worth asking whether, in contrast to Judges which looks at what happens in society when God's covenant is constantly flouted, Ruth is presenting a picture of a society where God's covenant is known but largely seen as peripheral to everyday life. In both instances we are shown the possibility of individuals within that society following the path of righteousness, justice, obedience and concern for the marginalized, but we are also presented with a picture of the wider society where for the majority of individuals, and for the community as a whole, that does not generally happen. Ruth can only be viewed as an idyllic pastoral story that contrasts with the very negative picture of society presented in Judges if this failure of the wider community in Bethlehem to fulfil its obligations is ignored.

d. Recurring motifs

Although in a straightforward narrative like this one it is possible that motifs may recur simply because they are part of the story, it is worth looking at what the recurring motifs are and asking what significance they might have.[4]

i. Goings and comings

Journeys, long and short, play a significant part in this story. The major journeys take us from Bethlehem to Moab and back. These journeys were completed in 1:19, but there are three further references to the fact that the characters had come back from Moab (1:22; 2:6; 4:3). Once in Bethlehem, Ruth goes out to the field, which turns out to belong to Boaz, and back; this was obviously repeated many times, but the text does not focus on that fact. She goes to the threshing-floor, and back, and Boaz goes from the harvest floor to the town gate. The writer does seem to be emphasizing these comings and goings and the conversations that take place at the starting and finishing points. It is possible that readers are being invited to consider the fact that life does involve movement and to question how far God's purposes are reflected in the various movements described. This involves asking both what part, if any, a knowledge of God's will or God's covenant played in the decisions to journey made by the characters and how far God's grace and mercy are illustrated in the events described.

ii. Attitudes to women and foreigners

There are three primary characters in Ruth, two of whom are women. It is not surprising therefore that the narrative keeps

---

4. There are obviously a variety of ways in which such recurring motifs can be identified and the points the writer is drawing out classified. Driesbach (2012: 504–508) chooses the categories of loyalty, honour, wisdom, reversal and redemption, blessing, and human and divine cooperation.

returning to events in the lives of those women. However, the interest in the attitudes and feelings of Ruth and Naomi and those of the townswomen of Bethlehem goes beyond a simple record of events. The writer seems to be deliberately emphasizing that women are significant members of the covenant community: what happens to them and how they behave matters. Similarly, from the beginning we are made aware of the fact that Ruth was not an Israelite, but the six further references to her as *Ruth the Moabite* do seem to indicate that the writer wants to highlight Ruth's nationality as a relevant factor in the attitude of the Bethlehem residents to her and to Naomi. In the legal negotiations described in 4:2–11 Boaz twice refers to Ruth as *the Moabite* when the key factor at this point was, as he also mentions twice, that she was the widow of Mahlon. Readers are clearly being encouraged to consider what attitudes and behaviour are appropriate when relating to foreigners, and how far can and should those foreigners who identify themselves with God's covenant community be acknowledged as full members of that community. L. J. M. Claassens (2012) picks up on the link with another foreign woman, Boaz' ancestor Tamar, who, like Ruth, was living in difficult circumstances. She argues that both of these women are faced with situations in which their dignity or worth is threatened or potentially violated and both take action to resist this dehumanization. Her conclusion is that in both cases it is the women's 'resistance' that 'compels the male characters . . . finally to see and recognise the humanity of the female characters, whose basic rights, needs and desires have not been recognised by their respective societies' (660–661). Whether or not this is so – and the explicit reference to Tamar in 4:12 could support this view – it seems clear that the writer is intending readers to identify and correct threats to the dignity and well-being of any people who might be being 'dehumanized'. It is worth noting here that the reference to David in the epilogue can just as easily be seen as included to further emphasize the points the narrative brings out – for example, that even foreigners can be in the ancestral line of someone like David – as it can be seen as the key, with the narrative simply giving background to David's ancestry.

iii. Family responsibilities

Related to the above, but adding a slightly different touch, is the question of what is family and what does being family involve. We have considered the implications of this in section 3c above, but it is worth noting at this point the way in which these interests, in particular the responsibilities of both the immediate 'nuclear' family and those of the more distant family-guardians, frequently come into focus.

iv. Food

Another repeated interest in Ruth is the question of food. No food in Bethlehem led to travel to find food in Moab. Hearing of food available in Israel led to the return, and the whole story revolves around Ruth and Naomi finding food to eat and eventually a descendant who will ensure permanent provision. Thus the symbolism of empty turning to full applies to both the provision of food and to the provision of an heir. T. J. Stone (2013) sees the references to barley seed providing food as emphasizing this link with what became the royal seed. Certainly both point to the assurance of God's eventual provision for his people.

ANALYSIS

A. Preface (1:1–5)
B. The returns (1:6–22)
C. Boaz and Ruth: first encounter (2:1–16)
D. Naomi and Ruth: conversation at the end of the day (2:17–23)
E. Seeking a marriage partner (3:1–18)
    i. Naomi and Ruth: making plans (3:1–6)
    ii. Boaz and Ruth: a close encounter (3:7–15)
    iii. Naomi and Ruth: further conversation (3:16–18)
F. Marriage and birth (4.1–17)
    i. Boaz takes action (4:1:10)
    ii. 'Naomi has a son' (4:11–17)
G. Afterword: the genealogy (4:18–22)

COMMENTARY

A. Preface (1:1–5)

Context

The concerns of the book of Ruth are not international or even tribal relations, although we are given a picture, incidentally somewhat different from that in Judges (e.g. Judg. 3:12–14, 30), of the relationship between Israel and Moab. What we have here is an account, largely based on dialogue, of the life and concerns of one small Israelite family. The first few verses introduce us to the family and provide a very brief account of the life of Naomi and Ruth before they travel together to what they hope will be a better life back in Israel. There is no doubt that the book is intended to be read in the context of the book of Judges. It is therefore legitimate for readers to approach the book with a question in mind related to the same question that has been of interest to the writers of Judges: will we see here anything about the way in which this family lives and interacts with the community that provides evidence of how far they, both the family and the community, are living in the light of the covenant relationship with Yahweh?

Comment

1:1–2. There is a remarkable amount of information in verse 1. First, the context is firmly set for us *in the days when the judges ruled*. The term that the NIV has as *ruled* was traditionally translated as 'judged' but is almost certainly better understood as simply 'led'. However, Moore (Harris, Brown and Moore 2000; 309) is probably right to suggest that the dual use 'when the judges judged' or 'the leaders led' rather than just 'in the time of the judges' is deliberately proposing that the writer is interested in concepts relating to justice and/or leadership. In either case the general time period is clear. These events are set somewhere in the time covered by the book of Judges. However, there is little information that would help us determine at what stage these particular events took place. The book begins with the primary characters based in Moab, situated on the south-eastern side of the Dead Sea, but it seems unlikely that it occurred during the time described in Judges 3:12–14 when Israel was 'subject to Eglon king of Moab for eighteen years'. However, although there are no indications in the book of Ruth of subjection in either direction, it could conceivably have taken place after the actions by Ehud when 'Moab was made subject to Israel, and the land had peace for eighty years' (Judg. 3:30). Whenever it was, it does seem clear that we are being asked to approach Ruth with a prior understanding of the events described in the book of Judges and the message presented by the writers of that book.

The situation faced by Elimelek and his family, while still in their home town of Bethlehem, was severe famine. There is irony in the fact that Bethlehem means 'house of bread' and yet food was not available there. There is no indication as to whether the famine was simply a result of natural weather cycles or had been exacerbated by the actions of oppressors – as for example described in Judges 6:3–8 before Gideon was called to take action – or was a specific act of judgment by God such as that suggested in 2 Samuel 24:13. In either case the famine seems to have been a fairly long-term situation. The stories of the patriarchs present travel to a different country as one way to cope with famine. Abram and Sara travelled to Egypt 'to live there for a while because the famine was severe' (Gen. 12:10), and Jacob's family also went to Egypt for help during an extended time of famine (Gen. 42). It is interesting that both of those journeys eventually resulted in trouble, but it is understandable if this couple assumed that this was a legitimate action for Israelites to take. There is no way of determining how old the two boys were at this time, but as neither of them was married, it is likely that they were still young. We know that ten years later they were married, so they were possibly teenagers or younger at the time of their migration. There is no indication here, or anywhere else in the book of Ruth, that there was anything other than friendly relations between Moab and Israel at this time. Whether the phrase translated in the NIV as *for a while* in verse 1 suggests that they had always intended their stay to be temporary, or whether it implies living as 'a resident alien' with no indication of timing, is debatable (see Hubbard 1988: 87). In either case, and even if Moab followed the Israelite pattern with a recognized status of 'resident foreigner', there would have always been a level of insecurity. In verse 2 we learn the names of the family: Elimelek, Naomi, Mahlon and Kilion. The fact that they are not named in the first introduction could mean that the writer is intending them to be seen not just as individuals but as a typical family, a microcosm of the way Israel viewed life. The statement in verse 1 that they went to live in Moab *for a while*, followed by the repetition in verse 2 that *they went to Moab and lived there*, could be intended to raise the question as to whether they should actually have headed back to the land God has given them a long time before they actually did. They originated in Bethlehem in Judah, and we are also told that they were Ephrathites. Ephrathah is sometimes seen as an alternative name for Bethlehem, as in Micah 5:2 where the phrase Bethlehem Ephrathah is used, or as referring to a village outside the town. However, it is also possible that it refers to the particular clan that Elimelek came from. What we can be sure of is that the family were Judeans coming from the area in or around Bethlehem. In these verses Elimelek has been the key character, the primary decision-maker in the family's move to Moab. But with his death the focus moves to Naomi. It is interesting that whereas in verse 2 Naomi is referred to as Elimelek's wife, in verse 3 he is referred to as Naomi's husband. (see Block 1999: 628). It was not usual to refer to a husband in terms of his wife, even after death, and here it is a strong indication that the writer at this stage is deliberately focusing on the lives of women (see Driesbach 2012: 513).

3–5. These three verses cover the period of more than ten years when Naomi stayed in Moab. We are not told how long they were there before Elimelek died, at what stage the two sons married or how long after their death the decision to move back to Israel was taken. None of those things is relevant to the writer's purpose. The fact of the three deaths is presented with stark brevity, which emphasizes rather than masks the devastation involved. The sons apparently married after Elimelek's death, presumably with Naomi's approval, and we do learn the names of the sons' wives, Orpah and Ruth. Mahlon, Ruth's husband (4:10), was apparently the elder as he was named first in 1:2, so it is not clear why Orpah is named first here.

Evidently, neither couple had any children, which could imply that
the two young men died very soon after their marriages or that there
might have been a problem. However, any suggestion of this is very
much implicit. As the marriage of the two sons is mentioned prior
to the statement referring to the ten-year time gap, it is possible
that the sons were married for ten years before they died, in which
case the lack of further children would be very significant, but the
point is not made explicit and we cannot be sure exactly when the
ten-year time period began. The final sentence of the section shows
that Naomi is to be seen as a key character in the ongoing narrative.
She is now there, in Moab, without husband or sons to protect her.
The question is clearly being deliberately raised in the mind of the
reader. What is going to happen to her next? The family had moved
to Moab to enable them to survive a famine. How is Naomi going to
survive now that she has no direct family to support her?

Meaning
In one sense in a family narrative of this nature the story and the meaning are so intertwined as to be inseparable. The story is the meaning.
However, it is worth noting at this stage that the book of Ruth picks
up on the teaching found in Judges that God is concerned about the
lives of ordinary people, including women. It is not just leaders who
are to be seen as significant. Maybe the fact that so far God has not
been mentioned, and neither Elimelek nor Naomi seem to have had
any idea of seeking God's perspective about their actions, is meant to
be an indication of the lack of concern, of the couple rather than of
the writer, for the purposes of God in the lives of ordinary Israelites
in general. It is also possible that readers are being encouraged to
consider that this family who had left the Promised Land searching for
life and blessing in the end found only death and bitterness.

B. The returns (1:6–22)

Context
Having provided the necessary background details of the original
emigration and the deaths of the three men, the writer turns to the
main focus: the ongoing life of Naomi. Genesis 2:24 says that a man
does/should separate from his parents in order to make a life with

his wife. However, there is little evidence that this was ever common practice in Israel or in any of the surrounding lands. In general, girls when they were married went to live with their husband who would normally be still living with his parents. This is certainly the pattern we see reflected here. There are at least ten references in this section to returning or going back. (The different terms used and the varying translations make it difficult for those reading in English to determine just how many references there are.) This does indicate that the writer has an interest in the concept of returning – whether to the land that God had given to them or to the covenant that God had made with them.

Comment

6–7. There is no indication that Naomi faced any kind of prejudice or persecution in Moab. The reason for her move was the news that the famine in Israel was over and life there was now much more tolerable. Naomi assumes that it was Yahweh who had brought about this renewed state of prosperity. It seems inconceivable that the famine had lasted for the whole of the ten years. Perhaps news of the deaths of Elimelek and his sons had been sent back to his home town and she had received specific information back from there which influenced her decision. With the death of her menfolk and no other family support in the region, it is likely that the need for back-up in her old age became more relevant to her. Her two daughters-in-law were clearly still living with her after the death of their husbands, and the first assumption is that they would go back to Judah with her. They all set out on the journey together – presumably after packing up their house and deciding what to take with them. For a journey like this, it is unlikely that there would have been any thought of return. The fact that there does not at this stage seem to have been any discussion of who should or should not go indicates a good long-term relationship between the three women and also reflects the apparent consensus that Naomi, as mother-in-law, was the one who would make the decisions.[1]

---

1. Schipper (2013) argues that the preposition usually translated as 'with' in v. 7 and also in 1:11, 22; 2:6, 19 (x2) could perhaps better be translated as 'under the authority of'.

8–9. As Naomi began to think of the reality of her return, she apparently realized that her daughters-in-law would be in the same situation in Judah as she had found herself in Moab – with no male providers. There would certainly be no guarantee that they would be able to find new husbands. Naomi realizes how difficult it is likely to be for them and therefore, again acting as decision-maker, instructs them to return to their parental home, gives them her blessing and kisses them goodbye. It is interesting that she refers to their return to their *mother's home* rather than their 'father's home'. Any significance of that is hard to determine, although the suggestion that she has lost confidence in men as decision-makers and providers is perhaps worth noting. However, Boaz' comment in 2:11 about Ruth having left behind her father and mother probably implies that the reference here is incidental. Naomi's request is that Yahweh will bless them, which probably indicates that the family has continued to worship Yahweh. She takes it for granted that the two young women will know who Yahweh is and understand the significance of her prayer. The syntax in verses 8b–9 is unusual in that 8b (in the LXX and some Hebrew documents) has no object and verse 9 begins with an imperative: 'find rest in the home of'. It may be an indication of Naomi's disturbed state of mind that she begins one sentence and then moves on to another without really finishing her first train of thought (see Schipper 2012). Naomi's words to the two younger women provide further evidence that life in Moab seems to have been happy and settled for all of them – characterized by mutual kindness. The second blessing follows the assumption that life for a young widow in that culture would be tolerable only if she married again. The thought of parting was difficult for all of them and tears were shed. At this point Naomi is taking it for granted that they will accept her decision.

10–14. In many cultures appearing to dispute the kind of decision that will make life more difficult for the decider is a formal require-ment. Both girls assert their willingness to continue on their journey with her. However, when Naomi makes it clear that there is little likelihood of their finding another husband, Orpah accepts the sense of Naomi's instructions. After more weeping and kissing she does return to her own home and we learn no more of what happened to her. Naomi's statement perhaps reflects an understanding that no

Israelite man would want to marry a foreigner, even one who had previously been married to an Israelite. The text goes on to praise Ruth's loyalty to Naomi, but there is no indication that Orpah's behaviour is seen as in any way blameworthy.

Naomi's understanding of, and relationship with, Yahweh is clearly mixed. In 1:6 she recognizes that the renewed hope brought about through the end of the famine in Israel had come because Yahweh had *come to their aid* and she later blessed the girls in his name, clearly assuming that he is capable of answering those prayers for blessing – even in Moab. However, for herself she finds only bitterness. It is difficult to determine the precise meaning of the second half of verse 13, and this difficulty is reflected in the different translations. Some see Naomi as speaking only about her own pain: *It is more bitter for me than for you* (NIV); 'Things are far more bitter for me than for you' (NLT); 'it is harder for me than for you' (NASB). Others assume she is expressing concern for her daughters-in-law: 'it grieveth me much for your sakes' (KJV); 'It is exceedingly bitter to me for your sake' (ASV, ESV); 'For my intense suffering is too much for you to bear' (NET Bible). Whichever of these is correct, Naomi takes it for granted that it was Yahweh's responsibility that circumstances had become so difficult for her. He, because he is sovereign, must be the cause of the deaths of her husband and sons, therefore she draws the conclusion that *the LORD's hand has turned against me* (v. 13). It remains to be seen whether the ongoing story will reveal that she was right or wrong to draw this conclusion. Block suggests that Naomi's statements 'offer no hint of human causation behind her tragedies. Instead of repenting of her own and her people's sin, she accuses God of injustice toward her.' Putting this alongside Naomi's encouragement to the girls to return to their own gods (although in fact her reference in 1:15 to Orpah returning to her own gods does not necessarily imply encouragement to do so), he concludes, 'Her theological perceptions at this point seem no more orthodox than those of many characters in the Book of Judges. If she represents the highest level of faith in Israel, it is no wonder Yahweh had sent a famine on the land' (Block 1999: 637, 639). This might be over-emphasizing the negative but is worth noting in the context of the question of how far ordinary Israelite families understood and kept to the covenant.

15–18. It is made very clear that Ruth's refusal to accept Naomi's instruction was by no means a formal disclaimer. She physically holds on to Naomi (v. 14) and, when faced with Naomi's repetition of her instruction to Ruth to follow Orpah's example, pleads to be allowed to stay with Naomi. The theological discussion in these verses is interesting. Naomi knows that in returning to her own family Orpah will also be returning to their gods – the implication is that Ruth and Orpah both left those gods behind when joining Naomi's family. Ruth's response may focus on her relationship with Naomi and her desire to go where Naomi goes, but she does this in the full knowledge of what is involved. Her identity will change. She will be joined to Naomi's people permanently, accepting that she will die and be buried well away from her own birthplace. And Naomi's God will be her God. Her specific reference to Yahweh in verse 17 indicates that she did have some understanding of who Naomi's God was and makes the NIV translation of *elohim* as singular (in v. 16) more likely to be correct. There are few signs that God's will had been sought about decisions relating to the location of residence, but it does seem as if teaching about God had taken place within the family. Indeed, Ruth makes an oath in the name of Yahweh that she will not be separated from Naomi even by death. Smith (2007: 256) points out the linguistic links between Ruth's words and those of the Judean king Jehoshaphat in the covenant agreements he made with the kings of the northern kingdom of Israel. Jehoshaphat states that they will act as a common people, 'my people as your people' (1 Kgs 22:4; 2 Kgs 3:7). Smith suggests that whereas Ruth's original relationship with Naomi through her husband had been broken by his death, Ruth is now joining Naomi's family not by marriage but by a covenant agreement.[2] Presumably, she is insisting that even if Naomi were to die, she would still remain in Israel. With this kind of commitment expressed, Naomi accepts that Ruth is not going to return to her roots and removes her objections to Ruth accompanying her. It could be that Ruth's speech is deliberately presented in such a way as to emphasize her understanding of God and perhaps to

---

2. See also Siquans' discussion of Ruth's legal status (2009).

suggest that that understanding at least matched and possibly out-
matched that of Naomi.

19. There is a lot that we do not know about Naomi and Ruth's
journey. We have no information about where in Moab the family
had settled; we do not know their method of travel, whether they
had a donkey, were able to hire a place in some kind of cart or walked
the whole distance. Neither do we know whether they took the route
round the south end or the north end of the Dead Sea. Thus we are
not aware of the distance, although it is likely to have been somewhere
between forty-five and ninety miles, and we have no knowledge
about how long it took. We are not told about the mood of the
women on the way. Was there much conversation or did they travel
in silence? Was there a sense of hope at times, even though despair
was clearly also present and eventually predominated? What interests
the writer is that eventually they did arrive. Apparently, the whole
town was aware of their arrival. The interest in, and recognition of,
Naomi perhaps indicates that before they left, the family was notable
in the town. The later picture of Elimelek's relatives being landowners reinforces that view. Whether the townsfolk being *stirred* implies
excitement or disturbance is not made clear; the word could be
understood either way.

20–22. Naomi reacts to their greeting with what might be
described as anguish: *Don't call me Naomi* [meaning pleasant] . . . *Call
me Mara* [meaning bitter]. However, it is interesting that there is no
evidence that the writer or the townspeople ever took her up on the
plea to call her by this rather negative new name. The sense that
Yahweh had *come to the aid* of his people, which Naomi had recognized in 1:6, seems at this point not to have influenced her to think
he might also have come to her aid. She has come back to Bethlehem,
but apparently only in despair rather than in hope – in spite of Ruth's
presence with her. It is possible that the fullness she had taken with
her and the emptiness with which she has returned refer solely
to the presence and then loss of her husband and sons. However, again given the ongoing story, she might also be saying that
whatever resources they took with them to Moab have now disappeared. Having been told of this, the townsfolk, if they had been
living according to God's covenant with Israel, would have had
a responsibility to do more than simply greet Naomi with interest

(e.g. Lev. 25:35ff.). As we have been informed that *the whole town was stirred* by their arrival, it seems inconceivable that close relatives would not have been aware of their presence. At the very least, they might have been expected to provide hospitality. The reason for the apparent isolation of the two women is not made explicit. We do not know whether it was a result of prejudice against Ruth as a Moabite, an assumption that 'the family will take care of them', a belief that as Naomi was quite clear that her misfortunes had been sent by Yahweh she must have deserved it, or simply a selfish unconcern. In any event the scene is set. The two of them have arrived in Bethlehem and have no apparent means of support. They arrived *as the barley harvest was beginning* – that is, somewhere around the end of April. This information is probably given simply to prepare us for the story that follows which is set in the harvest field, but it is possible that the reference in verse 22 to the harvest and to Ruth's accompanying Naomi are deliberately drawing the reader's attention to the fact that Naomi's despair had not taken all the relevant facts into account.

Meaning

If verses 1–5 present the broad-brush picture of the background to Naomi and Ruth's arrival back in Bethlehem, this section gives a more detailed view of the immediately preceding circumstances. We are now prepared for the ongoing story of their life in the town. We know that Ruth is a Moabite, we know why she is there and we know why her sister-in-law Orpah is not there. We have been informed that Naomi has returned with no resources and with a sense of resentment against Yahweh, and that the townsfolk, in particular the townswomen, took note of their arrival but did nothing to provide them with aid. It seems likely that the writer is intending readers to draw conclusions as to how far the community *in the days when the judges ruled* was adhering to covenant principles regarding community living, and that there is an expectation that those conclusions will not necessarily be positive. Driesbach compares the situation in Ruth with that in Judges and draws a contrast: 'Against this backdrop the characters and tone of Ruth stand out as calm, orderly and upright. A simple, rural dignity seems to pervade the little town of Bethlehem . . . there is danger, but society is unified in common values and people look out for each other' (Driesbach 2012: 501). However, the evidence for drawing such a positive assessment of the culture and society in Bethlehem seems more than somewhat lacking! In this chapter the writer is also encouraging ongoing consideration of the question as to whether God is or is not intending blessing for Naomi, and how this will affect Ruth – or even, how Ruth will affect this!

C. Boaz and Ruth: first encounter (2:1–16)

Context

The key character in chapter 1 was Naomi. In the next chapters she remains significant but the focus moves to Ruth and Boaz and the encounters between them. It is a characteristic of the book of Ruth that the story is predominantly narrated through dialogue between the different characters. In this chapter the story is told through five separate conversations, including the report of a sixth, with only brief interruptions (vv. 3, 17–18) for narrative comment, with the first and the final verses providing a preface and a conclusion. Dialogue is common in biblical narratives as a whole, but the extent to which it is used in Ruth is unusual.

Comment

2:1. It is possible that this verse should really be seen as part of the first chapter. It simply provides us with an introduction to Boaz so that as the story unfolds we know whom we are talking about. The technique of introducing people before they actually enter the narrative is a fairly common one in Scripture. (We see an example of this in Gen. 11:27–32 when Abraham and Sarah's background is given before they actually emerge as characters in the narrative.) Here we learn that Boaz was a relative of Naomi[3] – note how it is

---

3. Hubbard (1988: 132–133) argues that the term used here is more likely to imply friendship rather than blood relationship, but Boaz' recognition in 3:12 that although he was not the closest of the relatives he was part of the kinship chain perhaps speaks in support of the traditional interpretation.

taken for granted that a relative of Elimelek is to be seen as also
related to Naomi. This may or may not imply that Elimelek and
Naomi actually belonged to the same clan – maybe as cousins,
whether close or distant. Clans seem to have been fairly large sections
of tribes described by the name of the tribe itself, of an early
ancestor or a significant clan leader (Num. 36:1; Josh. 7:17; Judg.
13:2; 17:7; Zech. 12:12–13). Whether the reference to the clan of
Elimelek means that Naomi's husband was the clan leader, was
named after the clan leader or simply that Boaz and Elimelek
belonged to the same clan cannot be determined. We are also told
explicitly that Boaz was a *man of standing*, which may be a reference
to the fact that he was obviously wealthy, owned land and apparently
had many employees, but it may also imply that he was a leader
within the community. Within early Jewish literature there are many
stories and legends about Boaz. The Talmud speaks of him as a
widower with sixty children and identifies him with the minor judge
Ibzan (*b. B. Bat. 91a*; cf. Judg. 12:8). Moore gives more details of this
(Harris, Brown and Moore 2000: 326). However, although the picture
of Boaz provided within Ruth is of a very positive character, there
is no support in the book for the kind of heroic reverence that
developed later.

   2–3. Conversation 1: Ruth and Naomi. The relationship between
the two women is well illustrated in this little episode. Ruth is
thinking strategically and taking the initiative, but as Naomi is the
elder and therefore, at least theoretically, the leader, her permission
is necessary for Ruth to follow up on her idea. It seems obvious that
going out to glean in the fields during harvest might help them to
find basic resources, and perhaps the fact that it was Ruth who
thought of it is an indication that Naomi's return home had increased
rather than helped her sense of depression and had reduced her
ability to think clearly. This may also explain why there seems to be
no question that Naomi, who has apparently had no particular
problems in journeying back to Bethlehem, does not volunteer and
is not even asked to accompany Ruth in the task. She agrees that
Ruth should *go ahead*, but at this point 'she neither warned Ruth of
imminent dangers nor wished her well' (Hubbard 1988: 139). Specific
instructions for the practice of gleaning are found in Leviticus
19:9–10 and 23:22. During harvest the grain at the edge of the fields

and whatever was not picked up during the main harvesting activities was to be left for 'the poor and the foreigner'. Ruth came into both of those categories! This may have been a common practice in the Ancient Near East in general, or it may be that the poorer women of the town had informed her that this was an acceptable practice.

Verse 3 tells us that she acted on her idea and turned up in the field of Boaz, *from the clan of Elimelek*, that is, the Boaz whom readers have already been told about in verse 1. There is no mention of God's activity at this stage, but that the writer is pointing readers to the assumption that her decision was overseen by God's providential care cannot be avoided. In other words, it was a 'coincidence' from Ruth's perspective but not necessarily unexpected in the context of Yahweh's concern for his people. As Younger puts it, 'The NIV phrase "as it turned out" . . . is used in this sentence as a rhetorical device, hyperbolic irony. By excessively attributing Ruth's good fortune to chance, the phrase points ironically to the opposite, namely to the sovereignty of God' (2002: 441).

4–7. Conversation 2: Boaz and his workers. We learn here that Boaz was apparently not involved with the day-to-day work on his farm but was keeping an eye on what went on and was concerned for the welfare of his employees. The traditional greetings, *The LORD be with you* and *The LORD bless you*, may be not much more significant than the use of 'goodbye' (originally meaning 'God be with you') would be today, but are probably included again to remind readers that Yahweh is Lord of the harvest and perhaps to show a good relationship between employer and employees. Boaz knows his people well enough to identify that someone was there who was not part of the usual crowd. His question – not 'Who is she?' but *Who does that young woman belong to?* – may imply that there was some reason to identify her as a foreigner or that he is assuming that any female involved in independent gleaning must be a slave. It is just possible that there is also a hint of 'is she married?', which would alert the reader to future questions to be raised (see Hubbard 1988: 147), but this suggestion can only be speculative. The overseer's reply indicates a previous conversation between himself and Ruth that enabled him to know who she was and what she was doing. He had also noted that she was clearly a hard worker. That the overseer had been quite happy, and by inference assumed that Boaz would be quite happy, to let Ruth work in that way is a further indication that Boaz' *standing* reflected kindness and adherence to the law and not just wealth. There is some debate concerning the difference between Ruth's suggestion to Naomi that she go to pick up corn behind the reapers and the overseer's comment that she asked to glean *among the sheaves*, which would not normally be permitted. Whether this was simply an indication of Ruth's inadequate Hebrew or whether the overseer was intimating that she was making an inappropriate suggestion cannot really be determined (see Grossman 2007) – in either case Boaz picks up the point and specifically allows her extra privileges. The Hebrew in verse 7 is complex. One interpretation is the suggestion (Harris, Brown and Moore 2000: 330; Hubbard 1988: 153) that Ruth actually waited around until Boaz came on the scene to give his permission, but that is not the only way of looking at it and seems unnecessary.

8–14. Conversation 3: Boaz and Ruth. This is by far the longest of the five conversations and provides the main focus of the chapter. Boaz' address to Ruth as *my daughter* may be a recognition of age difference or the relationship between them, or may reflect, as his further words make explicit, that she is now to be viewed as part of his own workforce, an employee rather than a beggar, under his protection and able to use his resources. The reference to *the women who work for me* could be implying that there were actually no other unemployed gleaners in the field. There is no need for Ruth even to bring her own water to drink. Her surprise at his kindness to *a foreigner* may indicate that the people of the town had not in general been kind. Boaz replies that he has heard about her return, which does raise the question as to why he, as a fairly close kinsman, although not the closest, has made no more attempt than the rest of the townspeople to discover whether Naomi was actually provided for or to offer help. Boaz makes it clear that he realizes that Ruth has committed herself not just to Naomi but to *the God of Israel*, and commends her to God's care. The language he uses indicates that his awareness of, and allegiance to, Yahweh was more than just lip service. Ruth's recognition that there was no compulsion for him to treat her as an employee again focuses on Boaz' good character, which is further emphasized by his allowing her not just to snack on the grain she has collected but to share in the lunchtime rations of bread and pre-roasted grain. He may not have been in the fields until lunchtime, but he clearly interacted with the employees at that point. His statement to Ruth that he had told the men *not to lay a hand on you* ('not touch thee' KJV; 'molest you' JB) may indicate his suspicion that something negative (the varying translations indicate the difficulty of deciding exactly what he was afraid might happen, but it was clearly negative) could happen and had perhaps already happened to her.[4]

15–16. Conversation 4: Boaz and his workers. Here we see Boaz functioning as the 'boss'. It is a communication of instructions rather than a genuine conversation and it follows on from his concern for, and conversation with, Ruth. His men – note again the implication that for most of the time he will not be with them in the fields – are not simply to tolerate Ruth but actively to assist her in her work. The instruction for them deliberately to pull out stalks for her to pick up goes far beyond the requirements of Leviticus and is possibly being seen by Boaz as the fulfilment of a family responsibility to ensure Naomi's well-being.

D. Naomi and Ruth: conversation at the end of the day (2:17–23)

17–18. The rest of the day involved more hard work. There was perhaps a corner of the field where threshing was done. It would not be sensible to carry the chaff back to the town along with the grain. Threshing of the main harvest would have been done with the assistance of animals, but it is likely that Ruth used some kind of manual method. An ephah of grain was probably around 27 pounds

---

4. Although the Hebrew roots are different (*ngʻ* in v. 9 and *pgʻ* in v. 22), the same difficulty in translation arises in relation to Naomi's reference to 'harm' in v. 22. Shepherd (2001) and Carasik (1995) provide fuller discussions of the nature of the possible 'harm' in both cases. Younger (2002: 443–444) suggests that Boaz' repeatedly urging Ruth, *don't go, don't go away, stay here*, followed by the reference to the young men not harming her, probably implies that she was already about to leave because of something bad that had happened to her. This can only be speculative but is certainly a possibility.

(12–13 kg). This seems a very large amount to have collected and threshed in one day and would have been heavy to carry home after a day's work. Of course, it is important to realize that a whole year's supply would have to be found in just a few days.

19–22. Conversation 5: Naomi and Ruth. Naomi's reaction shows the extraordinary nature of the amount of grain that Ruth has managed to glean in one day. She rightly concluded that this could only have happened if the farmer involved had shown extraordinary kindness – such a man certainly deserved to be blessed. On learning that the man involved was Boaz, her reaction was not only to call down Yahweh's blessing on him but to recognize that, in spite of her having felt that Yahweh had deserted her, actually that was false. In reality, Yahweh had *not stopped* caring for her and her family. The explicit mention that Yahweh had *not stopped showing kindness* (*ḥesed*) does indicate that the writer at an earlier stage really had intended readers to consider the question of whether he had or had not deserted Naomi. The repeated mention of the *favour* that Boaz would and did show to Ruth (2:2, 10, 13, 19) reinforces that view (Harris, Brown and Moore 2000: 333–343 expand on this point). Yahweh's kindness to Naomi and Ruth was shown through the kindness of Boaz as well as through Ruth's kindness to Naomi. The 'coincidence' that Ruth had happened on the field of a close relative, indeed *one of our guardian-redeemers*, is now clearly ascribed to Yahweh's intervention. Guardian-redeemers were close family members who had the responsibility to buy back land that had been lost in order to ensure that it did not pass out of the family (Lev. 25:25–55). By extension, that came to be understood as those who ought to take responsibility for caring for needy relatives. The nearest that modern Western cultures come to this is the concept of next-of-kin, those who are called upon to make decisions on behalf of someone who, usually because of illness, cannot do so for themselves. But the concept here is much stronger than that and perhaps reflects a more solid sense of the importance of wider family ties. The writer may be suggesting that Boaz should really have taken action before Ruth 'happened upon' his field, but as far as Naomi is concerned, the fact that he has now assumed responsibility is the significant thing. Driesbach's suggestion (2012: 529–530) that Naomi is using the term here in a non-technical sense and is simply saying that he has behaved in the way a *kinsman-redeemer* would be expected to behave is worth considering. But Boaz' later acceptance of the technical role might be seen as evidence against this view. Naomi's use of *our* in verse 20 is probably significant. In describing Boaz as *our* relative, she now identifies completely with Ruth as family.

Ruth's report of Boaz' instructions to her indicates that he told her to *stay with my workers* (i.e. young men), whereas he had actually said, *with the women who work for me* (2:9). This may be a further indication of inadequate Hebrew on Ruth's part. Lim (2011) argues that the change is easily explained from the differences with the Moabite language. Naomi reiterates Boaz' instruction to Ruth to stay with his workers because otherwise she *might be harmed*, a thought that had apparently not occurred to her when Ruth originally asked for her agreement to the gleaning. Boaz seems to be taking it for granted that without his intervention she could have been in danger even from his own workers (although the only indication in the account that this might have been a problem is his instruction recorded in v. 9 that his men should not harm her) and was even more likely to be treated badly if she went to work for less ethical landowners. This presents a rather sad picture of the state of Israelite society at this time, suggesting that the mistreatment of women seen in Judges was endemic to the whole nation – that it would happen is taken for granted. However, although we may be intended to notice that fact, it does not seem to be the focus of this particular account.

23. The chapter closes with the information that Ruth and Naomi continued to live together and remained to some extent under Boaz' protection not only for the length of the barley harvest but also during the wheat harvest that followed. Ruth is named eight times in this chapter, six times simply as Ruth and twice as *Ruth the Moabite*. Both of these occur in the context of her conversations with Naomi: Boaz learns from his overseer that she is a Moabite, and Ruth refers to herself as a foreigner, but the ethnic ascription is not actually used in her contacts with Boaz. Whether this is significant and what any significance might be is debatable.

Meaning

The extensive use of dialogue may be just a literary technique, but it could be the writer's way of making a point. It emphasizes the fact that people, and what they say to each other, are to be seen as significant. Within the context of these dialogues we are presented with a clear understanding of the different characters. There is also much information included on the culture of the time – the way work is done, the way people relate, and apparently the background of endemic violence. However, the underlying focus seems to be that in spite of Naomi's previous experience of disaster, God is still with his people and still with this little family, still showing kindness, still acting as their covenant God. The concept of God conveying his blessing through the kindness of his people – in this case Boaz – may also be being deliberately introduced.

E. Seeking a marriage partner (3:1–18)

Context
Chapter 3 also contains a significant amount of dialogue, if not quite as much as we have seen in chapter 2. Only three conversations are recorded here, as opposed to the five of chapter 2, and there is much more explanatory narrative. In this ongoing study of family life which began with the deaths of Naomi's husband and sons and will end with the birth of Ruth's son (4:13ff.), it is not surprising that here we have a discussion of marriage. It would be wrong to try to extract a full picture of Israel's understanding of marriage and the processes involved from this one illustration any more than we can do so from the various discussions in the Samson narratives (Judg. 13 – 16). However, it is worth noting the way in which the wider family was involved in the marriage arrangements. In chapter 3 Ruth, Naomi and Boaz remain as the main and, apart from a reference to the unnamed closer relative, the only characters.

Comment
i. Naomi and Ruth: making plans (3:1–6)
3:1–4. The *one day* with which the chapter begins gives us no idea of how much time had elapsed since Ruth had worked in Boaz' fields. It is the equivalent of 'some time later'. It seems to have been long enough for Naomi to get over the worst of her depression as she once more begins to take the initiative. However, the reference in verse 2 to the fact that Boaz would be involved in the winnowing

of the barley harvest probably means that it was not such a long time – days rather than weeks if the barley harvest was winnowed before the wheat harvest began, but weeks if it was not. Threshing, or removing the grain from the rest of the plant, would normally take place immediately after harvest. Winnowing was a bit more thorough, taking away the rest of the chaff and making sure there were no pests getting through into the grain store. It could have happened a little while later.

It would normally be a parental responsibility to make marriage arrangements for their children, with the father usually taking the primary role. Ruth clearly has no parents of her own in this situation, but Naomi's initial address of *my daughter* may be included to show that she has deliberately accepted that responsibility. Again, it is taken for granted that it is only in marriage that a young girl will find 'rest' (translated in NIV as *a home* but cf. 1:9). Naomi wants to make sure that Ruth will be provided for, even after her mother-in-law has died. Naomi's fears that Ruth would never be able to find someone in Israel to marry seem to have faded into the background! Boaz has already assumed some of the responsibilities of a 'guardian-redeemer' in spite of Ruth's foreign heritage. Therefore, Naomi has decided that he will clearly be a good candidate to take over the further responsibility of marrying Ruth in order that the name of his dead relative, Mahlon, will be carried forward via the first-born son of the new partnership. It is worth noting that although the only reason that Boaz as a relative might have a responsibility actually to marry Ruth would be to keep Mahlon's name alive, at this point Naomi's primary concern seems to be for the welfare of Ruth (see Block 1999: 681). Naomi's recognition of Ruth as a member of her own family is further shown in her reference to Boaz as *a relative of ours*. It is interesting to note that although Ruth has already been described as *the Moabite* four times (1:22; 2:2, 6, 21) and has referred to herself as a *foreigner* (2:10), her ethnic origin is not mentioned at all in chapter 3. In the legal discussions of chapter 4 Boaz twice makes reference to her as *Ruth the Moabite*, showing that he recognized that this was a significant factor to those in the wider community. However, the lack of reference in chapter 3 may be deliberate and indicate the writer's intention to show that this was not actually something that Boaz himself saw as a particular problem.

Moore's conclusion that 'Finding Boaz may seem serendipitous (see 2:3), but not for Naomi. Naomi sees the hand of Yahweh at work' (2000: 347) may be correct, but there is nothing in Naomi's words at this point to confirm it. Block (1999: 680) seems to assume that Boaz was already thinking about marrying Ruth but was holding back for reasons of sensitivity:

> One may speculate that Naomi hoped that Boaz would take the initiative in establishing a relationship with Ruth . . . Perhaps he was being sensitive . . . not willing to impose himself on her until she was emotionally healed . . . Obviously he was not making any moves so . . . Naomi took it upon herself to overcome his inertia.

However, the text reflects only the fact that Boaz took no action! Perhaps Rowell is correct in asserting that the writer was pointing out that Ruth is showing more evidence of acting as Naomi's 'guardian-redeemer' than is Boaz (2003: 60). Naomi is clearly aware of what goes on in the winnowing hall. The work will be done, after which there will be some kind of corporate meal or feast. Then those present will sleep in situ – perhaps when the amount of drink consumed means they can no longer stay awake. She instructs Ruth to prepare herself with good clothes and perfume – possibly the kind of preparations that would have been made when a marriage introduction was taking place in normal circumstances. There is no specific mention of wedding garments or jewellery, so the idea that she was dressing as a bride stretches the evidence too far. It is worth considering Younger's suggestion that the change of clothes only implied that Ruth put off her mourning garments and moved forward into the future, presenting herself not as a grieving widow but as a potential bride (Younger 2002: 459). Ruth is to keep out of the way until Boaz is asleep and then go, uncover his feet – presumably to ensure that as it got colder in the night he would then wake up – and lie down. It is not at all clear why Naomi did not feel able to approach Boaz herself with the request or why she believed that he would immediately realize what action he was being asked to take. It may have been culturally impossible for Ruth to have a private conversation with Boaz, but there appears to be no reason why Naomi should not have contacted him. It is possible that there were

local traditions of which we know nothing. To modern readers it
might look as if Ruth was being asked to offer herself to Boaz in the
manner of a prostitute. The common assumption that *feet* (v. 4) is
being used as a euphemism for other parts of the body and that there
are specific sexual implications is possibly correct, but can only be
speculative. Naomi's reference to seeking a permanent home for Ruth
and her knowledge of Boaz as a relative with responsibility make this
less likely. However, perhaps Naomi did not think that anyone would
offer to marry *Ruth the Moabite*, so she is arranging a situation where
Boaz is being encouraged to sleep with Ruth, believing that his
integrity is such that he will then provide *a home* for her.

5–6. Ruth, who has come across as such an active, resourceful
character so far, here is pictured as simply acquiescing in Naomi's
instructions. Perhaps she is glad that Naomi is now taking initiative
herself or perhaps she recognizes Naomi's better understanding of
the Israelite culture. In any event we are told that she agreed and *did
everything* she had been told to do.

ii. Boaz and Ruth: a close encounter (3:7–15)

7–8. Boaz finished the feast *in good spirits*, indicating that he had
eaten well and possibly drunk heavily and was likely to sleep deeply.
We are not told what it was that actually wakened him, but it is not
unlikely that the cold feet could have pulled him back to full con-
sciousness. He awoke to find Ruth lying there. As noted above, it is
possible that *at his feet* is a euphemism for 'beside him' or 'very close
to him' and could have sexual connotations, but we cannot presuppose that. There was enough light for him to see that there was
a woman there, but presumably lamps had been dimmed and there
was not enough to recognize who it was. Hubbard's suggestion that
the lack of light has other significance is worth noting: 'Like the
human characters, God himself seems incognito, unrecognizable,
throughout the scene. One even feels that God is looking the other
way, thereby leaving the actors completely on their own' (1988: 195).
But as elsewhere in the book, sometimes the writer's failure to bring
God into the foreground does not mask their intention that readers
should be aware of his presence and involvement.

9–13. Ruth reveals her identity and stresses her relationship to
Boaz as *a guardian-redeemer of our family* (see comment above on

2:19–22). If Naomi had, with motivation that she saw as good, been encouraging Ruth to seduce Boaz, then at this point Ruth moves away from her adherence to Naomi's instructions and refuses to deceive Boaz, but rather makes her requirements explicit. Boaz' question, *Who are you?*, confirming that it was too dark for recognition, is answered briefly: *I am your servant Ruth*. But this is then turned on its head as she says in effect, 'but it is who you are that counts, you are a guardian redeemer' (see Block 1999: 692). Her instruction to him to *spread the corner of your garment over me* or 'spread your skirt over me' is generally taken to imply that she is laying it on the line that she wants him to marry her. Boaz' response shows that he certainly understood it in that way. Whether or not those who pick up on the vague allusions suggesting that the thought of marriage to Ruth had entered Boaz' head are correct, he had taken no action. It is Ruth who takes the initiative, going beyond Naomi's instruction to listen to whatever Boaz said. It is possible that Ruth has picked up Boaz' own thought (although not expressed in the same words) in 2:12 where he speaks of Ruth having placed herself 'under Yahweh's wings'. She is inviting Boaz to be the representative of Yahweh's *ḥesed* towards her (cf. Atkinson 1983: 102). E. A. Jones (2014: 658–662) identifies links between this chapter and the deception of Isaac by Jacob in Genesis 27. He thus sees the guileless Ruth as a deliberate contrast with Jacob the deceiver. Halton (2012) also argues that Naomi's plan involved 'sexual entrapment', but that by following Naomi's instructions but then also revealing herself to Boaz Ruth manages to show *ḥesed* (faithful kindness) to both of them. It may be significant that in this chapter Ruth is identified as a member of the family, and this may be the reason why her foreign origin is not actually mentioned. The race issue is clearly an important motif in the book as a whole, and the writer may be encouraging reflection on the relationship between, or the relative importance of, ethnic origin and family connections. Hubbard appears to support the idea that readers are being directed to view Ruth as the real 'guardian-redeemer': 'In demonstrating remarkable initiative and defiance of custom, she not only embodied the Israelite ideal of *ḥesed* but also, if successful, set herself up to be the true bringer of salvation in this story' (1988: 213).

Boaz immediately grasps what Ruth is asking. The fact that he does so, particularly in the light of Naomi's apparent confidence that he would, does point to some kind of known tradition. There is no indication that Boaz had even considered the thought that Ruth might be looking for some kind of 'one-night stand' or that he would have been ready to accept such an offer. It seems unlikely that he would have called for Yahweh to *bless* Ruth for her actions (v. 10) or refer to her as *a woman of noble character* (v. 11) if he had understood her to be presenting herself as a prostitute offering her services. The word used here is the same word used of Boaz himself in 2:1 where the NIV translates it as *a man of standing*. The word can have its primary reference either to status or character (as in the 'woman of noble character' or 'virtuous woman' of Prov. 31:10, which is the only other occurrence of the exact phrase used to describe Ruth), so both the *man of standing* and the *woman of noble character* are acceptable translations, but it seems odd not to bring out the connection by translating them both in the same way. It is possible that the writer is deliberately indicating that Ruth and Boaz shared the same social status, which makes sense of his view that she was doing him a favour by agreeing to marry him, and her view that he was doing her a favour!

Ruth refers to herself as *your servant*, which could be a formal recognition of his status but may be acknowledging her role as having been employed by him. He again refers to her as *my daughter* (cf. 2:8), which may be simply a formal address but could be either emphasizing the age difference or acknowledging the family connection. He alludes to Ruth's ongoing *kindness*; his reference to the earlier evidence of this presumably means that her actions are showing kindness to Naomi rather than to himself. Her willingness to marry him, which he seems to assume is a sacrifice on her part, is viewed as a way to ensure Naomi's well-being as well as her own. She could have ignored the guardian-redeemer role and sought her own younger husband. He did not seem to share Naomi's concern that this would have been very difficult if not impossible to do. The specific reference to *rich or poor* could indicate that Boaz is aware that his wealth is a factor in the decision to approach him rather than the closer relative of whom Naomi must have been aware. However, he immediately agrees to take action. His willingness for the closer relative to act if he so desires is a clear indication that what we are talking about here is an acceptance of a formal responsibility rather than a 'love-match'. There is no evidence that he actually did *spread the corner of his garment* over Ruth as she asked, such an action signifying his firm commitment to marry her. Rather at this stage his commitment was to ensure that she did find a husband (see Hubbard 1988: 219). He confirms this commitment with an oath. His action will happen *as surely as the LORD lives*, interestingly, the only actual reference to Yahweh within this chapter. His repeated instruction to her to *stay here for the night* and *lie here until morning* is to be seen as a further indication of his concern for her welfare. To send her home in the dark could be dangerous.

14–15. We are told that Ruth got up before it was light enough for anyone to be recognized. Boaz was clearly awake as well; perhaps reflecting on his future course of action had outweighed the effects of the previous night's drinking. It is not clear whether his instruction about keeping it quiet that Ruth had been there was addressed to her or to any of his other employees who rose early. The comment does seem to indicate that it would have been possible, or even likely, for her actions to be misconstrued by anyone hearing of what had happened. Knowledge of her actions could in this case bring negative effects to either or both of them. His donation of a further large portion of, presumably newly winnowed, barley was a further indication of his good intentions and possibly a message to Naomi that he had received her message. The liveliness of the narrative is seen in the inclusion of incidental details like the use of Ruth's shawl to carry the grain. The fact that she was still 'wrapped in' this shawl, large enough to carry the amount of grain that Boaz was providing, is further evidence supporting the view that she was not dressed for seduction. The textual variants at the end of verse 15 are understandable. It makes more sense to read that 'she went back to town', although most manuscripts read 'he'. It is not really of great significance which of these is original. Block may be right in suggesting that it is obvious that Ruth left the scene but Boaz had further work to do on the winnowing floor, so it needs pointing out that he left to go into the town, setting the scene for the next chapter.

iii. Naomi and Ruth: further conversation (3:16–18)

We learn nothing new in this little section, which simply rounds of this part of the narrative as Ruth returns home to Naomi and reports on the events of the night. We do see confirmation of Ruth's commitment to Naomi, Boaz' kindness and Naomi's complete confidence that Boaz will now fulfil what she sees as his obligations. It is interesting to note the extent of this confidence in the light of the fact that Boaz had taken no action on their behalf on his own initiative but had simply responded to the circumstances as they arose. Naomi's question on Ruth's arrival – 'Who are you, my daughter?' (e.g. KJV) – seems strange, and the NIV's translation – *How did it go, my daughter?* – is understandable. But if Jones (2014) is correct, then the wording provides a further deliberate link with Genesis 27 where Isaac asks first Jacob (Gen. 27:18) and then Esau (Gen. 27:32), 'Who are you?' It is possible that the question is confirming the fact that it was still too dark for anyone to be recognized or that Naomi was genuinely surprised that Ruth had come back at this stage. Another possibility is that, given Naomi's original suggestion, she is asking whether or not sexual intercourse had taken place and Ruth had actually become Boaz' 'wife', thus, in effect, acquiring a new identity.

Meaning

Chapter 3 ends with both hope and expectation. Although readers do not yet know how the situation is going to be resolved, the narrative conveys the impression that it will be. The depression and despair of earlier times has now gone. On the surface it looks as if the source of this hope is Boaz. However, his own words make it clear that he recognizes Ruth's *kindness* as the source of Naomi's renewed sense of well-being. Possibly with the mention of Boaz' oath in the name of Yahweh, the writer is also subtly drawing our attention to the fact that God is standing behind all the events that have been recorded, and cares for Naomi, Ruth and Boaz. The ongoing discussion within the book of both the significance of ethnicity and the meaning of family – that is, the question of whether family should be defined by blood or by commitment – is continued within this chapter. This section could be seen as evidence of the writer's concern as to whether or not the covenant with Yahweh is being observed in Israel. The reference to Ruth's kindness (ḥesed) and to Boaz taking up a responsibility to observe the law would support the view that although in general Israelite covenant observance was not great, there were still those who followed Yahweh, in this case Ruth the foreigner and Boaz the Israelite landowner.

F. Marriage and birth (4:1–17)

Context

The story is moving towards its climax. Ruth and Naomi play no part in the first twelve verses of the chapter as Boaz follows through his negotiations with the men of the town. The patriarchal nature of the society is made clear here, but again, the way the story is told indicates that the writer is pointing out that in God's world the rights, needs and even opinions of the women do count. Their omission at this point only emphasizes their involvement elsewhere in the book. There are two questions hanging in the air from the previous chapters: first, will Naomi be looked after (i.e. have a male heir who will take responsibility for her) and second, will it be Boaz or the nearer relative who will actually marry Ruth? Both will be dealt with in this chapter although the second question is addressed first.

i. Boaz takes action (4:1–10)

Comment

4:1–8. Boaz takes immediate action to fulfil his commitment to Ruth. The account of the meeting at the town gate is again lively and evocative. Readers can almost feel as if they were present and watching! We are given a very clear picture of the cultural understandings and behaviour of the time. It is probable that the town gate was the place where business transactions of all types were conducted. It may also be where the men gathered to chat and socialize on a regular basis, but the specific invitation to ten of the elders to act as witnesses makes it clear that on this occasion we are talking about an official civil court case. A decision is to be made, by the men, about what is to happen to the property and persons of Naomi and Ruth, neither of whom is required or invited to be present. It is possible that the writer is drawing attention to the women having been sidelined by the culture, but it could simply be informing us that this was how it was at that time. The fact that none of these men has taken any action so far to help Naomi or to push the unnamed close relative into doing so is also possibly significant. However generous and helpful Boaz was being, the fact remains that the women were viewed primarily in terms of property.

Verse 1's statement that Boaz sat down, just as the nearer relative passed by, reminds us of the 'chance' occurrence in chapter 2 when Ruth happened to enter the field of Boaz. But 'against chapter 2, choice, not chance, will guide events' (Hubbard 1988: 230). Boaz has so far been seen as reacting to events as they occurred, but now he is showing himself to be very capable of taking initiative. The NIV translation *my friend* masks the fact that his name seems to have been deliberately missed out. The phrase is better translated as 'so and so', or perhaps as Hubbard puts it, 'Mr So-and-So' (1988: 232).[5] Boaz first challenges the closer but unnamed *guardian-redeemer* regarding the land. This is the first mention of the land. It may be that Boaz is just being legally careful that all things are done properly and in accordance with the law, but there is a strong impression given that he is manipulating the situation to reach a predetermined conclusion. We are not told whether the *piece of land* that had belonged to Elimelek had been allowed to lie fallow and had possibly become overrun by weeds, or whether it had been used by other local farmers while the family were away. The fact that it now needs to be bought back may imply that Elimelek sold the land before they left for Moab, noting that any sale of inherited land within Israel was automatically what today would be termed 'leasehold' (Lev. 25:25–28). The fact remains that it had been the legal family property of Elimelek and his sons, and therefore measures should be taken to ensure that it was retained or reclaimed as the property of the wider clan.[6] At first sight this looks like an excellent business deal. The land will be added to the portfolio of the relative, and even if Naomi and Ruth are allowed to continue living there, it will bring in extra income. He is

5. The same expression is used in 1 Sam. 21:2 and 2 Kgs 6:8 in reference to unnamed places, and the NIV translations there are 'a certain place' and 'such and such a place'. (see Younger 2002: 474).

6. Hubbard (1988: 230–252) provides a detailed discussion of the legal niceties contained in this section.

pictured as jumping at the chance to buy, perhaps suspecting that Boaz, who might be thought able to spot a good deal, was trying to keep him out of it. The impression that the motivation was profit rather than any sense of responsibility for, or care of, Naomi and Ruth is very strong. Readers might be a little surprised at this turn of events; were things going to turn out badly for Ruth and Naomi after all? The writer's skill in maintaining the tension here is very evident.

At this point Boaz brings in the second requirement, and the ten witnesses provide no opportunity for the relative to ignore or sidestep this extra responsibility. Whoever buys the land is agreeing to marry *Ruth the Moabite*, and the land will be given to her first son to *maintain the name* of her dead husband Mahlon (cf. Deut. 25:5–10). In other words, the whole process should be seen as an act of charity rather than as a profitable business deal. Just how this would endanger the relative's own estate is not clear other than that it would cost him money rather than bring in a profit. We cannot tell whether the renewed emphasis on Ruth being a foreigner also played a part in his decision. It is possible that the relative knew about the responsibility of a *guardian-redeemer* to undertake a levirate marriage (where a brother was required to marry a dead brother's childless widow, and the first son of the second marriage would be legally seen as the son of the dead brother) and was deliberately ignoring it, hoping to get away with a good bargain, but that was not now going to be possible. The provision in Deuteronomy for a widow to be remarried gives the responsibility only to the dead man's brother, and Mahlon had no living brother, so it is perhaps not surprising that this more distant relative did not at first consider the possibility of marrying Ruth. But once Boaz had introduced the concept in such a public way, it would have been very hard for the relative to buy the land without marrying Ruth. In any event, he decides not to go ahead with the deal, indicating this by taking off his sandal. This custom had clearly gone out of use by the time the account was written up (v. 7). The NIV places verse 7 in brackets to indicate that it is an editorial comment rather than part of the ongoing narrative. Such comments are rare in Ruth, and on other occasions (1:1, 22 and 4:1 could be seen as examples) are used to add extra information to the unfolding story rather than providing the extraneous details for later readers that we find here. It is interesting that in Deuteronomy 25 the taking off of a sandal is seen as a way of shaming the one who refused to carry out his responsibilities, but here it is simply a way of turning down an opportunity.

It is possible that Boaz was genuinely giving the closer relative a chance to fulfil the obligations of a guardian-redeemer and would have been happy to have backed down if he did so. However, the way he presents the situation does make it appear that he was deliberately leading him towards a refusal. We cannot be sure whether this was because he suspected that the relative's concern for profit – and as a member of his family in a relatively small town Boaz would certainly have known something of his character – would have outweighed any concern for Ruth, and Boaz' sense of responsibility for her had already developed, or whether it was because Boaz really did want to marry Ruth. K. L. Younger points out the parallels between the withdrawal by Orpah after the discussion in 1:8–14 and the relative's withdrawal here. In that early section Naomi's concern for her daughters-in-law to be able to find a home and security is expressed. Ruth turned down that opportunity, but now it looks as if she is going to find both the home and the security in abundance (see Younger 2002: 472–473).

9–10. After the relative's refusal, Boaz uses legal language, addressing not only the assigned witnesses among the elders but *all the people* to confirm his commitment to buy the land and to marry Ruth. He again brings to the fore Ruth's Moabite nationality and the fact that the point of this marriage is to maintain the *name* of her first husband Mahlon through the birth of the first son that Ruth will bear him. There is no going back on this deal; Boaz has made sure that everyone knows exactly what he is doing. In the light of that, it is noteworthy that the last mention of Mahlon's name is in Ruth 4:9. In the genealogy found in 1 Chronicles 2 Boaz is listed as Obed's father, and this is followed by both Matthew and Luke in the genealogies at the beginning of their Gospels (Matt. 1:5; Luke 3:32). The concept of *maintaining the name* of the dead husband seems to have been little more than a formality, although the provision for the surrogate son of that husband, and thus for the care of the widow, was not. In verse 10 Boaz mentions for a second time (cf. v. 5) that the marriage involves 'acquiring' or 'buying' Ruth, again emphasizing the fact that women in this society were viewed as property. However, it is possible that the relational tone of the rest of the narrative is the writer's way of indicating that, although this was the view of society, it was not how they or Boaz, or by implication Yahweh, really saw it.

ii. 'Naomi has a son' (4:11–17)

11–12. This section of the narrative closes with the acknowledgment of the whole crowd around the gate that they are witnesses. The rather fulsome blessing that they then bestow on Boaz may simply be a formal recognition by fellow citizens that he is already a man of status and a sign that they want to keep on the right side of such a man. However, it could also show that they saw his actions as particularly praiseworthy, probably as much because he was willing to marry a foreigner as the fact that he had followed through on legal responsibilities that others had avoided. The prayer for many children (as with Rachel and Leah) may indicate a hope that he will not only father a surrogate son for Mahlon but will have children of his own. We have no evidence as to whether Boaz already had other children, but the lack of any mention of such and the inclusion of a blessing of this nature may indicate that he did not. The reference to Perez ties in with the genealogy at the end of the chapter. Boaz was a direct descendant of Perez, and there may be a hint of 'may you have children who are as high in status as the descendants of Perez – that is, as you are'. Whether either the crowd or the writer is intentionally pointing out that unorthodox unions had already taken place in Boaz' family tree – and the birth of Perez can certainly be described as 'unorthodox' (cf. Gen. 38) – cannot be determined, although the specific mentions of both Judah and Tamar as Perez' parents may point towards this. We have already noted several implicit references to other Old Testament passages within the book of Ruth. In this little section there are two explicit intertextual links to Rachel and Leah and to Tamar, Judah and Perez. Possibly the writer is pointing out that ancestral stories were known, and therefore also noting that the requirements of the covenant law regarding community responsibilities should also have been known. Levenson (2010) notes both similarities and differences between Ruth and the women referred to here. Rachel and Leah bore children as the citizens hoped Ruth would, and Tamar was apparently a Canaanite, a foreign outsider. However, whereas Rachel and Leah sometimes cooperated but were often rivals, and Tamar used deceit to ensure she had a child, Ruth and Naomi are portrayed as consistently cooperating with each other and having a good relationship. The elders' reference to Rachel and Leah having *together built up the family* [house] *of Israel* is interesting, emphasizing as it does that the various tribes came from both women – and the slaves who bore them further surrogate sons.

13–17. These verses provide a brief summary of what happened next. The bare facts, that they got married and had a son, are followed by a return to the focus on Naomi that we saw in chapter 1. However, whereas in chapter 1 the townswomen's only comment was *Can this be Naomi?* before they apparently left her and Ruth to fend for themselves, in contrast they take centre stage in this little section as the only speakers. The phraseology, stressing that the Lord enabled Ruth to conceive, could simply be a formal acknowledgment of God's involvement, or it could be a comment on the fact that Ruth had had no children with Mahlon and there is no mention of any other children belonging to Boaz. Another link with chapter 1 is that Yahweh is described as intervening in events only in 1:6 when *the LORD had come to the aid of his people* and in 4:13 when he *enabled* [Ruth] *to conceive*. Perhaps these two references at the beginning and end of the book are intended to direct us to look for, or even assume, Yahweh's involvement throughout the narrative.

However, the writer's main interest at this point is how the new situation affected Naomi. The women of the town are delighted by her new circumstances and now show a willingness to welcome both her and Ruth into their community. Their adherence to Yahweh may have been somewhat limited, but their recognition that Yahweh is the one who is to be praised as having blessed Naomi in this way shows that allegiance to Yahweh was not totally forgotten. Naomi now has a *guardian-redeemer* of her own. The prayer that he will become famous and the affirmation that he will sustain her in her old age almost certainly means that they are referring to Ruth's son Obed, who will have a legal responsibility for Naomi as his legal grandmother, rather than to Boaz, whose responsibility has been voluntarily assumed. The fact that the child is seen as belonging to

Naomi because her daughter-in-law Ruth gave birth to him is significant; Ruth is now firmly acknowledged as Naomi's *daughter-in-law*.
The praise of Ruth, with no further mention of her Moabite origin,
is interesting. She is *better than seven sons* – seen as the ideal number
– for one Ruth is worth even more than seven sons! Naomi, having
lost her own sons, saw herself as *empty* (1:21), but, in fact, even at
that stage she had Ruth who has proved herself more than capable
of fulfilling the role normally held by a son. As we have already
noted, it is possible that the writer here is suggesting that it is Ruth,
even more than Boaz, who has consistently acted as Naomi's *guardian-redeemer*. It is unlikely that the townswomen saw it in quite that
way, but it is not inconceivable that the author did. It is also possible
that the author is deliberately contrasting the women's attitude at
the beginning, when Naomi and Ruth were poor childless widows
and Ruth a foreigner at that, to that at the end when they were related
to a *man of standing* and Ruth had given birth to a child. The covenant
with Yahweh gives the community particular responsibility for caring
for the poor and needy in their midst, but these women seem to be
willing to support only those who might be seen as having social
significance.

The ascription of the child as 'Naomi's son' is probably a recognition of his identity as a surrogate son of Mahlon, although this
factor is not mentioned again. The boy, who is named Obed, became
the father of Jesse, who in turn fathered David. The book of Ruth
was clearly not written up in its final form until well into the reign of
David at the earliest (see pp. 231–232). It is not clear whether the *they*
who named Obed refers to the family or the women of the town.
We can't be sure of the traditions of the time for naming a child.
Many years later the women in the time of Zechariah and Elizabeth
expected to have some role in the naming of their son (Luke 1:59),
although the father's preference clearly took precedence.

Meaning
As elsewhere in Ruth, separating out the story and the meaning is
not a particularly helpful activity. However, it is possible to say that
this chapter is emphasizing that life goes on, that God continues to
care for his people and that society functions best when those people
take responsibility for caring for and supporting one another. The

importance of taking responsibility for those who are weak and lacking support is particularly stressed.

G. Afterword: the genealogy (4:18–22)

Context

The question arises as to whether this little section is an appendix, added to link the book of Ruth to the later accounts of David, or to show that the blessings called down upon Ruth in 2:12 and 4:11 were definitely fulfilled through the birth of her famous descendant. The alternative suggestion is that this section is really the point of the whole book, providing a background for David and giving information about his ancestry. The genealogy itself does not answer this question directly, although it clearly indicates that the final form of Ruth was not produced until well into the reign of David at the earliest. The mention of Perez in 4:18 does seem to show that the writer was following through on the link with Boaz' family. We learn of his ancestors and his descendants. Genealogies were important markers used in identifying relatives and responsibilities and confirming identity. It is likely that people, as in many countries today, would have been able to quote the list of their ancestors back through many generations.

Comment

18. Genealogies can start at any point, and it is not entirely clear why the writer should choose to start with Perez, as opposed to Judah, Jacob or Abraham. If the intention in 4:12 was to emphasize Perez' unusual birth circumstances and stress that this did not prevent him from doing well in Israel, then the same point may be being made here. Obed might have been born to a foreign woman, but there is no reason why he should not do just as well. Hezron was apparently a fairly common name; Reuben also had a son called Hezron (Exod. 6:14). The suggestion that the main point of Ruth is to show a direct link between David and the patriarchs seems to be undermined by starting with Perez rather than Abraham, although of course every Israelite could theoretically trace their ancestry back to Abraham.

19–22. We learn a little more about this Hezron and his descendants in the genealogical material found in 1 Chronicles 2. Apart from that chapter, nothing of Hezron, Ram, Amminadab, Nahshon or Salmon (recorded in some manuscripts as Salma) is mentioned again until the genealogies of Matthew (1:3–4) and Luke (3:32–33). In 1 Chronicles 2:10 Nahshon is described as 'the leader of the people of Judah'. We read in Numbers (1:7; 2:3; 7:12, 17; 10:14) of his leadership role during the time of Moses as the one chosen from Judah to assist Moses and to take command of that tribe during their trek to Canaan from Sinai. It may be that this explains the prosperity of Boaz in the time described in Ruth. Mentions of Obed after this time are also restricted to 1 Chronicles 2, Matthew 1 and Luke 3. On each occasion he is described as the son of Boaz, so the thought of maintaining the name of Mahlon clearly did not have any permanent effect. Matthew 1:5 tells us that Boaz' mother was called Rahab, possibly referring to the Rahab mentioned in Joshua. Matthew's intention seems to be to emphasize the extent of unorthodox births in Jesus' lineage. However, this information is not found anywhere in the Old Testament, and we cannot be sure where this information came from. If it is the Rahab of Joshua, then it would explain why Boaz was unfazed by the thought of marrying a non-Israelite but not why her existence is not mentioned in Ruth. Hubbard suggests that the list is formulated to make Boaz the seventh name, which is traditionally seen as 'the spot for the ancestor of special honor and importance' (1988: 283). However, if this is so, it again speaks against the view that sees the whole story based on an interest in David. Having said that, the chapter and the book close on the mention of Jesse and David as descendants of Boaz and Ruth.

Meaning

Readers are clearly meant to notice the reference to David at the end of the book (see the discussion on this point in the Introduction, pp. 228–230). What goes before is intended to be read as part of David's background. But that does not mean that this invalidates or even minimizes the lessons that the book of Ruth as a whole presents. We are also intended to notice the way in which this particular set of people lived their lives *in the time when the judges ruled*, to consider issues relating to the treatment of women, perhaps especially widows, and of foreigners, and to accept the challenge to reflect God's 'kindness' in the way that Ruth did. The challenge to the original readers of Ruth to question whether they were living in relationship with Yahweh and keeping their covenant with him – which is clearly intended to have implications for the way in which they relate to the marginalized and at-risk people within their society – remains a challenge to modern readers who have received the New Covenant.

Printed and bound by CPI Group (UK) Ltd, Croydon, CR0 4YY

25/03/2025

14647340-0004